To fellow Southgate
Sir John Bourn, On
school's more spec——— ic
successes from one of the school's
more spectacular academic
disasters. Hope you enjoy a
good read

Kind regards and very
best wishes

Bryn Williams

JUNE 2008

Red Tails in the Sunset

by

Bryn Williams

Bound Biographies

Foreword

by

Water Rat Barry Cryer, OBE

I've known Bryn Williams for many years, and he's known me for nearly as many. He is the definitive toastmaster, a man who will keep your functions moving – in fact, I once christened him, "All Bryn".

His admonishing "Hush", breathed with innate style into the microphone can reduce any gathering to respectful silence – the man has presence and if he's not there, the absence is painfully obvious.

To sum up, the safest pair of hands in the business. He's met them all and most of them are in this book. He should have called it: "Name Drops Keep Falling on my Head!"

Sit back, relax and read – you'll think you're there. And I often was and it was always a pleasure.

My Lords, Ladies and Gentlemen, I give you (Plus VAT)

THE TOASTMASTER'S TOASTMASTER – BRYN WILLIAMS.

Baz

Produced in association with

Bound Biographies

Heyford Park House, Heyford Park, Bicester, OX25 5HD

www.boundbiographies.com

ISBN: 1-905178-08-5

Dedication

To Ann

And to the memory of my parents

Toastmaster Bryn Williams BEM

"My Lords, Ladies and Gentlemen," – that's how they usually begin,
"Pray silence for the Toastmaster," a sort of red-coated 'whipper-in'!
We all know the script: "Dinner is served – top table, this is your call,"
Today we pay tribute to Brother Rat Bryn, for he is the best of them all.

When Bryn is in charge, it's all systems go,
The arrangements are perfect; the events seem to flow.
No difficult moments – everyone at their ease,
"Ladies and Gentlemen, take your seats, please."

In these days when we're seeing some standards fall down,
And behaviour's less civilized all over town,
Thank goodness for Bryn – protocol's leading light;
His talent makes sure that all titles are right.

And no mumbled announcements that no-one can hear,
Bryn's stentorian tones make the info quite clear,
From, "Pray silence for Grace," to, "Gentlemen, you may smoke,"
Every word's crystal clear from this red-coated bloke.

The speaker's dilemma – will there be a mike?
Or even a lecturn… the sort that I like?
Who'll be on hand to see if I win?
Your problems are sorted if your toastmaster is Bryn.

He'll see that all's ready for you to succeed,
For he'll have provided all that you need,
From pop stars to Royals – Yes, Bryn's shepherded them,
The Queen was so pleased – Bryn was awarded B.E.M.

And so, Brother Rat Bryn, we salute you today,
This old Order joins forces – please allow us to say,
At your special Savoy Lunch, here in the Strand,
Toastmaster Rat – you're the best in the land.

Water Rat Peter Goodwright
Poet Laureate of the Grand Order of Water Rats

Contents

Acknowledgements

"…With your experiences you should write a book!" is a phrase I have heard in various forms thousands of times. With such pressure as well as encouragement from a doting, if somewhat misguided, wonderful and adoring wife, how could I not? So written it I have and here it is writ and proof-read a billion times and totally free of all blemishes! I wish!

But before you plough through its pages – wade through its waffle – slosh your way through it sludge – or subsume yourself with its superlatives here are a few, but very necessary thanks and the odd explanation. Order of importance is irrelevant as all the following are as deserving of my deepest and undying gratitude and most heartfelt thanks, which I give unequivocally.

Ann will receive plaudits elsewhere – as she certainly deserves them – has been quite wonderful and I cannot thank her enough.

I suppose the top of my list must come my editor and newly acquired friend Michael Oke of *Bound Biographies*. When he first agreed to edit and advise, he had absolutely no idea of the tome it was to become and was somewhat taken aback. But, over endless weeks and months he has proven to be patient, kind, encouraging, critical and downright rude all wrapped up in one little package and was great. Don't get me wrong; I wrote the thing but he – in cahoots with my wife Ann – connived, colluded, coerced, cajoled and bullied me, telling me what could go in and what couldn't, and I had to put up with it all. I'm deeply indebted to him – I think! I must also not forget to thank the whole team at *Bound Biographies* who had the mammoth task thrust upon them of proof-reading and picture-scanning, which they did with consummate skill. (God, what a way to earn a living!)

There are nearly 100 photographs in the book, the origins of many lost in the mists of antiquity. I know that photos taken by Peter Dyer, Marissa D'Alisandro, John Rifkind, Harold Baruch and Ivan Robin are in there somewhere and I am thankful to them for allowing me to take advantage of their expertise. David Gibbs is another great photographer who has meant a great deal to me as I've known him since he was a young lad. His mother's firm *Lawsons* did our wedding in 1957. He did our daughter Tracy's wedding and I cannot leave him out of my thanks. Others, regrettably, must remain anonymous and unheralded as I have no way of finding out their names. I can only hope they will forgive my publishing without their permission. But a huge number were taken over many years by my dear friend and Brother Water Rat Doug McKenzie who rejoices in the Rats-imposed soubriquet of Paparazzi Rat, which he loves. He gave me unconditional permission to use any I wished and I thank him most sincerely; if it's a show business snap, then it is almost certainly his as he has been at the very pinnacle of his profession for over 40 years.

Of course Ann has been the driving force behind all this effort and has shown supreme patience and fortitude, looking at my back as I pounded away for hour after hour at the computer throwing it together. Also her memory of events is far clearer and more accurate than mine and many of the stories were prompted by her reverse vision. She has been my pal, my guide, my mentor, my lover and my severest critic and, frankly, I couldn't have written the thing without her incalculable support. God bless and keep her – as I can't afford to!

Explanations! My father was an avid reader of *The Autocar* on the back page of which was a small item called *Disconnected Jottings,* little stories and vignettes about bits in the motor industry. I discovered that I had dozens of similar 'cameos' which didn't fit easily into any of the chapters, but felt that they were worthy of recounting. So I hit upon the idea of this disconnected jottings thing which my editor (God Bless Him!) thought were just right. So, at the end of each chapter is an extra little tale not really connected to that particular one. I have called them all D.J.s, which, co-incidentally, relates in three ways: 'Disconnected Jottings,' 'Dinner Jackets' which is the male garb I see most frequently and, of course, 'Disc Jockeys' who handle the music at many functions I now attend. Hope you enjoy reading them.

Rat Barry Cryer is another who is deserving of my warmest blessings for his superb foreword. He is such a fantastic and very funny wordsmith and I was honoured when he agreed to do it. Thanks Barry.

Rat Peter Goodwright's poem was written as a tribute to me for a special luncheon given by the Grand Order of Water Rats at the Savoy. He was kind enough to allow me to reproduce it here; thank you Peter.

My daughter Tracy-Jane Faulkner has also been a tower of strength. I had tried to keep the book a secret from everyone, but like all secrets, it leaked out and she agreed to proofread it with her legal-proofreader's hat on. I thought she'd tear it to pieces; she didn't but expunged hundreds of useless commas and 'ands' to make the thing much more readable. Thanks darling, you did a great job.

It is my fervent wish that I have not missed out any important people. The book has been a labour of love and fun to do. I am fortunate that I can type very quickly indeed and can literally think through my fingers on to the keys, which has made the task simple.

I hope you enjoy reading it as much as I enjoyed writing it – well most of it. Mind you, I like the bits that Ann and Mike chucked out that they won't let you see. So be warned... the seeds of volume two can be scavenged from the waste paper basket!

Chapter 1

In the Beginning...

"The moving finger writes; and, having writ, moves on..."

The Rubáiyát of Omar Khayyám
Edward Fitzgerald

On Thursday 20th August 1933 a number of highly inconsequential and singularly trivial events took place. In India, Gandhi was rushed into hospital on the fourth day of his fast; in Italy, Benito Mussolini met Austrian Chancellor Dollfuss at Rimini; in Berlin, an American surgeon was attacked for failing to salute Hitler. As I say, a whole load of totally unimportant and forgettable events occurred. Equally unheralded and unremarked, a mewling, puking infant umbilically attached to a recumbent mother, made a squalling entry into this cruel world in the North Middlesex Hospital, Edmonton. With the first of many slapped bottoms I eventually received, the nurse proclaimed that I had joined the human race at 9.15 am. Astrologically speaking, another Leo, sharing birthdays with Count Basie, Kenny Rogers, Orville Wright, Coco Chanel, Bill Clinton and John Travolta – albeit in different years – and Yoko Ono, born on the same day.

Proud parents, Ivy (née Heffer) Williams aged 23, and Hugh James Owen Williams aged 33, named this infant Brian – God alone knows why. It was intended to be either Trefor or Tudor, two good strong Welsh names, but with a cockney mum and a Welsh dad, why did they choose an Irish name? When the birth was registered, for some reason Brian and Owen were given. So I became 'B. O.' Williams, although, strangely, the reference and analogy to personal hygiene did not seem to be so important in those far-off days. Thus began, 'The Life of Brian'.

Confusion surrounds my father's name. The family surname was Owen and I can trace my lineage back to a certain Matthew Owen of Cwm Mawr near Betws-y-Coed in North Wales. Dad's father married and had several children, but then his wife had to be admitted to an asylum. He went on to have more children by another lady, my grandmother, but they were not allowed to marry in view of the fact that my grandfather was still legally married. Dad was the twelfth of these thirteen half-sisters and brothers. My grandfather could not write, and when he went to register my father's birth, instead of 'Hugh James William Owen', it was recorded as 'Hugh James Owen Williams' – no doubt something to do with the fact that my grandmother's surname was Williams. To compound the error, the registrar wrote 'father unknown' as he could not reconcile the names of 'Williams' and 'Owen' relating to father and son. Consequently, to all intents and purposes, my lovely dad was a bastard! When he became a professional singer, he chose to be known as Hugh Owens, although his family and English mates in his day job, necessary to pay the bills, called him Jim Williams... all except for Mum who called him 'Jim Duck'!

My father was a singer of no small ability, winning a scholarship to the Royal Academy of Music, from which he emerged with an LRAM. As a result of having Gilbert and Sullivan rammed down his throat there, he developed a hatred of operetta, which extended to opera. His favourite songs were Victorian and Edwardian ballads at which he excelled. Dad refused many offers to go on tour with operatic companies, and, as this limited his income, he found work as a tanker driver, which fitted in with his private singing engagements in the evenings. On one of his deliveries he had to report to a lady in the office, a certain 18-year-old Ivy Heffer. They married in 1928 in a double wedding with my mum's elder sister, Lillian, and her husband Bernard – they were a poor family and it saved money! During the 1930s my father managed to get a job 'On the Buses' which fitted in well with his evening singing work, the hours being flexible.

I am mindful of an incident that occurred around that time in my mother's family. Her parents, George and Florence Heffer, had seven children, Charlie, the eldest, dying in infancy. The others became, and remained until their dying days, close knit and loving. Grandpa was a soldier in the Great War, and one summer's day a Salvation Army officer put an envelope through their letterbox hoping for a donation. When he came to collect it, Nanna said that with six mouths to feed and her husband away, she had no money and so, sadly, returned it empty. On Christmas Eve, a large car pulled up at their front door and out stepped two Sally Army officers bearing the biggest hamper of Christmas fare you have ever seen. They simply said to Nanna, "We send you and your family God's blessing and hope you have a wonderful Christmas," and with that they left. My grandmother was speechless and so deeply grateful. That story moved me so much that I have made it my duty never to pass a Salvation Army collection box without making a donation - they ask no questions, they just deliver!

Within three months of my appearance into this world, my whole body became covered with infantile dry eczema, and I also had to put up with the attendant asthma as they are part of the same family. To complicate matters further, I also suffered from hay fever for which I ultimately needed medication. All this caused me no end of problems throughout my school life where I became known as 'the boy with old-man's hands' – not too pleasant for a youngster. The asthma was also a nuisance, as whenever I got excited about anything at all I would become wheezy and croaky and life was miserable. I took the Common Entrance exam to get into Mill Hill School, which I passed, but while my parents could struggle to pay the fees, the medical bills to cover my health would be enormous, so I didn't go to public school.

Hay fever was also a prevalent inconvenience as I was allergic to pollen, house dust and, worst of all, dogs and cats. It is a tribute to medical science back in the 1930s that the doctors, who reassured my parents that things would improve when I got to seven years old, were perfectly correct as I can clearly trace the improvement in my health every seven years until I was 28, by which time I was totally cleared of those allergies. It resulted in some of the happiest days imaginable when we discovered that we could own dogs, which we did for over thirty years.

We lived with my grandparents in a small house in White Hart Lane, Wood Green, but in 1939 my parents decided that we needed to move. Whilst looking in an estate agent's window one day, I chanced to glance up and saw a 'To Let' sign on the top floor of a block of flats. My parents contacted the agent, which resulted in us moving into No. 6, Gladstone House, Wood Green, London, N22. This was perfect as it was near the tube station and *Woolworth's* – two vital prerequisites for my mother! Who could ask for more?

It is to my great horror and dismay that my parents – and after Dad died, my mother alone – paid rent for that blasted place until I bought her a retirement flat in 1990. The financial imposition of paying rent for over fifty years still rankles with me, but the word 'mortgage' was one which terrified them as it implied 'debt' and regular repayments. This stemmed from a time earlier in their married life when they had tried to buy a *Rover* car on the 'never-never'. They had one final payment of £3 to make, which they could not raise, and such was the parlous state of the rest of the family's finances that no one could help. The car was reclaimed and they lost all previous payments. They swore it would never happen again, so the thought of a mortgage to buy a house was never even discussed.

In August 1939 we went on a rare holiday to *Butlins* in Skegness, returning home on 1st September with Dad looking forward to a full season of singing engagements. Sadly, that was not to be. On 3rd September 1939, Britain declared war on Germany. Hitler had raised his ugly head and everything stopped – yes, as abruptly as that. An immediate Government decree went out that all social events and gatherings of more than four people were illegal – my father's full diary had to be torn up. Nothing, zilch, empty – no income from that source whatsoever. It was a devastating blow for my parents.

To quote those immortal lines of Rob Wilton, "The day war broke out…" two of my uncles, who had already joined up, said to my grandma, "Right, Mum, we're at war now and Jerry's on his way over, so you're all going into the country – quick!" And that was that! Thus, at the ripe old age of six, and within a few days of war being declared, I found myself on a Welsh farm in Machynlleth, West Wales, with a reluctant grandma, a brace of aunts and a sprinkling of cousins.

My Welsh father had some influence on the destination and a kindly but suspicious Welsh farming community suddenly had a bunch of Cockneys dumped on them. It proved to be a mutually uncomfortable arrangement – they really didn't want us and no way did we want to be there. Three unhappy months later (having spent a term in a Welsh village school and not understanding a word), Jerry had not come over and the phoney war was proving peaceful. Nanna had had enough. In her feisty Cockney tones she told the world, "I'm London born and bred, an' no Jerry wotsit's gonna keep me out of me own bed!" And so we reversed the pilgrimage back to London. A few weeks later, London had its first air raid and the Blitz began. Wood Green was our part of London; we'd had our little taste of 'evacuation' and wanted no more of it, so we remained to take all the Hun could offer.

Mum, Dad and I braved the war years in our top-floor flat and throughout the entire war none of us ever went down an air-raid shelter. At that time, many of my family were dabbling in Christian Science and, with the arrogance of beginners, believed unquestioningly that 'We were God's Perfect Children' and therefore would be protected! Arrogant we may have been, but we regularly thanked God. It is either tremendous coincidence or Divine Intervention that not one single member of our large family was hurt or injured during hostilities. The worst we suffered was the odd broken window.

The siren announcing an air raid was a very loud wailing up-and-down sound emitted from a machine turned by a handle. This would continue for several minutes and it was not long before the cockneys christened these contraptions 'Moaning Minnies'. The 'all-clear' was one long straight wail, informing everyone that it was safe and that the bombers had gone away. The peeling of church bells throughout the war years was prohibited – they were only to be used to warn of invasion, so their silence was a blessing.

During the Blitz, Hitler sent over every available heavy bomber to drop thousands of tons of high explosives on London and other major cities. Night after night, for weeks on end, they droned over and chucked down everything they had. Herr Schickelgrüber's intention was to frighten the people of London into submission and get the Prime Minister, Winston Churchill, to surrender. Hitler totally misunderstood the guts and tenacity of the London cockney and the British public. We simply refused to bow down.

In order to thwart the efforts of the German Luftwaffe, London had to be totally dark at night, and I do mean totally. Houses and flats were supplied with blackout material for the windows and it was a legal requirement to comply. Air Raid Wardens walked the streets every night and if there was the slightest, teenciest, weenciest chink of light coming from the edge of the window, they would shout, "Oy! Put that ruddy light out!" or they would bang on the door and say to the lady, "Hey Missus, there's lights showin' from your window. Don't you know there's a war on?" Some of these wardens were absolute horrors, but they were only doing their job, and an important one it was too… even if they were somewhat on the officious side. Bill Pertwee's portrayal of a warden in *Dad's Army* was perfect. I little knew then that he and I and the writer Jimmy Perry would later become friends and members of the same order.

Petrol was strictly rationed as it was needed for 'the war effort' – an expression used when anything was taken away from us and given to the Government. However, someone ingeniously invented a gas-powered car. These were easily recognisable as on the roof was a huge gas bag which, when full, was like a small barrage balloon. They worked, although they were very slow. You may remember that episode in *Dad's Army* when 'Jonesy's' butcher's van had one – hilarious.

Dad was too old to be called up and working on the buses was a reserved occupation. The London Passenger Transport Board was a male-dominated organisation and the thought of 'women' on the buses was inconceivable. However, necessity meant that jobs which had hitherto been the sole preserve of men suddenly required the female touch and women soon found themselves in strange occupations. My mother applied and was accepted as one of the first 'Clippies' – the name given to bus conductresses who were required to clip, or punch, a little hole in the passenger's ticket with their 'pinger'. She was taught the bus routes out of Wood Green and Tottenham garages and started a career which she followed for many years.

There were various daily schedules: early-turn, late-turn, spread-over (four hours in the morning and four in the evening), and even 'all-nighters'! As I had to be looked after, my parents alternated their shift patterns and as a result rarely saw each other… which may explain why I was an only child! Becoming fed up with this separation, they decided that things would be better all round if they could be teamed on the same bus – Dad driving, Mum conducting.

There were two levels of inspector – the Silver Badge and the Gold Badge – who looked after timings and routings, and the general performance of the crews on the road. Many of them were 'right little 'itlers' who threw their weight around. When they became unbearable they became Gold Badges, with even greater powers of punishment and chastisement! Needless to say, they did not engender too much love amongst the crews.

My mother had the audacity to approach one such Gold Badge with the request, "Jim and I are both out of Tottenham; how about us working together?" "Lady," he replied with a laugh, "You ain't got NO chance of that. Go 'ome, Dear, and forget it!" She didn't. Instead, Mum made an appointment to see der Untergruppenführer at the Tottenham garage and put the request to him. "Jim and I want to work together, please. Can you arrange it as we're tired of being on separate shifts?" After almost having an apoplectic fit at the effrontery of her request, the inspector let his fury subside before saying in measured tones, "Mrs Williams, there is no way on God's Earth that we will ever allow husbands and wives to crew together. So just forget you ever asked!" Ever so politely, Mum said, "Thank you, Sir. Now will you please tell me who is above you in this garage, as I wish to speak to him?" The name was given with the rejoinder, "You're wasting your time, lady. They'll never agree to that, not in a million years!"

Their reasoning was not altogether illogical as it was felt that a husband-and-wife team could get up to any number of fiddles, but Mum was not to be thwarted and went to see the der Obergruppenführer with the same request. Her grit, determination and persistence were eventually rewarded as, after four attempts at increasingly higher levels and within six months of going on the buses, my parents became the first ever husband-and-wife crew, remaining together for the duration of the war. Many years later, I was pleased to discover that the newly-formed London Transport Executive (LTE) advertised for husbands and wives to work the same route to ease domestic arrangements!

Mum and Dad worked together throughout the Blitz. Nightly they would travel between North London and the docks, via the City, as, despite Hitler, the bus services continued unbroken. People had to be transported thither and yon, and my parents were there to take them. They returned home with countless stories of air raids, bombsites, buildings collapsing, miles and miles of water pipes across the streets, and of exhausted policemen and firemen crashing out fast asleep as soon as they sat down. But never once, throughout the whole horrendous business, did I hear them complain or become irritable with their toils. 'Jerry' had to be beaten and they were there to do their bit.

Before the war, Dad had always needed a car to get from job to job and he refused to sell his little *Opel 10,* registration number EXF 51, although as petrol was so strictly rationed it was almost unusable. When the war effort became a little easier, the Government needed vehicles and drivers to replace ambulances on non-emergency journeys as the younger men were away at war. They therefore devised a wonderful scheme called 'The Volunteer Car Pool' (or VCP) and, as quick as a flash, Dad volunteered. You simply registered yourself and your car with the local council and agreed to drive whatever or whoever to wherever and whenever in your spare time. Journeys mostly consisted of taking social workers, council officials or other dignitaries to various destinations to enable them to conduct their business. These places were usually obscure and frequently tucked away in the country. For quick identification, Dad was required to place a large white card with the letters 'VCP' on his windscreen – this was an important document as it opened doors and gates to all kinds of official places.

There were many occasions when Dad was called out in the middle of the night on an emergency mission. He really had a great time as he felt he was 'doing his bit' for King and Country. Dad also had to take patients for treatment. I clearly remember one regular Thursday trip where he picked up a nine-year-old lad named Alan who suffered from polio. Dad collected him from his home (in a caravan in a field behind a pub) and drove him to a therapist for treatment. He made this weekly trip for years and was thrilled to see 'Young Alan', as he liked to call him, getting better as he got older. It was a round trip of thirty miles for which Dad's petrol was supplied.

This work was unpaid and totally voluntary, but it had its perks... extra petrol coupons. The authorities agreed what the mileage consumption would be for his vehicle – which was round and bulbous rather like Noddy's little car, only maroon. Each journey was carefully measured and every week he would submit his request for coupons to cover those miles. During the war there was a great trade in black market coupons, but Dad would have none of this and indeed did not need it.

He was a very good driver and developed a clever technique to save precious petrol and preserve his 'gift' of petrol coupons. He would switch off the engine going downhill then coast as far as was possible before starting up again. He would also turn off the engine at traffic lights to nurture his 'Government Issue'! This cautious and astute driving meant that he built up a whole pile of coupons which we could use ourselves. Being Welsh, he was of course eager to get to his mother country to see his family. The average motorist could barely get to the end of their street, let alone Harlech in North Wales, but off we would go, sure in the knowledge that we had enough juice for the return journey. A pop down to Southend to buy a *Rossi* ice cream was also a regular treat.

It is hardly a surprise then, that when I began to drive after the war, this technique of 'saving gas' rubbed off on me, and when my impecunious mates and I went out for a spin, they relied upon my coasting abilities to stretch the petrol as far as possible – petrol was only five bob a gallon in those days (5p a litre!). There were many occasions when, in Dad's very old and very large *Oldsmobile* gas-guzzler, I would switch off the engine outside Alexandra Palace and coast the full three miles down the hill to our flat in Wood Green High Road… that's if the lights favoured me! More recently, in 2002, it became extremely useful in the fuel crisis as I would drive my wife's manual car and coast everywhere. I had no trouble at all in rationing my petrol during those weeks as I copied Dad's VCP talents.

During the Blitz, Jerry chucked everything on London. When the fires were at their height, we, living ten miles away in North London, could see a golden glow in the sky and knew that the East End was 'taking a packet' as the Cockneys would say. Fire engines and firemen were bussed in from all over the country, some from as far away as Devon and Cornwall. There were a number of nights when they actually ran out of water. The River Thames was at its lowest and they often had to wait for the tide to turn before they could continue. But the British spirit remained unabated and no one caved in.

Wood Green was not heavily bombed, but when it was, the bombsites were havens for kids with which no theme park could possibly compete. They were a morbid paradise of freedom, danger, mystery, discovery, excitement and amusement. Crab-apple trees could be 'scrumped' without fear of an angry or violent owner screaming at you to "B****r off, you little s**s!" – and many a gyppy tummy resulted.

Bonfires could be lit with impunity as there was plenty of fodder to feed them. Half-buildings and shattered stairways made perfect 'close-fighting' war grounds, and bits of metal and shrapnel lying around were wonderful pretend guns. We were too young to realise or even care that these had once been family homes, where people had lived, loved and laughed but which had now been destroyed. Indeed, the destruction had been so total that nothing we could do could make them any worse.

The Noel Park Estate in Wood Green was the pride of the 1920s. Long, straight, wide avenues of terraced houses covered vast acreages of beautifully designed and planned housing. Each had a small front garden fringed with iron railings and a gate for privacy. We moved into our flat at the top end of Gladstone Avenue in 1939 and I can only guess at their splendour when they were built. One morning we awoke to find that the entire estate had been stripped of all railings and gates. It was as though some giant magnet had been dangled over the top and drawn them all away. The resultant nakedness was as embarrassing as if one had seen an old friend standing before you in the nude. It then hit us that things were serious, as the Government needed every available bit of metal to melt down for the war effort. We kids discovered another 'toy' in the *Fleur de Lys*-style tops of the railings which had escaped the magnet. They made the perfect pretend pistols to scare our mates.

Towards the end of the war, we had another little bonus when the trams along the High Road were replaced by trolley buses. The metal tram rails were needed for 'the war effort' so up they came. These had been set in tar blocks and we soon learned that they made great fire fodder, not only for our bonfires, but also to heat our houses. We would load our little barrows and tote the blocks from door to door selling them at sixpence a load. This gave us welcome pocket money and cheap heating for cold houses. Sadly, it did not last long as they soon got cleared away.

Our next perk was transporting 'the bundles'! Most of London's tube stations had been converted into shelters, with row upon row of bunk beds being built along the platforms. Families were allocated their own site to which they were entitled to go at any time during an air raid. As the evening sirens wailed their monotonous and frightening wavering drone telling us we were in for another aerial beating from the Hun, from our kitchen window we would watch the mums and their kids trotting to Wood Green tube station – most of the dads were away in the war.

The nightly trek to the tube with nightclothes and bedding was both a nuisance and difficult to manage for the mums, grannies and children, so they wrapped the bedclothes into 'bundles' for easy carriage. Every evening during the Blitz, a group of volunteers, myself among them, would collect these bundles from a local depository where they were stored during the day, wheel them down to the platform and put them by the bunks. Each morning, someone – I never discovered who – would bring them all back again for storage. We earned about sixpence a week for this little job, which was a real service to these families… and another bonus to our pocket money. This ended as abruptly as it had begun. *Garners Depository* was a large furniture store immediately opposite the tube, adjacent to a wood merchant, a miserable sod called Denchfield. The Blitz had ended and the regular nightly air raids with them. However, the odd Jerry plane still came over and one dropped a bunch of incendiary bombs which scored a direct hit on *Garners Depository*. The resultant fire was as spectacular as it was total, taking with it the wood store and the remaining bundles. It was the best and safest bonfire we had ever seen, and the blessing was that no one was hurt and no serious damage ensued. At the time, I did not appreciate what a near miss this had been – our little flat was less than one hundred yards away and so a split second's difference in the dropping of those bombs could have spelt disaster for us.

The war was getting much worse for Hitler and he was clutching at straws for ways to beat us down. His armourers invented two unmanned bombs to send over to drop on London. The V1 or 'doodlebug' was targeted to fly very high, run out of power over London, and simply drop and explode. It made a very loud, harsh, coarse roar and was easily recognised, but as soon as the noise stopped everyone knew that it was about to drop – but not where. Thousands were launched. The radar at the coast was not too advanced and quite a number got through to London, creating havoc and destruction wherever they landed. However, as these were like conventional aircraft, in many instances RAF pilots were able to fly alongside, nudge the wing and deflect them off-course. There is a large map at Rye in Sussex which pinpoints where every one of them landed, and it is thrilling to see that hundreds were caught at the coast and crashed harmlessly into the sea or neighbouring fields.

The V2s were much more lethal. These jet-propelled rockets could not be intercepted and gave no warning. I remember a huge, almighty explosion one afternoon at about three o'clock. I had been squatting on my bedroom floor, reading, but I ended up on my bed – I don't know how. We had a charlady called Mrs Popper and when we looked down the road her house was all dust, smoke and devastation. She rushed to see what had happened – a house two doors away had received a direct hit and there was rubble everywhere.

Mrs Popper was a real cockney character who stayed with my mother until she was too old and frail to work. Her initials were 'E.F.' and I discovered that Evelyn was her first name. I always teased her and one day I asked, "What does the 'F' stand for? Is it Fanny?" To which she testily replied in true cockney fashion, "Fanny? Me bum! My name is Frances!" She couldn't win. Thereafter she was known, especially by me and my pals, as Evelyn Fanny-Me-Bum Popper. In the icy mornings of winter she would come in, make herself a cup of tea and proclaim, "I'm so cold; I feel like a frozen turd!" She was great. She gave two of my friends her own pet names. One, a certain Laurie Boyall, was rather fat and ungainly. He became 'Bulldozer'! In later life he actually became a professional ballroom dancer! The other, Kenny Mehrtens, once said in a pique of anger, "My farver looks after 'undreds of loonies in 'is job." He was forever after known as 'Fortyfahzand lunatics'.

After the V2 exploded, every shop along the High Road lost its windows and was wide open. A policeman called Jim Denyer was soon on the scene and took matters in hand. He controlled the crowds, helped the ambulance service, and personally went into the smoking ruins and carried out several people still alive. He was later awarded a medal for bravery, and was the father of my closest friend Jimmy whom I have known since we were six. Jimmy Junior later also became a policeman.

Shopkeepers had a great sense of humour and when the fronts of their shops were demolished, they would put up a chalk notice on a bit of cardboard reading, 'More open than usual!'

My final and abiding memory is of going onto the roof of our top-floor flat and watching the blaze as the City of London took its nightly pounding. The bright orange and red glow of fires against the dark night sky was both frightening and fascinating. Isn't it strange how one's childhood memories are more vivid than what one did last week! I must be getting old.

Curator Water Rat Jimmy Perry, writer of the immortal *Dad's Army* and other comedies like *Hi-De-Hi* and *You Rang, M'Lord?* has been a great supporter of mine over the years. He is also a member of the left-wing Scriptwriters and Authors Guild who, for many years, presented their own awards at banquets held in London. Political disagreements amongst the membership resulted in these being discontinued, but back in the 1990s, The Guild decided to run them again. The venue chosen was The Dorchester Hotel, Park Lane, and Jimmy, as organiser, chose me and a Water Rat colleague Tommy Draper to be the two toastmasters.

The evening took the form of a champagne reception prior to a four-course dinner, during which I organised a raffle for a chosen charity. After the Loyal Toast, the presentation of a dozen or so awards began and was handled by the Secretary of the Guild. The format was that he would read the names in each category and then invite a celebrity to come to a second lectern, read the four or five nominations, open an envelope and read the winner's name. The award would be presented by that celebrity followed by the winner replying briefly, sometimes very controversially, and then on to the next award. It was a fairly stereotypical awards presentation function.

The banqueting room at The Dorchester was full and, facing the stage, on the opposite side of the room, were TV cameras and spotlights. For no real reason, I walked around the room and casually noticed half a dozen men in black tie and dinner jackets just sitting against a wall but not at any particular table. In fact, I thought they were part of the production crew.

The awards ceremony continued with the Guild Secretary introducing each well-known presenter. To read the citations and announce the winner of the children's book award, he called upon Norman Willis, General Secretary of the TUC, who, to my surprise, proved to be one of the best and funniest after-dinner speakers I have heard – he was great. He read the names of the finalists in the children's book section and ended by saying, "The winner is... Salman Rushdie."

Now, it must be remembered that at this time Salman Rushdie was in hiding and under police protection because of the 'fatwa' placed on his life by Muslim extremists offended by his controversial book, *The Satanic Verses*. Consequently, after gentle applause from the audience, the presenter continued, "Regrettably, as we are all aware, because of political difficulties, Mr Rushdie is unable to be here tonight to collect his award. It will be collected by his agent..." – at which precise moment the six men I had noticed, looking like clones, rose from their chairs and walked across the ballroom floor. It was only then that everyone realised who one of them was... Yes, it was Salman Rushdie! I genuinely cannot remember any moment in my career which was so indescribably melodramatic. The reaction of that audience was quite astounding. It was one of total and complete astonishment and incomprehension. They rose as one, applauded, cried, cheered but were totally bewildered as precisely what to do.

Salman Rushdie went to the lectern whilst the five 'guards' flanked him. He took a sheet of paper from his pocket and read a prepared speech, touching briefly on the fatwa and how his life had been affected. They hung on his every word, but more in awe and amazement than anything else. The effect upon the whole room was cataclysmic astonishment that someone, somewhere, somehow had managed to locate him and persuade his protectors to allow him to come to that ballroom for that occasion.

At the end of his brief speech, he stepped down from the stage, was immediately surrounded by his bodyguards and marched swiftly across the floor and out through a kitchen exit and away. The guests went wild. Tears were streaming down the faces of many; some were laughing; others, who disapproved, were trying to hide their disgust – it was a total miasma of emotions which engulfed the room. For several minutes there was pandemonium at what had just occurred. But what slowly dawned upon them was that, as they had 'welcomed' him back into their midst in such a public way, all of them became subject to the same Muslim fatwa which was then vested upon all members of that Guild!

When something of such enormity happens in a function, whatever follows has to be an anti-climax. When everyone settled down, we all wondered who would be next and how would he react. The Secretary, having regained his composure, and Tommy and I having silenced the audience for the next award, he said, "And now to introduce the next award, will you please welcome John Cleese." It was he who had the unbelievably difficult task of bringing the event back to normal and we all wondered what he would say. We were not disappointed. He reached the lectern and said, with total composure and perfect timing, "…Thank God for that. I thought I was going to have to follow Dennis Norden!" He had had no longer than the length of his introduction and a short walk to the lectern to dream up what he was going to say, but it had the desired effect of bringing a bolt of humour back into the proceedings and the crowd roared their approval.

Several years later I introduced John Cleese to the late and much-loved and lamented Roy Castle whom, strangely, he had never met. I told Roy of that unforgettable moment and John related the story in greater detail. He also said that he had dined out on that one line for years. One-liners of that quality come so very rarely.

The sequel to Salman Rushdie making an appearance at the event rumbled on for weeks. Jimmy Perry told me that there was only one person in the whole organisation who knew it was going to happen, the Secretary of the Guild himself. He had kept it a total secret, only to be revealed at the time and with such dramatic success. The owner of The Dorchester, the Sultan of Brunei, himself a practising Christian, was absolutely furious when he heard. His anger, so I am told, was frightening. He ordered a thorough investigation of the senior management and security staff of his hotel and demanded to know why they had not been briefed, why no one had sought their and his permission to allow Rushdie in, and why they had not taken steps to prevent it. Salman Rushdie now has much greater liberty, but the secret remains as to how the Secretary managed to get him to come to collect his award.

Chapter 2

Early Education

"Schooldays are the happiest days...
the happiest days of your life."

Water Rat Cardew Robinson

I cannot remember precisely when I became aware of 'Show Business', but when I was very young I listened avidly to the wireless in my bedroom in our small Wood Green flat. It was either a case of the 'Light' or the 'Home Service' – I always tuned into the former because that's where I heard such wonders as *Happidrome*, *Monday Night at Eight* and the big band sounds of Bert Ambrose and Henry Hall. Personalities of the calibre of Derek Roy and Ted Ray ensured little chance of sleep until Mum threatened to pull the plug on me.

When I was not listening to the wireless, I was usually to be found engrossed in such highbrow literature as *Beano* and *Dandy*, along with *Film Fun* and *Radio Fun* where I could read about such famous names as Jewel and Warris, Petula Clark, Joe E Brown, 'Big Hearted' Arthur Askey (born, incidentally, on the same day as my father, 6th June 1900) and so many more. I loved them and could identify with them, but there was no way in my wildest dreams that I would ever come to know any of them, meet them, or possibly even see any of them on stage. The thought of working with them was a million miles away... but what did I know?

Dad's dearest ambition was for me to become his accompanist on the concert platform so, at a very early age, piano lessons were foisted upon me. I flogged myself silly at all my exams with the Royal Academy, eventually achieving a respectable Grade VII. I was adequate, not brilliant, but Dad did not mind. As long as I could accompany him whilst he sang his favourite Victorian and Edwardian ballads, he was a happy man. He simply loved singing, and memories of those precious hours together – father, son and piano – will live with me forever.

By this time my parents had left the buses. Dad took the huge risk of setting out on his own as a singer, while Mum worked over the road at the QS Restaurant where she met a whole variety of people. She had the knack of picking up 'lame duck' acquaintances at work, some of whom she would bring back to our flat. One I remember was a bloke called Fred Rocker, a right weirdo as I recall. I was learning to play the piano and he was a pianist particularly fond of Chopin – or 'Showpang' as they rather quaintly pronounced it. He would occasionally pop across to the flat just to play and talk music. It was all pretty odd really, when you come to think of it.

I vividly recall one character around Wood Green known by my chums and me as 'Dirty Ben', but Ben Wilson was treated more as a joke than anything serious. I doubt that he was aware of our nickname for him and we just kept him at arm's length. Occasionally one of the lads would turn up with a new pair of roller skates or a football, a 'gift' from Dirty Ben and we never really asked why! I was totally naïve in those days, but not stupid, and one afternoon he invited me to the *Gaumont* cinema to see the current flick. Nothing happened, but I began to feel uncomfortable and made an excuse to go to the loo. When I thought he wasn't looking, I tore out of the cinema and ran home. As our flat was opposite I didn't have far to run, but run I did. I often wonder what could have happened, but am pleased that I never found out. I saw him a few days later and in my usual courteous manner called him by what automatically came to me as his 'Christian' name. I said, "Oh, hello, dirty… er… Ben." He didn't comment.

Coincidentally, during the 1990s, I heard a brief news item on the car radio: "The Home Secretary has today refused parole for 84-year old Mr Benjamin Wilson, serving a thirty-year sentence for child molestation." I scoured all the papers to see if it was my 'Dirty Ben', but to no avail. If it was him, he must have died in prison as he was about twenty years older than me.

With much practice, I became fairly proficient on the keyboard and, at the grand old age of 14, my big day arrived. Dad decreed that I was good enough to go to a Masonic meeting to play for him. The *Master's Song* was, and still is, sung at many Lodge Installations and is quite easy to play but is ghastly and we both loathed it. However, if he wanted to earn a living, Dad had to sing the damned thing! This was my 'taster' into the magical world of entertainment and I was smitten. My mutilation of the keyboard must have gone largely unnoticed, as I was soon accompanying Dad at other Masonic meetings and Ladies' Festivals. My career in entertainment had begun!

Actually, I had dabbled in an amateur way before that. Every Saturday morning, the *Gaumont* cinema opened its doors to all the local kids. As it was only a penny or two, even *we* could afford to go in by the proper way… although it may also have had something to do with the fact that an usherette was always posted by the fire escape to thwart any other ideas we may have had! At the Saturday Morning Gaumont British Club, there were always a load of cartoons, the inevitable Cowboys and Indians, a main feature adventure film and other bits and pieces. As if this were not value enough, we were also treated to a 15-minute live show, courtesy of *The Dennis Scott Juveniles,* a troupe of youngsters who sang and danced between the two films. I just had to be part of that and went backstage to see the great man himself.

I knew that I could just about hold a tune and also hammer out something vaguely recognisable on the piano but it was my burning desire to 'perform' that I remember most. Unlike my contemporaries, I was not scared at the prospect of talking to a cinema full of noisy, ill-mannered kids. I don't know why, I just wanted to be there. I made a few announcements and I also clearly remember singing a duet with an equally untalented but quite pretty little 12-year-old girl. The song was called *Chewing a Piece of Straw* and for the reprise we had to sing whilst 'eating' a piece of string.

With my co-star at one end of the string and me at the other, we sang and ate until, gradually, our mouths were so close that we kissed! At the tender age of 12 I was in heaven... and performing in front of 500 raucous kids wasn't bad either, especially when they went wild at seeing 'live sex' on stage!

It would be wrong to say that we were poor, but money was tight and we had to be careful about our spending. My parents had a strong belief in good-quality education and struggled selflessly to get me to the best schools. I actually went to twelve, starting with Miss Hawes who ran a small primary school in Gladstone Avenue on the Noel Park Estate.

Education during and immediately after the war was ad hoc, with something of a ragbag of teachers. Many had been brought out of retirement and others came from the second division and were not totally up to the job. In the hope of improving my health and because of school closures, I moved around a lot during my early school years. Despite this upheaval, I consider Southgate County Grammar as my *Alma Mater*. It offered me a wonderful education, which I was both too lazy and too dumb to accept, remaining in the 'C' stream for four years. At the end of the year, when I was 15, my wonderful headmaster, Mr (Willie) Auger sent for my parents. He was a lovely man but almost totally crippled with arthritis and would take forever to mount the stairs to the stage for morning prayers, which he insisted upon taking. Everybody loved and respected him.

My parents and Mr Auger decided that I should leave Southgate County and seek education elsewhere. His parting words to my parents, which have remained with me ever since, were, "Don't worry, Mr and Mrs Williams. Brian (Lord, how I hated that name) will be a late developer." I'm still waiting.

Bob Griffiths, a radical Welsh schoolteacher with a wonderful sense of humour, was a lifelong friend of my parents. He knew them both before they were married and I remain convinced that he fancied my mother; I am equally convinced that she was so naïve that she never really knew! As recently as the year 2000, I took her to South Wales to see him when I was working there and even then he pestered her to visit again. He had a soft spot for her but she just accepted him as a likeable fool.

When I left Southgate County, I needed a job and Bob introduced me to a Mr Sidney Bafico who ran *The Victor Printing Company* in York Way, Kings Cross – it was based in the old York Way tube station, a listed building which is still there. At the time, the premises housed a wide variety of printing departments and after an interview I was accepted on a three-month trial. I loved every minute of it and thought that the world of printing was magic – it was productive, creative, varied and fascinating, and I felt that I could easily adapt to it. Sadly, I did not reckon with my health. The infantile dry eczema, which had plagued me well into my teens, now only affected my hands and ankles. I also still suffered from asthma, but much less seriously. Within the first week of working on the printing machines with paper-dust, oil, printing ink, lead from the compositors and the regular journey on the tube six days a week, my health began to deteriorate. After ten weeks, the doctor advised that I either give up printing or give up health! There was only one choice, and printing and I sadly parted company. I had loved it, but it was not to be. What to do next?

It was apparent that my future lay in the world of entertainment but as I appeared to have no obvious talent, we were at a loss as to where best to channel what little there was. Italia Conti was one of several stage schools around London and we called to make an appointment to see the then Principal, Miss Ruth Conti. This was in a building in Archer Street, Soho – the land of the ladies of horizontal entertainment (…who frequently invited me in) – and right next-door to Charlie Chester's Gaming and Night Club. I was to learn later that he was not proud of that association, to which he had only really lent his name; he eventually managed to pull out of all involvement.

Ruth Conti was the niece of the famed Italia and was now running the school. She was about five-foot nowt in her stocking soles and I was led to believe that she had been a drill sergeant in the Women's Royal Armoured Corps during the war. She was a right martinet - later in life, I often referred to her as the only woman in the British Army who had enemies on both sides. She was a real tartar but, boy oh boy, could she teach acting! This diminutive fireball would stand at one end of the long rehearsal room, as we puny would be Laurence Oliviers were destroying the immortal Bard's Othello, and holler: "For God's sake, speak up, boy! They've got to hear you at the back of the gods, y'know!" And speak up we did; she terrified us, but it worked.

I was there at the same time as the renowned Anthony Newley. He came from a particularly poor family, but his talent was recognised and he was offered a scholarship – this trust paid off, as he became an international star. Frequently we would all be sent to theatres to audition for parts in forthcoming shows. Guess who always had an offer! Anthony Newley was so charismatic that the rest of us stood no chance. I was once offered a part at the Theatre Royal, Drury Lane, in Mozart's *Magic Flute*, but when they discovered my age, I was told that I was too young for a regular slot at 15. Sad really. Who knows… I may well have been another John Gielgud! Ha! pigs might fly!

So, when I was given the opportunity to attend the Italia Conti Stage School, I jumped at the chance. I only went on Saturday mornings for a couple of years, but I loved every minute of it. Thanks to the hollering and machinations of the awe inspiring Ruth Conti, I was taught the absolute importance of projecting my voice using the diaphragm, a technique that stood me in good stead the first time I worked in the Great Room of The Grosvenor House: a dinner for 1,500 men. I banged my gavel on a small table supporting the sensitive microphone. The coil inside broke and it instantly went dead. I HAD to be heard and Ruth Conti's yellings came home to me in a big way.

I couldn't have been too bad as a student at the stage school because I was offered a kind of scholarship to become a dayboy. Again, my dream was short-lived, because Mum wanted me to have a commercial education, so Pitman's College, Palmers Green, became my home for the next 14 months. I enjoyed it enormously and took to the shorthand and typing like the proverbial duck to water. I received a good commercial education, achieving the commendable speeds of 140 wpm at shorthand, and 40 wpm 'accurate' (that's important!) in typing.

I vividly remember the fellow who taught the rudiments of shorthand. His name was Ted Goody and he was great, starting us off with the usual P.B.T.D.CHAY.JAY.K.GAY.F.V.ESS.ZEE. ISH.JEE.M.N.ING – the first basic outlines of shorthand. That lot won't mean anything to anyone who has not studied Pitman's Shorthand; anyone who has will know what it's all about. He also taught us that in the English language there are only five words ending in 'stitute' and he gave us a sentence to demonstrate it. "She constitutes a substitute for a destitute prostitute in an institute," a useless piece of trivia which I have never forgotten.

At Pitman's there were about 15 blokes amongst about 120 pretty, nubile, young women and being the born organiser my wife insists that I am, I managed to run a football team in the winter and in the summer both a cricket and netball team. We persuaded some of the more interested (attractive) girls to get a team together and we had loads of fun – both on the court and off! They were halcyon days.

I owe a tremendous amount to both Italia Conti's and Mr Pitman's genius, as throughout my life I have benefited from their guidance but, of course, for different reasons. I was quite proficient in the world of commercial practice and have remained a competent typist, having the ability to 'think through my fingers'. When reading this tripe, you may beg to differ.

Dad had a very brief career in films, which he hated. It was, however, fairly well-paid work and he was in a number of Government Information documentaries. He also had a colourful part in a period picture called *The Leading Lady* with Valerie Hobson.

Dad's character was a bewigged Major Domo with a long staff and he had to announce people into a glamorous banquet. The reason Dad hated filming was because of the very long hours of inactivity, sitting around drinking gallons of lousy coffee, reading newspapers and just waiting to be called.

Coincidentally, I met Valerie Hobson and her husband John Profumo at a dinner some weeks later and mentioned Dad's part in it. I vividly recall that Mr Profumo asked me to purchase a packet of *Gauloise* cigarettes for him as he smoked nothing else. They were the gentlest and most charming of couples with no apparent troubles in the world! The following morning the storm broke and everyone woke to the headlines blazing across every paper about his 'doings' with Christine Keeler and Mandy Rice-Davies. It was the sad and sorry end to a great political career of a delightful gentleman.

There are two utterly stupid stories about Dad's brief film career. Dad never smoked and was clean-shaven but was booked to play the part, in a Ministry of Information film, of a man with a moustache driving a car whilst lighting a cigarette – the car crashes into a tree and he is killed. For that, he was sent away for two weeks, just to grow the moustache – not only that, but he was a lifelong non-smoker. We just could not fathom out why they couldn't engage another driver who did have a moustache and who smoked!

Dad's agent was a chap called Ronnie Curtis, who was a 'fixer' for walk-on film extras, and as Dad had speaking parts he earned a bit more money. Ronnie was casting extras for a film and needed hundreds of them, so arranged an audition at a London theatre. "Right," he called out, "I need twenty policemen – you lot over there, you look like policemen, go and sign in. I need thirty nurses. You girls will do – go and sign in as well. I need a dozen firemen. You men there – yes, you'll be OK… give 'em your names. Now I need about forty passers-by," and he picked out a bunch of men and women as passers-by. At the end he said, "Thanks everyone, you can all go now." But still standing in the corner of the stage was one solitary man who had not been called. He shouted, "But

42

Ronnie, what about me? Can't I be a passer-by?" Ronnie came out with the classic line, "You don't look like a passer-by!"

My only reason for recounting this about my father was that I too ventured, very briefly, into the film world. Yes, my voice can still be heard on the silver screen. An agent called me and asked me to go to Pinewood Studios in Iver, Bucks. They needed a toastmaster to do a voice-over. Arriving at the prearranged time, I sought out the producer and was directed to a small cinema. As I went in, I noticed that they were screening a film and were dubbing the voice of one of the stars. It was then that I spotted Telly Savalas sitting with a script before him. I was introduced and everyone was very charming.

The star of the film was getting married at a big open-air ceremony and they needed me to announce the newly-weds over the hubbub of chatter and clinking glasses. The producer and I went to the plot where I was asked to holler the following phrase, "My Lords, Ladies and Gentlemen, the toast is, the bride and bridegroom... Mr and Mrs James Bond!" Yes, I had a speaking part in a James Bond film; it was called *On Her Majesty's Secret Service*. Every time I see that film, which is very rare as I don't like Bond films, I listen for my stentorian tones almost at the end of the picture... after which, the bride gets killed by Mr Savalas!

I learned an interesting secret about making films as I sat for some time in that little cinema watching them work. They went over and over the same section many times and Telly Savalas spoke words, almost 'in sync' to his lip movements on the screen, but they kept changing the words to get greater impact. So next time you see any film, watch very carefully to see if the actor is actually saying what his lips would seem to be saying; it certainly wasn't so in that Bond epic.

Chapter 3

Agar's Plough

"The Battle of Waterloo was won on the playing fields of Eton."

Arthur Wellesley, Duke of Wellington

In 1945, the war ended and singing engagements began to return, but at 45 my father's best years for stardom as a singer had passed. Nevertheless, his diary filled as he became in great demand for a new type of work hitting the country, especially London – the profession of toastmaster. Men were returning from the war complete with demob suit and gratuity and wanted to celebrate their newly-won freedom with every means at their disposal. Many of them became 'joiners'; they joined Freemasonry, Rotary, Round Table, The Royal and Antediluvian Order of Buffaloes, the Catenian Societies and any organisation that would admit them, all of which had celebratory dinners, dances and parties – resulting in work flooding in. Indeed, I was a member of Rotary, Round Table and Freemasonry, becoming Master of Waldeck Lodge, No. 1969, at the tender age of 31.

Despite the lingering wartime rationing of a few things like bread and sweets, the time had come to live life to the full – and that's when Dad's, and eventually my, career began to take off. The red tailcoat became our uniform, and we started each function at sunset.

Night after night Mum and I would wait up till Dad came home, usually on the last tube from town getting to Wood Green at five to one. One night Dad said, "You know, I really feel tired tonight.

They were a tough crowd." I jokingly quipped, "I dunno why you should feel tired, all you do is go out every night and have a good time. What's tiring about that?" His equally mild riposte was, "Well, if that's what you think I do, why don't you try it?" My rude reply was, "If you can, I'm damned sure I can!" What do they say about little acorns and great oak trees? The seed was sewn resulting in nightly chats about my future and could I ever conceive of doing work traditionally the realm of much older, mature men. I have often challenged friendly enquirers to see if they know of any 16-year-old they would send out to run a banquet. Not many do, but such seemed to be my destiny. But what about a name for myself; what would be a smart, professional, easily remembered name that would set the banqueting world alight? This was an important point.

During these seemingly endless nightly dissertations about my future, that subject was always at the top of the agenda. It was agreed that Brian Williams was a nothing kind of a name. 'Tudor' and 'Trevor', names planned whilst in my mother's womb, somehow got lost but were resuscitated for discussion and again dropped. We studied names of other toastmasters, among them Arthur Whitehead and Dennis Redhead. We had a load of laughs, especially when it was suggested that I be called Brian Blackhead... which I had in abundance!

Although a staunch supporter of the Spurs, at that time Arsenal had a brilliant inside forward named Bryn Jones. To please Dad I decided to keep the Welsh influence and felt that Bryn was more professional and memorable, and thus it was chosen. I feel that time has justified this although 56 years later some of my cousins still have difficulty with it and often lapse into the old name.

It was not long before the first opportunity knocked on the door – or, to be more accurate, the telephone rang and the Perforated Paper Company briefly entered my life. Firstly, however, another problem had to be addressed – the matter of costume and uniform. Red tailcoats have been synonymous with toastmasters since the 19th century, complete with full evening dress: white tie, stiff-fronted Marcella shirts, very stiff wing collars, white, equally stiff vests or waistcoats, evening dress trousers (double braided) and patent leather shoes, all of it topped off with pristine white gloves. As my Jewish friends would say, "The complete Megillah."

In those days Dad tipped the scales at a very portly 17 stones; I was a mere stripling of ten (my rather cruel family nickname during the war was Belsen Boy). So the thought of borrowing his garb was too ludicrous to contemplate. The only items I could filch from Dad were studs, shirt-front buttons and cufflinks. If I was to do any work at all I needed to be completely kitted out. Cost was a problem as we were 'borassic'. God Bless *Moss Bros* – not only did they have a hire department, but also a very good second-hand section and one misty, moisty morning found me in Covent Garden sifting through piles of 'once worn' – a euphemism for thin and threadbare – clothes of all kinds. Trousers, shirts, collars, bow ties, dress vests, all available and very cheap. The hire department had a plethora of ex-hunting pink and, yes, Royal Golf Club Past Captains' red tailcoats from mini to massive; all I needed to do was to try them on and pick one. Rental charge was three guineas (£3.15p), and so a few quid poorer but fully, if very ill equipped, I launched myself on the stiff, starchy, smart, severe and sinister world of banqueting. I certainly did not feel as confident as I looked, but what the hell, I had to do something with my life.

I did learn one trick which has stayed with me all my working life. I have always tied my own bow ties. I cannot stand the pre-tied ones that most of my colleagues use. Mine are individually tied and in my view look a great deal smarter than others. In fact, when I have to wear pre-tied black bow ties I find them almost impossible to hook up.

Wednesday, 15th March 1950 is engraved on my heart as the fateful day when I entered the Lyons Corner House, Coventry Street, Leicester Square to 'do' the Perforated Paper Company Dance – who can forget disasters that easily? I was just sixteen years and seven months old and must have had a giant-sized ego to think that I could do the job. Even the longest treks have to begin with one short step and I took mine that day.

The Perforated Paper Company produced paper products of every kind, especially toilet rolls! I used to delight in getting cheap laughs when talking to Ladies' Luncheon Clubs, telling them that I literally 'started at the bottom!' Dressed in a tailcoat with a gaudy gold-tasselled badge on my lapel proclaiming 'M.C.', I began my work after the dinner had ended. Nobody knew me or why I was there, and the band had won every *Melody Maker Dance Band Contest* for years and simply did not want to know me. I struggled through the evening with ever disheartening results, until 1.00 am when it was all over. Getting changed in the men's cloakroom a nice, kind-looking gentleman came over to me, pinned me against the wall, looked me straight in the eye and said, "Son, I've got some advice for you. Go home and pack it up. You're bloody useless!" I went home and cried.

Dad followed the old adage of what to do when you fall off your bike – get straight back on. Job number two soon came down the wire. A famous toastmaster named Harold Dean, unquestionably the doyen of the business in those days, needed a toastmaster. Dad already had an engagement, but he advised that I was available. Mr Dean said that if I had been trained by Dad, I had to be good. Oh dear. How little he knew.

> The venue – the RAC Club, Pall Mall.
> The job – a simple cocktail party with a couple of speeches.
> The time – 6.00 pm until 8.00 pm.
> The client – the RAC Club.
> The fee – three guineas.

Possibly the easiest job there is and absolutely impossible to screw it up! Well, they hadn't bargained for a teenage, wet behind the ears, beginner. Oh yeah, at the reception bit I introduced a couple of hundred names OK, but then I had to announce two speakers: the Rt Hon Michael Stewart MP and one other whom I forget. The devil was around that night and was playful. The Rt Hon Michael Stewart, Member of Parliament, suddenly became the Honourable Sir Michael Strutt. Gawd knows why. Well, actually I do know. I had been reading a golf book; that man had just won a big amateur tournament and his name was locked into my dizzy thoughts.

There was I covered in shame, embarrassment and in total disarray, and they were not amused. Two days later a letter arrived withholding my three-guinea fee – the precise sum I had spent on renting the outfit. It was ten years before the great Mr H. Dean entrusted me with another job!

Job number three was a Masonic Ladies Festival, the first of many thousands to follow during the years. The preamble, "Ladies, Gentlemen and Brethren" became so regular and commonplace that it frequently slipped out at non-Masonic events. Restaurant Frascati was in Oxford Street. Alas it no longer exists and like so many others has sunk under the weighty demolition crushers of the property developers' greedy demands. Wonderfully traditional establishments steeped in history, elegance and quality have vanished. The Trocadero, venue for many Wallis Simpson/Edward VIII *soirees*; the Café Monaco in Piccadilly; the Holborn Restaurant with 19 banqueting suites; all the Lyons Corners Houses and many others are now only remembered by old fogies like me. The Chaucer Lodge held its Ladies' Festival at Frascati and I was booked to officiate. I began badly and it didn't get much better, at least until the dancing began.

Dad had given me a gavel – well, not a proper gavel, it was actually a brewer's 'bung 'ammer' with a very hard leather head. I used it for years until it was pinched. But in Frascati, where to use it? Not on one of the tables, they were all glass-topped. Looking around the old-fashioned reception room, I noticed I was surrounded with beautiful solid oak panelling. "Aha," I thought, "that'll do!" so BASH I went with my bung 'ammer. The not so solid panel suddenly disappeared leaving a b.....y great big hole. I reckon it was the first demolition blow in the ultimate demise of that lovely restaurant.

One thing every toastmaster must do at the outset of any function is to inspire confidence in his clients or bookers. This I patently failed to do and the dinner toasts did not go well. However, my talents as a dance MC, even at 16, were good and I gave that Lodge a superb party and all my earlier aberrations were forgiven. Ten years later, by coincidence I got the Chaucer Lodge back and it stayed with me for many years until it closed for lack of numbers.

During our nocturnal ramblings, Dad and I talked at great length as to precisely what I had to say at these events. The correct wording for the introduction of The Grace, Toasts, both formal and informal, distributing table prizes and ladies' gifts, and any other regular announcements which may be needed were carefully chosen. Dad took me through an imaginary Ladies' Festival and I diligently typed every single word I would be likely to have to say. There were pages of notes and in those early days I read everything verbatim. I couldn't ad lib either 'hallo' or 'goodnight'; I read it. It was several years before I had the courage to tear them up.

These first three jobs were now history; I had learned from them and gradually acquired more confidence. I was on the roller-coaster ride of a professional toastmaster and I had not even been called up for my National Service. I duly received my 'call-up' papers a couple of years later and took myself off to the Army selection office in Wanstead, Essex. I, together with a whole bunch of similar aged spotty young men, was subjected to all the usual tests, both medical and academic and wondered what I would do if I passed muster. I had been sitting in a rather drafty corridor for what seemed like hours when a smart looking man in a uniform said to me, "What are you still doing here?" I told him that I was waiting to be called, but that nobody had spoken to me. He disappeared briefly before coming back and saying, "You can go home. You should have been told hours ago. You'll never get into the Army; you're not fit!" And that was that. I eventually received my 'medical card' which listed me as grade 'D', one degree above dead. This was due to that fateful word 'asthma' on my medical report; the army doesn't want you if you're likely to be a health hazard. So maybe my earlier illnesses proved to be a good thing after all.

Secretly and wholly unbeknown to my mother, I had nurtured a desire to join the RAF. Had she known she would have been furious. Whilst sitting in that busy, drafty corridor I had resolved that should I get in to HM Forces I would sign on for three years and 'pick' my own military (ha!) career. At that age I had three passionate and burning ambitions. Firstly, I had a strong yen to visit the USA, in my view a dream world; secondly, to learn to ski, both of which I eventually achieved. The third was to become a pilot, which I didn't. I thought that in joining the RAF that wish would come true. Who knows what would have become of my life had not my babyhood disabilities manifested themselves? There is no doubt that my toastmaster career would have foundered. One can only but wonder!

In those days, the Wood Green Chamber of Commerce held monthly dances in a hall at the back of *The Cherry Tree* pub in Southgate called The Selborne Hall. I had been attending Saturday morning classes at the Italia Conti Stage School in Archer Street, Piccadilly, being taught to act and sing and dance. I had achieved a modicum of success and, despite my tentative first engagements as a toastmaster, discussions about me entering the profession in partnership with Dad had by now reached serious levels.

He told the organisers of these monthly soirées that I needed to gain experience and, despite my still being a student at Pitman's, wondered if they would allow me to run one or two of them... and they were daft enough to agree. It was at these gentle, local events that I made my first, very nervous, appearances before an adult audience. I was just 16 years old and did them for free! Everything seemed to go well. Of course, I received criticism and advice as I was an absolute beginner, but I did not find the experience too terrifying. At the end of the evening, receiving the plaudits of the audience was great... even now, after 56 years in the business, I still find it very pleasing.

In the final months of the war, with a general feeling of victory in the air, the Government introduced a scheme called Holidays at Home. Families who could neither afford the time nor the cost of going away were given the opportunity of being entertained in their own town or city. In conjunction with local councils, committees were formed all over the country to arrange galas, parades and carnivals for the entertainment of the local community. Slough's was staged on Agar's Plough, the playing fields of Eton College, and these became an annual event for many years.

My father and I had built up a large Masonic clientèle in Windsor and worked regularly at the three major hotels, The Castle, The White Hart and The Old House. We worked at one of those hotels virtually every week throughout the winter season, often both of us on the same night, enabling us to share the car. It eventually turned out that we both worked over the Christmas period, me at The Castle Hotel and Dad at The White Hart, engagements which lasted for many years. Indeed, when I began Christmas work at The White Hart I was just married; when it all came to an end, my son was 16, a time-span of nearly twenty years.

The success of any good Master of Ceremonies depended entirely upon the talent and co-operation of band leaders and musicians. They can certainly make or break any MC trying to get a bunch of Masons or similar Ladies' Festival party-goers, their wives, girlfriends and mates to do silly things on the ballroom floor under the mystical guise of 'having fun'. He may have all the bright ideas in the world, but with an incompetent – or, far worse, unco-operative bandleader – a euphemism for a bloke with a telephone who rang a few mates with different instruments for a gig – life was hell. Throughout the early years of my career I met 'em all and soon learned the art of diplomacy and tact. To enable me to achieve any success on the dance floor I had to persuade talented musicians to dance to my tune for part of the evening. They would be asked to play a variety of disparate melodies not normally in their repertoire whilst I persuaded the unsuspecting revellers to do soppy things to make them laugh. The whole idea of all this was to send everyone staggering home at the end of the evening having had the time of their lives.

In Windsor there was one particular and very special bandleader who was a pure joy to meet, Jack Marshall. In his day job he was a boffin for the Ministry of Defence; a highly intelligent, well educated man of letters who simply adored playing the piano with his 'knock-about' band and who knew Dad's and my programme inside out. For me to make Christmas successful over a four-day period Jack had to be totally co-operative and helpful and he never failed. Even now, at 93, Jack is still playing at hotel restaurants, local operatic societies and at any place where decent piano music is appreciated, travelling the world, visiting jazz clubs, and he is one of life's genuine characters. I still enjoy our long nostalgic chats about not-quite-forgotten events – and especially songs and their lyrics.

He and many other helpful and willing bandleaders around the country contributed to Dad's and my successes as dance MCs. In the end everyone benefited: we shone as MCs, the band shone as a super entertainment with their choice of dances and music, and finally the crowd benefited because they had been given a great evening's fun through our concerted endeavours.

At a Masonic dinner I met Bill Groome who organised the Slough Holiday Carnival on Agar's Plough. He said that I would be perfect as the arena announcer and would I be interested? Assuming I would be earning a fortune at the same time as learning another facet of entertainment, I jumped at it. But what was the format? And, more importantly, what was the pay? August Bank Holiday Monday was always the first weekend of that month. The Carnival opened on the Saturday before and remained open until the following Saturday night. As well as the large fairground with all the usual rides and sideshows, they organised a huge arena show, twice daily; it was this that I was to compère.

The arena was vast, at least the size of a football pitch but oval in shape, with all the entertainers performing in the centre. Marquees and sideshows flanked either side and at the lower end was a special tent for VIPs, entertainers and me! The marquees were supplied by Derek Lane of *Harts of Windsor*, whose job it was to set everything up for the eight days of the Carnival. I once asked him how he managed to get the tentage so precise, as nothing seemed to vary even a single inch from one year to the next. He pointed to an ash tree amid all the others and said, "Everything comes from that tree. I simply pace it out every year, place my markers, and my boys erect the tents accordingly. If they ever pull that tree up, I'm buggered!" And so, for about 15 years, Slough Council organised Holidays at Home for anyone in the neighbourhood to visit.

As well as all the fun of the fairground and the arena entertainment, many local charities benefited from raffles and competitions and other fund-raising activities and sideshows which ran all week. The largest of these was the Horticultural Show but there were several others, including Fur and Feather, Local Produce, The Prettiest Garden and Floral Decoration; in short, there was a great deal of local interest and involvement.

Bill Groome had the unenviable task of booking acts to appear twice daily for seven days (spanning eight, but it did not open on Sunday!), with a very limited budget. It always had to include a high-wire tightrope walker or a swaying pole act, so that people only needed to look up to the heavens to see the show. In short, he needed to find as many and varied circus acts as he could. On the ground he needed clowns, with or without cars or motorbikes, which invariably went wrong and anything else to amuse the audiences. He also managed to secure a number of military acts like dog-handlers, motorcycle formation teams and the RAF Regiment gun display team which boasted '150 different movements without a single command!' There were two ninety-minute shows, at 2.30 and 4.30.

In between each show, Bill managed to add another great entertainment called tent-pegging. It was set up at the bottom end of Agar's Plough where there was much more room away from the large crowds. It consisted of soldiers on horseback trying to pluck a small tent peg out of the ground at full gallop – they were from the mounted guard at Buckingham Palace, the Blues and Royals and the Life Guards. The competition was intense but their riding talents were supreme. The peg was about six inches tall and about four inches wide, being hammered into the ground at an angle facing the rider. There would be a mounted soldier at either end of the joust about 100 yards apart, each tightly holding a ten-foot lance with a very sharp point. On the order from me, as the umpire, they would set off at full gallop and gently lower the point of the lance to spike the tent peg and hoist it out of the ground. It was extremely dangerous for the riders as a misjudgement could result in a dislocated shoulder or throwing the rider off his horse... both of which often happened in training, but it was invariably 'alright on the night'.

Points were scored thus: a full hoist and lift merited five points, a hoist just out of the ground was four points, a single touch, which I would have to confirm, was two points. There were several bouts, during which I would keep the score and announce the winning team who received plaudits from the crowd and a modest prize. It was enormously exciting but typical of the high quality of military entertainment for which this country is world-famous.

We were always dependent upon the weather and if it rained or was very windy, most of the aerial acts could not perform. In such circumstances we had to rely on the ground acts to fill in the lost time. The most important day as far as the weather was concerned was the last Saturday. A sunny day would bring the crowds flooding in and significant amounts of money would change hands. However, if the final Saturday was rained off, as occasionally happened, the committee only made just enough to cover all expenses and very little went to the charities.

Eric Stowe was the man who had the task of providing the public address system, which was always superb. He ran a wireless shop and his young assistant brought along about a dozen shellac records. One of these was Eric Coates' *Dambusters March,* which I have always loved, and I decided it would be the ideal way for me to begin every performance. It was agreed that immediately prior to my walking the thirty or so yards into the middle, the *Dambusters March* would be played... and so it was, twice a day for seven days for eleven years. I still call it my signature tune.

Two acts are imprinted on my mind above all the rest. The first was called 'Little Beaver and Marie'. 'Little Beaver' was a small, swarthy, pig-tailed 'Indian' – actually from Burnley – who erected a steep sloping wire to halfway up the post used for the high wire act. He was assisted by his daughter... whose name was not actually Marie! Little Beaver would ride a clapped-out 125cc *AJS* up this slope, where Marie would perform acrobatics from a trapeze suspended below. The problem was that the bike, which was probably older than him – and he wasn't a young man! – kept refusing to start. I cannot count the number of times I had to make a PA announcement to the effect, "Is there any motorcyclist in the crowd who has a carburettor for a very old 125cc *AJS*?" and he spent all breaks between the shows repairing the damned thing.

The other act was a girl called 'Gina – The Girl In The Moon'. Her act consisted of sitting on a crescent-shaped moon, which slowly hoisted her up the tight-wire pole from where she performed acrobatic poses, in slow motion, suspended below the 'moon'. The walk from her tent was about fifty yards, which she took very slowly indeed, draped in a huge silver and gold-sequined cape which dragged along the ground and which she gracefully doffed before 'going to the moon'. Unfortunately, she did not have any records or music of her own and so our own PA man took it upon himself to decide. His choice was the *Theme from a Summer Place,* which he played endlessly whilst she performed her little trapezy tarradiddles below the moon. We had to endure this twenty-minute act twice a day for the whole week, which nearly drove us barmy. Gina was very pretty and my wife thought that I fancied her. Not true but, anyway, she was one of the untouchables as her mum and dad always used to chaperone her everywhere! Any thoughts I might have had in that direction were pie in the sky... or dare I say it, moonshine!

One rather damp, overcast day just before the arena show was about to begin, Derek Lane, a couple of other chaps and I were walking through the as yet unopened fair. As we passed a small tent housing the 'Clairvoyant! Let Mystic Mabel Reveal your Future!' she called out, "Hi there, fellas! What's the weather gonna do today?" to which one of them replied, "You tell US, mate. You're the clairvoyant!"

Bill Groome's *pièce de résistance* at the end of every show was professional wrestling; this was magnificent and, as the arena announcer, I was the automatic choice for timekeeper. Derek and a few of the lads always came and sat with me at the table and we literally had a ringside seat. *Dale Martin Promotions* from Brixton was the company commissioned to find two different wrestlers for each bout – fourteen in all every year – and a referee... and, boy oh boy, what a character he turned out to be! His name was Lou Marco and there cannot be anyone around who witnessed these bouts who does not remember this unbelievable and totally charismatic man.

Lou stood about 5' 4" in his stockinged feet, a feisty, cocky little Jewish man from London's East End – he was the unquestioned 'guvnor' of the wrestling fraternity. No matter how big or tough these hefty wrestlers were, all of them were scared of Lou Marco. He and I got on like the proverbial house on fire, and it was my job to get the audiences ready. In the last few years we allowed them to come inside the ropes encircling the whole area, for atmosphere. With small crowds 20-30 yards away, it was difficult to create any competitive spirit between the wrestlers, so the audience came to the ringside. The two combatants and Lou would climb into the ring, at which point I would hand the 'mic' to Lou to introduce the contestants, which he did as though he was introducing Mohammed Ali. "Fiiiiiive rouonds of five minutes each, twooooo faaalls or two submissions, or one knock-out to decide the winner!"

I would ring the bell, set my stopwatch running, and all hell would be let loose in the ring. The two wrestlers had carefully rehearsed what they were going to do in the bout (I mustn't call it a fight), whilst little Lou danced and pranced around them like a ferret with a rabbit. It was huge fun and we loved every minute.

There were great wrestling names like Jackie Pallo, Mick McManus, 'Dropkick' Johnny Peters, Johnny 'Black' Kwango (actually a school teacher from Dulwich), Tibor Tschachkzi (yeah, you try to pronounce it), and The Royal Brothers (Bert Royal and his younger brother Vic Faulkener!) on the rare occasions Lou brought along tag-wrestling. These and countless others gave of their all to entertain the noble Burgesses of Slough. Sometimes things were very rough indeed and if one of them got hurt and became angry we saw some REAL fighting, but there was the ubiquitous Lou jumping in between to separate them before things got out of hand. Because of the proximity of our table, there were several occasions when one of them got slung out of the ring and landed in our laps. The language then was ripe and quite unrepeatable.

I recall making one particular announcement. Lou had introduced the two wrestlers – the skin of one was as white as snow, while the other was a well-educated and very black gentleman. Just before ringing the bell, I said through the microphone, "Now don't forget, ladies and gentlemen, pick your favourite and shout encouragement. And just to remind you so that you can recognise them, Johnny Black Kwango can be easily spotted as he is the one… pause… wearing the GREEN trunks!" He thought I was going to say something rude about his skin and nearly choked with laughter.

As the bouts progressed, one of the wrestlers would throw the other onto the canvas, leap on him and try to hold his shoulders down for a count of three. Lou would then lie flat on the floor, slide his hand under the shoulder of the bloke underneath and, in a huge voice, which his tiny size and stature belied, holler, very slowly indeed, "Onnnnneeeeee, Twooooooo, Theerrrreeeeeeee," lasting all of a minute when it should have lasted ten seconds. I always left the mic open and his counting could be heard all over the ground – all over Eton so far as I could judge. If Lou thought that the bout had not gone on long enough, he would extend that count until the under wrestler could wriggle out. Who said it wasn't all fixed and a sham? Not I! But great entertainment it certainly was.

Agar's Plough was great experience for me. On the major days – the first Saturday, the Bank Holiday Monday and the last Saturday – crowds could be as large as 20,000-30,000, although during the week, especially if the weather was unkind, the numbers were usually down in the hundreds.

Bill Groome told me that one reason why I was given the job was because previously they had had an announcer whose stock phrase was, "GIVE 'EM A BIG 'AND… COME ON NOW, GIVE 'EM A BIG 'AND," which drove all the workers around the ground absolutely potty. This taught me a couple of lessons. The first was never to use that phrase as there are always others that can be adopted, and the second was to seek variations of saying the same thing.

I also learned a third lesson concerning use of microphones and PA systems in vast spaces. The speakers were placed about fifty yards apart at the far end of the arena immediately opposite the fairground. They were also about fifty or so yards away from where I was making the announcements, resulting in a half-second delay in me hearing what I was saying – very disconcerting. In a closed environment like a ballroom, where the sound is instant, it is easy to adjust your volume and speech, however, hearing your words echoed moments later can be incredibly off-putting and requires tremendous concentration. After a while, it became easier to handle, but it was a wonderful learning curve for a young announcer.

Oh yes. What about the pay? In those days I was earning between six and ten guineas for each evening job. Bill Groome said, "I'll pay you fifteen quid for the whole week. Take it or leave it!" I took it – not only did I need the money, but traditionally in midsummer there is little work around and fifteen quid is fifteen quid!

For some years after the war I worked at the London Welsh Association Dances in the LWA Hall, Grays Inn Road. I seemed to be popular with the newly-formed London Welsh Youth Choir and I spent much time with them. At one of these dances in 1953, a certain Margaret Jones saw me working and, apparently, had a mild crush on me – I doubt it, but it's a nice thought. Her sister, Ann, was approaching her 21st birthday and Mr and Mrs Llewelyn Jones were planning a party for their eldest daughter. During these years, such events were prolific and Dad and I worked at many of them. I later learned that when the Jones family were discussing the matter of a toastmaster for the birthday party, Margaret was enthusiastic about me, my youth and my perceived abilities, and it was agreed to engage me for Saturday 11th July, 1953.

Back in little old Wood Green I spent most of my leisure time with several mates: the aforementioned Jimmy Denyer, John Dickens who I'd met via his sister Molly at a local youth club, and Paul MacDonald, whose father was a tough senior police officer in our district. We lads had decided to go to *Butlins* in Skegness for a two-week break in July and I was to drive as I was the only kid around with a car.

When Ann Jones telephoned to ask if I was free for her birthday party, my mother, who dealt with all our bookings, had to tell her that I would be on holiday. After discussion, it was agreed that Dad would do the job and all was settled… this was one of the first occasions when HE would deputise for ME! However, a week or two before we were due to go to *Butlins* an event occurred which not only changed our holiday plans, but affected the whole course of my life. Paul's brother Duncan had recently been to *Butlins*, had got involved in a bar brawl and had been beaten up. He was a right mess and when he got home, Paul's mother put her foot down with a firm hand, saying, "Right, Paul. That's it. Your holiday's off. You are not going to *Butlins* and that's that!" And so we cancelled. Although she was married to a hard-headed copper, at 4' 11" tall Mrs MacDonald could be a real cow when it mattered.

I telephoned Miss Jones to inform her that I was now available for her party, and she seemed pleased that I would be there after all. She asked me to meet her at the Orient Café in St Mary Axe in the City, where she worked, to discuss arrangements for the party. It transpired that Ann's father Llew owned the Orient Café along with a dairy and sandwich bar in Cullum Street. He had also owned two other establishments but had had to close them during the difficult war years.

I first saw the lovely Ann Jones walking back into the restaurant, having delivered some coffees to offices and I thought to myself, 'This little lady ain't too bad! Who knows… I may just get lucky!' The post-luncheon interview lasted well into the evening because, when she closed the café at around 5.30, she invited me to her home in Dulwich Village to meet her parents and talk about the job. It was a lovely evening. I was fed and wined in great style and met the whole family. I returned home at 10.30 pm… where my mother was doing her nut. She still treated me as her 'little boy' and anything past nine o'clock was enough to call the police. It was quite stupid. I could come home from work at any time of night or early morning and nothing would be said, but go out socially and after nine o'clock there was total and unreasoned panic… she was certain that I must have come to a sticky end!

Many large stores used to convert their restaurants into ballrooms in the evening for extra revenue, and Pyne's Restaurant in Lewisham was chosen for Ann's party. I had worked there a few times and remember that the manager rejoiced in the rather unusual name of Mr Shrubsall. While it was a very pleasant evening, there was nothing particularly special that I recall, except that Ann had invited four serious boyfriends…! A band had been engaged, as had I, to give them all a happy time with the traditional speeches, cake-cutting and novelty dances. Dad and I were experts in this field and had built a reputation of being able to make the evening go with a swing. The party ended at midnight and that was that – the 120 or so guests went home.

I had worked at many such occasions but felt that there was something a bit special about Ann; I don't really know what, but I had that feeling. And so, the following morning, I cajoled my friend John Dickens to come with me all the way over to Dulwich. Having met the family the previous week and done a good job the night before, I knew that I would get a reasonable welcome. Ann seemed pleased to see me, and so began our friendship. Ann's best friend from the City of London Girls' School was Jean Cave; she and John also became friends and in due time we went out as a foursome.

Ann was a very popular girl and, as I mentioned above, had several boyfriends. She nearly became engaged to a highly qualified and respected Welsh doctor, a gynaecological specialist. Other suitors included a Welsh rugger-playing policeman who eventually married (later to become Dame) Gwyneth Jones who sang in the same amateur Welsh choir as Ann. There was also an LCC (London County Council) lawyer, and others who might have become more serious. The chance of me making it much further with Ann was slim, but I became very fond of her and was most persistent. You must remember, that because of my mother's 'protection' of her little boy, I had been closeted, never really being allowed to have a regular girlfriend, only a few female 'chums'.

The Agar's Plough engagement was offered to me when Ann and I had been seeing each other fairly seriously for about three years. After much badgering and persuasion – believe me, it was not easy – I proposed to her. Eventually she agreed to marry me… she had firmly, but kindly, discarded the others along the way. I was now number one in her book, a position I enjoyed then and still do today, fifty years later – but it took a lot of persuasion!

For me, our courtship (oh, what a funny old fashioned word that seems nowadays) was four years of deep anxiety. As I have always been a somewhat jealous person, the thought of four boyfriends in her past, and in the first few months as well, worried me like hell. I was never completely able to convince myself, as we continued to see more and more of each other, that she really did care for me and I worried myself silly. On reflection, I can now see that my fears, especially in the last two years, were unfounded but that was how I felt. I suppose I should have been more confident because every time she went on holiday, either by herself or with her parents, Ann would write to me every day, very long, detailed and loving letters, and bring me nice welcome home gifts.

I never actually proposed to Ann, you know – like going down on bended knee with a bunch of roses in my hand and saying, "Darling, will you marry me?" When we went out for the day, in our quieter moments I would broach the subject of marriage and ask whether she was interested. Ann has always been cautious about making snap decisions, especially important ones… and getting married is pretty important. When I did mention it, she would say, "I don't know. I'm not certain. I have to be sure," and I would go away miserable. Eventually, my persuasive powers won the day and she agreed to marry me.

An interesting comment on the morals of then and now is that at no time during our four-year courtship did we ever go away together by ourselves. It was totally inconceivable (no pun intended!), and neither of us would have wasted our breath mentioning it to our parents. "What! Go away together? On your own? Don't be so silly. Of course not!" and that was that… and, don't forget, we were both over 21! It didn't matter; we were not allowed to go. We did occasionally go away with our parents and one year Mum and Dad took us to North Wales where we stayed in separate but adjacent bedrooms in my Aunt Dwd's small cottage. We were chaperoned – however they did not watch over us all the time... so we did have our moments!

Stephen Llewelyn Jones was an extremely shy man and he really only shone in the company of his male friends and fellow-dairymen. He was known to all his Welsh friends as Llew but to all his English mates as Clow! Notwithstanding his diffidence and nervousness, he was an active Freemason and Almoner to two Lodges – not an easy job – and Ann used to type all his letters for him.

I have heard thousands of 'mother-in-law' gags, but none of them apply to mine as she was a super lady and very special. Elizabeth Dilys Jones was a delightful and handsome lady; we have a photograph of her as a young girl and she was a stunning beauty. She was a happy lady with the most beguiling laugh and smiling face; she laughed a lot and it shone through her eyes. We spent many happy times together over the years.

Dilys had a large collection of friends from 'The Boro', as we called The Borough Welsh Congregational Chapel in Southwark Bridge Road. London Welsh Chapels were the social centres of their communities and were hives of activity. Each had its own choir competing fiercely in the annual *Eisteddfodau*. They also held outings, holidays, nativity plays, concerts, prayer meetings, Sunday School, whist and beetle drives... the list is endless. Mrs Marjorie Byron-Jones – Auntie Marjorie to everyone – was the catalyst at The Boro. She founded a choir of around thirty called 'The Gwalia Girl Singers', which travelled extensively all over the UK and made many broadcasts. Two of their sopranos achieved greatness: Gwyneth Jones, and Anne Evans, the latter a member of The Boro from childhood. Both became Dames of the Order of the British Empire for their contributions to the world of opera. Auntie Marjorie's husband 'Byron' was also very active and wrote plays in Welsh. Ann regularly appeared in these and spent many evenings rehearsing at The Boro.

Ann's mum gave us her blessing to get married, although the erratic nature of my profession caused her some anxiety and she once said to Ann, "Why doesn't Bryn go out and get a REAL job?" Having secured her support, it was then up to me to ask Ann's father for her hand in marriage. Actually, Mr Jones (I never called him anything other than that!) was Ann's stepfather – her real father, David Rheidol Powell, had died on the day Ann was born. Dilys married Llew a couple of years later and Ann took the Jones surname. When I went to get her birth certificate from Somerset House, I was told that she did not exist; the lovely girl I was engaged to marry was not there! After much searching of soul, memory and records, it dawned on me that Ann was actually born 'Powell'. It transpired that she had not really been adopted and was, in fact, still Ann Elizabeth Rheidol Powell. Indeed, whilst at the City of London School, Ann won a Grocers' Company Scholarship and the certificate hangs in our office. It proclaims that Ann Jones had won it – wrong!

I had to plan when to ask Mr Jones formally for Ann's hand in marriage and the only time he was available to discuss it was in the evening. However, being in the dairy business, the Jones family went to bed very early as they had to be at the shop by about 5.00 am and needed their sleep. My planning for this momentous meeting had been poor as I chose to seek Mr Jones' permission during the week I was working at Agar's Plough. I usually managed to leave the grounds at around 8.30 pm, but it was a good hour's run to their lovely house in Dulwich Village. Ann and Dilys agreed to keep the old man occupied for as long as possible, while I rushed like billy-o through the traffic to try to get there before he went to bed. They tried everything possible to keep him up and for three nights in succession I simply belted – ignoring speed limits – in my rather quick car to their house, only to be met at the door with... "Sorry, he's gone up. It's too late."

On the fourth night I left the ground a little earlier – I nipped out and tore like a maniac to Dulwich. Ann opened the door with a gleam in her eye and said, "Hurry! He's just going up." They had tried every ruse they knew to keep him from going to bed and he was actually at the foot of the stairs with his hand on the banister, dressed only in his pyjama bottoms, baring his rather hairy chest, when I breathlessly stopped him – all 5' 4" of him – a thoroughly unprepossessing sight. I blurted out in an embarrassed gabble, "Please, Mr Jones, Ann and I would like to be married. Will you please give us your consent and permission?" It was obvious that it was as acutely embarrassing for him as it was for me. He must have known that marriage was in the offing, as undoubtedly Dilys and he had discussed it, but he kept his composure and said to me, "Well, if that's what Ann wants, and Dilys agrees, then I suppose I shall have to agree as well. I must say, that you are not the person I'd have chosen for our daughter, but if you're the one she wants, then it's OK by me!" The words may have been slightly different – after all, it was fifty years ago – but who cares? I had gained his support, and the rest, as they say, is history.

Ann and I set the date for our wedding for Saturday 6th July 1957, exactly four years to the day when we met. For me, money was more than tight – even at the age of 23. I was not just impecunious, I was flat stony-broke and when it came to buying the engagement ring, I just did not have any money. As Ann had been working regularly, she happily agreed to buy her own engagement ring from the Goldsmiths' and Silversmiths' Company in Regent Street, saying as she did so, "You'll pay me back for it one day!" I hope I have. I wanted to marry Ann so badly that I had to swallow my pride and let her buy the ring. It seems funny now and we laugh at it, but at the time I felt dreadful. At least it laid to rest any doubts I may have had that she was still holding a candle for one of her former *enamorados,* something that had long rankled in the back of my mind.

Mr and Mrs Jones were extremely kind and, despite the fact that doctors, lawyers and policemen had been seeking the hand of their daughter, they accepted me without question into their midst. The fact that I too had been an active Freemason meant that I met Mr Jones on the same level, which made it easier. They were still worried about my ability to look after their daughter in the manner to which she was accustomed, but they did not let it show.

I was becoming well-known in the banqueting world, especially in the five-star hotels in London. The Grosvenor House, Savoy, Dorchester, Hyde Park, Café Royal and many others had become accustomed to my style of working and I had gained a good reputation. The question of our own wedding reception was now occupying our thoughts and it was established that the Joneses were perfectly happy to consider a glitzy West End reception. They were not 'rich' but were comfortably off as they had owned their very successful restaurants and dairy for years and had invested wisely. I was given the task of trying to find the best 'deal' in London and immediately went to the Banqueting Manager at The Grosvenor House, Mr Gibbs, to ask if he would consider taking it on. His advice was that The Grosvenor House did not really specialise in weddings – the most reputable hotel in the West End for such functions was The Hyde Park and he suggested that I pay them a visit. I was not too well-known there, but made an appointment to meet their Banqueting Manager one very hot day in August.

Mrs Jones, Ann and I duly arrived at the agreed time, asked to see the Manager and ordered afternoon tea. Despite our appointment, he kept us waiting for over half an hour and his whole attitude was one of almost total disinterest. He was snobbish, offhand and really could not be bothered with the possibility of a 300-guest champagne wedding reception the next summer. His manner was dreadful and, when he departed, we were presented with a bill of thirty shillings for the afternoon tea. Mrs Jones paid this, but we were disgusted and left the hotel swearing never to return.

As it was a beautiful day, I suggested that we stroll up Piccadilly to Park Lane Hotel to get a brochure of the privately owned establishment with a beautiful ballroom. I was only casually known there and was not on the regular list of toastmasters they used. Nevertheless, I picked up the house telephone and asked to speak to Mr Eric Bishop, the Banqueting Manager, not expecting him to come down to speak to me personally. I misjudged him.

Mr Bishop, the archetypal English Banqueting Manager – charming, polite, charismatic and thoroughly professional – briefly shook my hand and Ann's, and then turned his full charm onto Mrs

Jones. She had pure white hair, smiling eyes, a ready laugh, and looked bewitching that day. Eric fell under her spell. He took her under his wing and said, "My DEAR Mrs Jones. How delightful to make your acquaintance," as he slowly led her away from Ann and me. "Would you like a nice cool glass of champagne on this hot afternoon? Do, please come this way and we will have some refreshment." Ann and I need not have been there. It was the cleverest ploy imaginable and from that moment the wedding reception at that hotel was assured.

Saturday 6th July 1957 dawned and the temperature rose to over ninety degrees on the Centre Court at Wimbledon for the men's singles final between Lew Hoad and Ashley Cooper. Our wedding service was planned for 2.30 pm, and some 350 friends and family squashed, sweatily, inside the Boro chapel where the Jones family had worshipped for many years and which was their spiritual home.

The Reverend Dr Ivor M Edwards, BA, BD, officiated. One of the great baritones of the day was the well-known Raimund Herincx who sang *Panis Angelicus*; Maurice Hughes, the accompanist to the Gwalia Girl Singers, played the organ and the whole service was quite magical. Twenty members of The National Association of Toastmasters gave us a Guard of Honour of gavels, the sun shone and we all sweltered. In a traditional symbol of good luck, Mr Hardidge, the Chapel-keeper, dressed as a chimney sweep complete with brushes and soot all over his face, welcomed us and gave Ann a sooty kiss. Hire cars from a friend of mine took us all to the cool air-conditioned Park Lane Hotel, where Eric Bishop pulled out all the stops for us.

(I, along with Eric's many other friends, was desperately sad when he was sent to prison for alleged Income Tax fraud because of the cash tips he received to dispense amongst the catering staff through the 'tronc' system – he was the scapegoat for a system rife in the hotel world at that time. Eric spent less than a year in Ford open prison and we were all happy to see him, after his incarceration, attending functions at the Park Lane Hotel. So sad. So unnecessary.)

Our health was proposed by Clifford Thomas, the father of Margaret's boyfriend, Ieuan, whom she later married. Mr Clifford Thomas was the Headmaster of Dulwich College and delivered one of the most amusing and wisest speeches I have ever heard at a wedding. He was a kind, rather 'cuddly' gentleman whom everyone adored and he always had a twinkle in his eye. I spoke after Mr Thomas, in a speech that went on for quite a while, so I am told… but that won't surprise anyone who knows me! It was a wonderful day and at 6.30 pm we departed for London Heathrow for an overnight flight to Zurich for our honeymoon. The Hotel Schweizerhof in Engelberg was our destination and my first trip abroad.

I used to run a number of functions for *Thomas Cook's* Foreign Exchange Department and as a gesture of goodwill they gave us a good deal on the trip. Sadly, our planning was not the best, and having a flight at 9.30 pm meant that we flew through the night. I often complain that I spent my honeymoon night sitting upright in an aeroplane! Additionally, we had left the Park Lane Hotel dressed in smart clothes and stupidly failed to make any provision to change into more casual gear.

Arriving at Zurich airport in the early hours of the morning, we took a coach, a train, a bus, a lake-steamer, a taxi and, finally, a cable car to the hotel where we arrived, mid-morning, still in our smart clothes, very hot and sweaty. All we wanted to do was to get to bed… to sleep! When we undressed, we discovered thousands of bits of confetti stuffed down our clothes by well-wishers who had come to see us off. There were no secrets from the hotel staff as to why we were there but, to add to my chagrin, they had given us two single beds. We pushed them together, but could do nothing about the solid wooden edges down the middle! We coped, and still have very happy memories of a wonderful honeymoon. It rained every day... so we were told!

To complete the story of Agar's Plough, Ann did not often come with me but, when she did, it was principally to see the wrestling, which she loved. She and I will never forget the time when she brought our three-year-old son Timothy along. Ann was holding him whilst watching two great wrestlers knock hell out of each other. The crowd loved it and Ann was shouting herself hoarse for one or other of them, or sometimes both. At a lull in the wrestling, my small son was heard to shout in a tearful voice, "Why doesn't that man go home and tell his mummy?" The crowd roared, and so did the wrestlers!

All good ends must come to a thing, and so it was with Holidays at Home and the Slough Carnival at Agar's Plough. In fact, it was brought to a sudden close by the Government moving the August Bank Holiday Monday to the end of the month. Eton College needed the ground to mark out the pitches and so a new venue would be required. With everything getting more expensive and with it becoming increasingly difficult to gain commitment from people on the sidelines, the tireless, devoted and dedicated volunteers decided to call it a day. It was the end of an era. I had had a great time, learned a lot, met some lovely people and was left with many fond memories. I was now happily married with two lovely children, Timothy Dorian and Tracy Jane, and my career was taking off nicely.

A charity dinner, concert and dance was arranged at The Astor Club, a small nightclub in the West End. A lovely George Mitchell and 'Black and White Minstrel' singer Tony Mercer was the main act. He had a gorgeous, deep, velvet voice and charmed all his audiences. He was also a Water Rat and sadly died very young. He was sorely missed.

HRH Prince Charles was the guest of honour at a tribute dinner to the American lyricist and composer Sammy Cahn. It began with the cabaret, after which dinner was served. The conversation was genial and Prince Charles congratulated Sammy on his writing talents. Sammy said, "Well Prince!" (Yep, that's what he called him all night and Prince Charles didn't seem to mind). "Well Prince, writing words ain't too tough. I just think of something and the words pop out." As an example, off the top of his head, he composed a little musical poem to the tune 'Three Coins in a Fountain' which he had written about Prince Charles. He sang this and Prince Charles was thrilled. "That was lovely," he said, "Would you mind writing it down and letting me have a copy?" "Sure, Prince," was Sammy's laconic reply. "I'll write it tomorrow and send it to you... By the way, what's your address? Where shall I send the goddam thing?" to which, with a smile on his lips, the Royal Gentleman quietly replied, "Well, if I were you, I would try Buckingham Palace. It should find me there!"

Chapter 4

Married Life

"Behind every successful man… is a surprised mother-in-law."

Bryn Williams

Prior to getting married, Ann and I had noticed that 53 Bounds Green Road, Wood Green, N22, was for sale. It was just up the road from where I was living in a tiny little two-bedroom flat with my parents and was an easy walk to the tube station – a vital prerequisite as Dad and I frequently came home on the last train.

The house was a large, Victorian, end-of-terrace, leasehold property with sitting tenants, Jack and Josie Boorer and their two children (Felicity) Flicky and John occupying the first floor, for which they paid rent of £2 per week. The downstairs consisted of two bedrooms, a huge 40-foot lounge-dining room, bathroom, toilet and the smallest kitchen I had ever seen, 8' x 8' in which we virtually lived. The price was £650. I didn't have 650 pennies, but my parents came to the rescue, dug into their savings and bought it for us. Within a couple of years the Church Commissioners, who owned the freehold, sold this to us for about £400 and the house became totally ours… along with the sitting tenants, of course. In the Deeds, it was interesting to read that the income from the ground rent was to pay 'The Living of the Vicar of Lower Peover', which, in one of our many ambles through the Midlands countryside, we actually discovered and wondered what the vicar was like.

We carpeted the 40-foot lounge in a bright green *Kossett* carpet (who remembers the lovely white cat in their ads?). The room was vast and, as we could not afford furniture, it looked rather like a football field. We had a dining room suite with six chairs, our bed and that was all. One evening, we decided to entertain our parents to dinner. When the meal was over, Mr Jones was dismayed to find that there was nowhere comfortable to sit – so he went to bed! The following day he said to Dilys, "Go out and buy Bryn and Ann some furniture so that the next time we go, I've got somewhere to sit!" He was that kind of man and we were delighted to go out and choose a three-piece suite, thanks to my very generous pa-in-law. Actually, I never referred to them by their first names, but always Mr and Mrs Jones, until the kids arrived. Then it was much easier as they automatically became Nain (Grandma) and Taid (Grandpa) – in Welsh, of course.

Ann and my father got on well together, possibly because he was 100% Welsh; he was thrilled that I had chosen to marry a Welsh girl – albeit a *Cardi* – someone who hailed from Cardiganshire! There has always been light-hearted antipathy to Cardiganshire natives – the county that divides North and South Wales and the one that neither wishes to own!

Not only had I been umbilically attached to my mother at birth but, because of my profession and living at home, I was attached in virtually every way. Mum was then, and remained so for over forty years, our secretary and dealt with all of Dad's and my business. She only relinquished this when she was in her eighties and even then with great reluctance. So, in effect, Ann not only married me, but also my family – believe me, a very tough situation, which gave us many discordant moments over the years. It is a great tribute to Ann and our love that she managed to stick through it all, and this year we celebrate 48 years of marriage. It also meant that we needed to be in north London rather than the luxurious surrounds of Dulwich Village where Ann had lived for years following a move from a flat over one of their shops in Cullum Street, deep in the heart of the City of London.

My mother dominated our lives and, as she was Dad's and my secretary, it was pretty well unavoidable. 53 Bounds Green Road was about half a mile from Gladstone House and she insisted that we had a direct telephone line from her kitchen – the office – to our

72

home! This meant that every call, both in and out, had to go through her. If Ann or I wanted to call anyone at all, even Ann's mother or sister, we had to pick up the phone and say, "May I have a line out please?" If she was in a bad mood she would ask why and who we were calling. It was none of her damned business and made us both mad; her interference in our lives was palpable.

When we were house-hunting, we had seen one for which we intended to make an offer but, when the agent called to speak to us, my mother told him that we were out, and added for good measure that we were not interested anyway; we lost the house and were furious. When we eventually moved to another house the telephone company informed my mother that it was exactly two point two miles away (albeit measured in furlongs), so she demanded that we continue with the extension. By now Ann had had enough and insisted, rightly, that we have our own private line as well, for which we paid. Mum was furious but could do nothing about it. This maternal protectionism was equally active when Ann and I were courting, as frequently Mum refused to pass on messages Ann had left. On the plus side, she was a wonderful secretary who protected me from 'my public' and negotiated much higher fees for my services than I would have been able to do, as I have always been a softy in money matters – and still am!

By this time Ann's father had sold the Orient Café. While this was a sound commercial decision, it did mean that Ann was now out of a job as she had been joint manager there with her lifelong friend and childhood nanny, Marie Lloyd.

E B Byron-Jones was a Deacon of the Chapel where Ann's family worshipped, and had been a friend for years. He and his wife Marjorie virtually ran the place and became known as Uncle and Aunty to all the children. Uncle Byron, who was the solicitor in charge of the Legal and Parliamentary Department for the LCC at County Hall, came to the rescue when he heard of a job vacancy in his office. Ann had an interview and got the job, which was a godsend to us as it meant a regular income for years while I was still a struggling, impecunious toastmaster barely scraping a living. "It 'elps to 'ave a mate in 'igh places," so the fact that her knowledge of legal and parliamentary work was nil didn't matter a fig – she got the job and spent the next few years doing compulsory purchase and tree-preservation orders.

Our son Timothy Dorian was born on 7th April 1959, exactly one year and nine months after we were married, precisely as we had planned. Tracy Jane came into the world two years later on 11th June 1961. Our family was complete and it became necessary to find a larger house.

I was driving my golfing mother and some of her team-mates to a representative match for Muswell Hill Golf Club, when I learned that Masie and Len Hoskins, brother and sister members of the Club, were selling Masie's house. I called Len, a London stockbroker, who was kindness and helpfulness personified – we discussed prices and the deal was made. So, in September 1962 we moved into 35 Vallance Road, Muswell Hill, thanks in great part to the vendors' generosity as they had offered us a very good deal. It was a lovely four-bedroom house with a large living room, separate dining room, scullery and kitchen, which we later enlarged, but no garage. Houses built between the wars rarely had garages as everyone travelled by bus and train in those days.

We were able to keep the house in Bounds Green which we rented out to a succession of tenants over the years. The rent was fixed at £2 per week as we had sitting tenants and in those days the law was on their side, especially if the flat was unfurnished. We now owned the freehold and had enough money to put down a deposit on another house and so were able to keep this one. We decided to go into the rental business and were able to let it out fully furnished, a much better proposition than empty. We kept this property for a few years with the attendant earnings and problems. We quickly learned that owning flats was not all it was cracked up to be; oh sure, it made money, but it was also a daily problem needing constant attention.

The Gwalia Girl Singers were still quite active but some of the members decided to form a small cabaret act as the choir was reaching its 'sell-by date'. There were five of them, all close friends. As well as Ann, there were the Byron-Jones sisters Wenna and

Glenys, Ann Knight and Hedydd Hanaby. Wenna's husband, Morris Hughes, became the accompanist; he had trained as both a vicar and a music teacher but music won the day.

David Morris Hughes (known as Morris) was a lovely man, a school teacher in Battersea and a Fellow of the Royal College of Organists. His métier was classical and choral music, but at the insistence of his very persuasive mother-in-law, Auntie Marjorie, he was bludgeoned into becoming the Gwalia's accompanist and arranger. Morris was put in charge of all the music for the new cabaret act and, after much discussion between us all, songs were selected for him to arrange. He was quite brilliant and much of what he wrote was magical. Deep down he hated it, but he had to comply. At rehearsals for both the choir and the cabaret act, he would sit at the piano and do the *Daily Telegraph* crossword until he was asked to play. He was totally disparaging about the material, which he described as 'musically vapid', but he did enjoy the cabaret performances with 'his girls'. Nevertheless, he couldn't wait to get home to his favourite glass of red wine with a bar of milk chocolate straight from the fridge – he had earned it.

The newly formed group needed a name and my mother came up with the brilliant 'Harmony Hi-Lites' – corny and naff by today's standards but at the time it sounded OK. Finding work for the group did not present too many problems and after weeks of discussion about music, costume, choreography, and everything related to the new show, they were in business. Costumes presented some difficulties as the two Anns were both 5' 2", while Glenys was 6' 1", but with clever design and dressmaking, the disparities were not really noticed. The act consisted of a full thirty minutes of close harmony singing. Songs from the shows, folk songs, traditional airs, country and western and operetta were all included. A super dancer named Terry Brent choreographed movements to go with the music and the whole production was very musical and attractive.

Many clients asked my father and me to provide artistes, toastmasters and bands for their functions and so I became a registered theatrical agent with the title 'Owen-Williams

Entertainments' – well actually a Theatrical Employer as they had different licences and there were laws governing this distinction. We applied for a licence to make the bookings legal and were told that we needed to be able to display a small plaque outside our premises. Living in a flat, this was impossible; also the laws and financial dealings governing agency licences were complicated and restrictive. We were then told that we could apply for a Theatrical Employer's Licence, which was substantially different but was legal and sufficient for our requirements.

The Harmony Hi-Lites entertained and delighted audiences all over the UK for ten years. They performed on radio and made several appearances on television, particularly on *The Ivor Emmanual Show* from Cardiff, Hughie Green's *Opportunity Knocks*, which they won hands down, and others. There are still many people today who remember them with great affection as their singing and production really was superb. Alas! time and ever-growing families – they boasted twelve kids between them – meant that it had to end. And in 1975 it did.

For many years, Auntie Marjorie ran concerts for The Boro involving all the children. Ann and Glenys were regulars and performed various hilarious and ridiculous routines. One of these involved Ann trying to look as tiny as possible, wearing a bowler hat, horn-rimmed glasses, a shapeless pullover and bushy moustache, while six-foot-tall Glenys wore six-inch heels and a feather boa. They did a pastiche on a great old number called *Madam, will you walk?* with Glenys looking down on Ann from a great height, singing the words, "Cecil, will you walk?" They were a riot and very popular with London Welsh audiences. For an encore, complete with blackened teeth, they sang *Nobody Loves a Fairy when she's Forty*, waving two broken wands and wearing tutus.

Charlie Lewis owned a company called *The Hanover Grand*, which was run by his son Joe and a manager named Tony Gorbutt. Joe Lewis is now about the third richest man in the world, boasting a fortune in excess of a thousand million pounds, but in those days he ran a catering establishment in three places: The Hanover Grand in Hanover Square (originally called Selby's Restaurant), The

Tavistock Rooms in Charing Cross Road where I worked many times, and The Cockney Restaurant. They were all super guys, great to work for and extremely generous.

Tony Gorbutt was a remarkable man whom we all loved dearly; he was extremely handsome, gentle, kind and a wonderful boss. As a boy, he had escaped from communist Eastern Europe on foot. He walked, scrounged lifts and eventually stowed away on a boat to England, and when he landed, he went into a telephone box, looked down the list of names and chose Tony as his first name and Gorbutt as his second. Arriving by the same method in London, he eventually became the manager of Selby's Restaurant in Hanover Square and remained there after it was sold.

I knew Tony through my work as a toastmaster and he called on me one day to discuss a new venture that the company was proposing. It was to be a theme restaurant in Ivory House, St Katherine's Dock, in London's East End. He knew about *The Harmony Hi-Lites* and told me that he was looking for 'singing wenches' for a project to be called *The Beefeater by The Tower* – a new, mediaeval-style restaurant in the period of King Henry VIII. He asked if I knew where we could get singers to act as waitresses and to entertain and invited Ann and me to see the place.

As it was being totally converted and redecorated, we entered the building by the kitchen door and saw what was to be Ann's place of employment for the next twelve years. Ivory House was built nearly two hundred years ago as an ivory store. It was subterranean, consisting of a very long, wide centre aisle from the kitchen to the entrance stairway. Off the centre aisle were nine very long bays for laying down the ivory tusks. Bench seats were being built around the walls and long wooden tables would occupy the centre. When full, it would seat over 500 – or, if they were all Japanese, 600 as they would all squash up together!

The idea was to engage a rotund actor as King Henry, with as many wenches as were needed to act as waitresses as well as singers and dancers. It was also planned to employ special acts to entertain between courses of the set meal, or 'Removes' as they were to be called. Tony showed us around and asked if we would be interested in getting involved – we were.

The venture was still at an embryo stage and entertainment was needed for the official opening in a few months' time. Our task was to provide wenches and, of course, we asked the 'girls' in *The Harmony Hi-Lites* first. Only Wenna was interested and, even then, only casually although later on she became a regular and enjoyed the work. Ann agreed to take on the role of finding and providing as many wenches as needed, at the same time acting as their 'Mother Bunny' each evening. She had no idea what a huge task this would prove to be. The journal *The Stage & Television Today* turned out to be her saviour as it attracted dozens of young aspiring dancers, singers and actresses, desperately needing to earn money. From this Ann easily found the required wenches.

One of the first managers at *The Beefeater by The Tower* was a young, recently qualified graduate from Sussex University called Robert Earl, the son of a very successful singer of the 1960s by the same name – I had worked with Robert Earl Senior at *Selby's* years before. At 23, Robert Junior came to the job with no background or experience whatsoever, but this was no barrier to such an enterprising young man. He and Ann began a working relationship which lasted many years before he left to form his own business. He eventually became another mega-millionaire founding the Hard Rock Café, Planet Hollywood and other great theme restaurants. Robert Earl Senior is a Water Rat, his son eventually becoming a Companion Rat.

At the age of 8½, Tim was at my old prep school, Franklin House in Palmers Green. He was unhappy as the other boys played the teachers up and he couldn't work, so wanted a change. Ann, an avid reader of newspapers, noticed a small ad in *The Daily Telegraph* saying that the founder and principal of a school in Leicestershire was looking for two boys for whom he would give a bursary in his last year before retirement. His name was Serrille Phillips and the school was Nevil Holt, near Market Harborough; we phoned and made an appointment to see him.

The school was an old King John hunting lodge in the most idyllic of settings on a hill in vast acres of Leicestershire countryside. Serille Phillips was just like Clifford Thomas, the headmaster of Dulwich College who had spoken at our wedding – gentle, rotund, 'cuddly' and most charming, and treated us with the greatest courtesy. He was obviously very proud of the school which he had founded many years before and which he was pleased to hand over to his son David, whom we also met.

We were conducted ('interviewed') around the school and grounds and sent on our way. Timothy loved the place and we duly received a formal letter accepting him and offering a bursary. Still being inept about financial matters, I asked Mr Phillips to spell out the precise terms. We did our sums and then posed the most difficult question of all to Tim: "Do you want to go to that school and board away from home?" Without hesitation, he said, 'Yes'. We decided that we could afford it – just – especially if Ann continued to work at the *Beefeater*, and that we would send him there. We were then reminded of a brief word from Miss Myrnahan, a teacher at Franklin House, who had said to us, "Don't worry about his future; Timothy is definitely scholarship material."

I remember with painful clarity what I felt at the time was the worst day of my life. Tim was to start in the January term and the only way we could get him there was by train from London, escorted by a teacher and some boys returning from holiday. We put our eight-and-three quarters little boy on this train, seemingly on his own, and watched with tears flowing down our cheeks – but not Tim's since he was so excited – as we waved while the train pulled out. I do not know how I managed to work that night, I was so miserable. Pagliachi comes to mind: "Laugh clown, laugh, though your heart be broken." It proved, however, to be one of the best decisions we made. Tim spent four of the happiest years of his life at that wonderful school, not only receiving a fine education, but also learning the joys of cricket and skiing as well as other sports.

Ann and I rejoiced in our regular visits, either to collect him for holidays or exeats, or take him back there afterwards. We attended sports days and celebration evenings and simply adored the place and everything about it. Ron Deas was the master who arranged several skiing trips which I went on... but Ann only once! She had a lousy ski instructor and, having ended up up-ended in a very snowy bush, said, "What sort of sport is it that has a blood wagon waiting at the bottom of the hill to pick up the pieces? Never again will I put those stupid bits of wood on my feet!" And she never did; but I did and loved every minute.

Tim took his Common Entrance exam and won an Exhibition to Mill Hill; believe me, this really did help our finances. He did very well there, playing some good-quality cricket for the First XI as an opening fast bowler. He became head of his house and a senior prefect, eventually going to Brunel University to read Economics and European Studies.

Our daughter Tracy was totally different. From the age of 4½, she attended Palmers Green High School for Girls, one of the better ones around at the time, and there she stayed. We have always said that Tracy is happy in a rut. Get herself into a comfortable, untroubled groove and there she loved to stay, and no persuasion or coercion on our part could shift her. Queenswood is a wonderful girls' public school nearby which would have given her the same type of education as Mill Hill gave Tim and which we offered her. No way! She loved her school, her friends and everything about it and did extremely well.

One day Tracy came home and broadcast the news that she had become Head Girl in partnership with her close friend Tessa Row. Our cup of happiness was full and we were thrilled that she too had achieved something akin to Tim, who always seemed to be winning things. The two girls had very good alto voices and sang in the school choir led by Miss Venus. Each year they would sing at the Royal Festival Hall in the Ernest Read Christmas Concert for Children on the first Saturday morning in December. We never missed, and it was highly amusing that when they left school, John Railton, the very charming conductor, persuaded them both to continue to sing in the concert as he was desperately short of altos. They did this well into their twenties, still dressed in PGHS uniforms! The wonderful song which ended each concert was

Parry's *Ring out wild bells*, one of the greatest secular year-end songs ever written and which, every time I hear it, sends a tingle down my spine. If ever I am invited onto Roy Plomley's desert island, that would certainly be one of my eight records.

Palmers Green High School did not have a sixth form at that time. Tracy did not consider that she was university material, as bright as she was, so went to St Godric's Secretarial College in Hampstead, which boasted a great reputation, not only as a secretarial college but also as a kind of 'finishing school'.

At the *Beefeater*, the cloakroom had to be guarded and our kids worked there occasionally, earning themselves tips. In Henry VIII's theme show, Master Trenchermen were appointed, as were 'Keepers of the Food' and 'Keepers of the Wine', the reward for which was a scroll upon which their names were written. It had to be in Olde English writing and we all developed a kind of talent for it which has never left us. Tracy's handwriting was never brilliant and on the day she sat the scholarship for secretarial college, we asked how she had fared and if her answers were legible. She dropped the bombshell that she had written the entire four-hour paper in genuine Olde English script, illuminating the first letter in every paragraph and producing an epic. The teachers were absolutely astounded. She won her scholarship.

Incidentally, Ann recalls one delightful occasion when Tracy was about six years old. At an open day, Tracy's favourite teacher, Mrs Loudon, sidled up to Ann, very conspiratorially, and said in a quiet voice, "Er, Mrs Williams. May I have a private word with you please?" And, after a pause said, "Do you mind if I ask you a very personal question which has been worrying us?" Now very puzzled and intrigued, Ann agreed. "Would you mind telling me what you do for a living? Oh, this is so embarrassing." Ann simply said, "I'm a singer in cabaret. Why?" "Oh, thank heavens for that!" Mrs Loudon replied, obviously deeply relieved. "You see, we asked the children to write a little story about their parents and Tracy wrote, 'My mummy goes out at night to earn pennies!' and we just wondered what on earth she meant!"

High in the beautiful mountains of North Wales, close to Harlech, was a small but prosperous sheep farm called *Cwm Yr Afon*, which translates to *The Valley of the River*. An extended family, including eleven children, lived in the big, whitewashed farmhouse looking back over a lovely pair of mountains, *Rhinog Fawr* and *Rhinog Bach* (Big and Little Rhinog). Dad boasted that his father would send his two sheepdogs out of the farm, down the valley and up the far hillside to round up his 100-fold flock of sheep and bring them home. Simply by whistling from the farmhouse door he could control them with consummate ease and herd them in. As a youngster, Dad would accompany his father as they 'drove' the sheep from Harlech about forty miles to the market in Bangor, taking them along the foothills around Mount Snowdon where they would sleep rough overnight and watch the sunrise. He said that no two sheep are alike "…and, *Huw bach,* I will give you a shilling for any two you can find that are identical!" He never did.

My grandfather had an amazing way of counting, in *farmers' Welsh*, the sheep in pairs as they ran through a gate, and he was never wrong. It is called 'sheep-scoring' and originated with the Welsh language! Sadly, I only met him once when I was a baby and do not remember him. The only language spoken on the farm was Welsh. Indeed, none of Dad's older relatives spoke any English at all and, although it was never mentioned, I believe that he only learned English in the army in the First World War. I vaguely remember a sepia photograph of Dad in uniform, but for some reason the subject was taboo.

In 1919 he won a scholarship to the Royal Academy and English became his main language. He boasted that he totally lost his Welsh accent; Ann had other ideas and noticed vestiges of it whenever they spoke – he used to enjoy his little Welsh chats to Ann.

For over 170 years, the Welsh community in London have held what is known as the *Gwyl Dewi Sant,* the St David's Day Dinner at The Savoy Hotel, and discovering a true, Welsh-speaking toastmaster in their midst, my father was booked. He was in his element as it meant that he was amongst his fellow-countrymen and could make all the announcements in both languages and enjoy the predominantly Welsh speeches. At that time there were a number of Welsh County Societies holding dinners in London at which both he and I were in demand.

Regrettably, Welsh was never spoken at home as my mother was English so I never heard it. When I met and married Ann, I occasionally went to her Chapel, The Borough Welsh Congregational Chapel (where I met my doom!), where the services were nearly all in Welsh. Even then I did not learn to speak it, but fortunately I have a flair for languages and in particular, pronunciations. Dad died in 1983 and the *Gwyl Dewi Sant* was offered to me, with the condition that I make every announcement in Welsh and English. This I have steadfastly managed to do, with the help of Ann and other members of that organisation, especially The Hon Gaenor Howells, who actually invented a Welsh word for Toastmaster, '*a Llwnc Destynwr*'. I relished the challenge and feel proud that I am carrying on a family tradition and, in a very small way, promoting the Welsh language. In fact, I am honoured to have been asked to be President in 2007 – God help them!

I have had other occasions when my scant knowledge of the language has been put to good effect. One memorable occasion was the formal opening of the second Severn Bridge. It was to be opened by HRH The Prince of Wales and I presided over the inaugural ceremony held in a large marquee on the Welsh side of the bridge. The arrangements were as follows: Prince Charles arrived on the English side, had a brief walk along part of the bridge and met officials and VIPs in the presence of hundreds of schoolchildren, to whom he chatted. Having completed the introductions, the National Anthem was played, after which he got into his limousine and drove to the middle of the bridge, where he stopped and unveiled a plaque. He then continued over to the Welsh side and met the important dignitaries, again in the presence of children from local schools. As he got out of the car, a 21-gun salute was fired honouring his arrival and they played and sang the Welsh National Anthem, *Land of My Fathers*. These ceremonies were shown on television screens in the marquee where hundreds of officials and guests were assembled awaiting his arrival.

When HRH arrived, he recognised me and came and shook my hand. I asked if everything was OK as he looked windswept and, uncharacteristically, a bit dishevelled – he is always immaculate. He whispered to me, "No, it damn well isn't OK… I'm furious. The person who sited those guns for the salute must be an idiot. They were placed right under the bridge where the children were standing. It was absolutely deafening, the children were frightened and the blast blew back all over us!" He then paused, as he never really allows his emotions to show in public, and then added with a smile, "… but otherwise, I'm fine, thank you!"

A consortium of English, Welsh and French contractors had collaborated to build the bridge and all were represented at the highest level at the opening ceremony. There were three speakers and it had been tacitly suggested that I introduce them in all three languages. Now, my French isn't too bad, but I was not *au fait* with some of the official words in the speech. Thankfully, Ann and I had arrived the day before and so we dashed to Monmouth to buy a French dictionary. However, this was useless as it did not advise on grammar, so we asked if the hotel had any French staff who could help. They sent a highly bemused and suspicious young French commis waiter to our room and we asked for a translation. He, too, had difficulty but eventually came up trumps. When I made the announcement, the French consortium was thrilled to bits and appreciated the gesture.

As he was about to leave, Prince Charles spotted me and came to say goodbye. His parting shot was, "I didn't know you could speak French!" I said, "Oh yes, Sir… but what about my Welsh?" "Well," he replied, "With a name like Bryn Williams I would have expected nothing less! If I can speak it, I'm jolly sure you can!" And, grinning broadly, he left.

Chapter 5

Round Table

"Order!... Order!"

George Thomas
Speaker of the House of Commons

The National Association of Round Tables of Britain and Ireland (RTBI) was founded in the 1930s in Norwich by a young man named Louis Markesi. The Rotary movement, founded in Chicago in 1905, was also very active. However, it admitted only two senior practitioners from any professional calling into their midst and therefore consisted of rather older gentlemen. Nevertheless, many Rotary Clubs actively assisted in the founding of Round Tables in their towns. Louis Markesi had the great idea that there were thousands of young, aspiring business leaders in every community, who were not quite eligible for Rotary. He gathered together a number of his younger business colleagues from many professions and vocations and eventually founded Norwich Round Table Number One. The badge he designed is round with 24 black-and-white segments; in the centre is the Rose of England with a gold King Arthur segment at 'twelve o'clock', based on the Round Table of Cornish legend. Everyone in Round Table is equal, but for management purposes a chairman is elected annually. Qualification was not restricted to only two in any profession, but encouraged all young, aspiring business and professional men to join. The motto of Round Table is 'Adopt, Adapt, Improve' and the organisation helps local and national charities.

As my profession began to burgeon and grow, I did more and more work at small functions in the Wood Green area. Mr Bob Mepstead told me that The Rotary Club of Wood Green was sponsoring the founding of a Round Table which would entail some functions and would I be interested? I certainly was and became quite friendly with Bob… until he was caught with his hand in the till of his employer and saw time as a guest of Her Majesty!

The founding of a Table in those days required two formal functions: an Inaugural Dinner followed by a Charter Night, the two being held about a year apart. Bob invited me to officiate at the first of these in November 1950, which was a huge success. However, Wood Green became and continued to be a somewhat rebellious Table and, instead of waiting the statutory twelve months, decided to hold their Charter Night nine months later in July 1951. The rules state that all who register as a member at the Charter Night become founders. I was 17 years and 11 months old! – too young by a month to become a founder! Tough! The Charter night was also a big success and at the first full meeting of the new Round Table in September, I became the first inductee at the very tender age of 18 years and one month.

Possibly the finest rule that Louis Markesi – whom I eventually came to know, albeit briefly – created was that 40 was the magical age at which everyone had to leave. Yes, everyone is kicked out at the AGM of the Table year after his fortieth birthday. (Regrettably, in my view, this has been extended to 45, but as the movement is now in serious decline, I suppose it was a rescue operation!) I was able to stay until I was 40 years and nine months old, a total of 22 years and eight months, which my Table claimed was the record as the longest period of membership of any Tabler at that time.

The '40 rule' eventually resulted in retired members not wishing to lose the friendship and camaraderie they enjoyed in Round Table, forming follow-on clubs they could join at 41. In the 1960s, a national organisation was formed, its full title being The National Association of Ex-Tablers Clubs, euphemistically and simply known as 41 Club, which ex-Tablers joined in their thousands. Many of these still exist, very happily and successfully today, but are mainly dining clubs with some community and fund-raising activities. Indeed, many 41 Clubs are thriving in areas where Round Tables have closed and cease to exist.

As a Tabler I worked at hundreds of dinners and ladies' nights, launching one of the most successful and enjoyable periods of my life. I officiated at National Conferences all over the UK, with the odd incursion into Europe. As a crowd, Round Tablers are very special and 'different'. All are highly intelligent, successful businessmen, many with huge egos and personalities and some are irrepressible 'would-be' comics and comedians who like to be heard. In short, they can be the toughest crowd that any toastmaster can encounter – or the most rewarding, as I found to my great joy. However, one of my criticisms is that they are somewhat – nay, highly – intolerant of non-Tablers who are trying to control them and so tend to give them a rough ride. Don't get me wrong, they are not unkind, they are just unthinking and ultra-critical if they think that someone is not performing too well, which is why many of my colleagues hated doing Round Table functions. Personally, I revelled in them because I was one of their number and knew how to handle them.

Peter Bush was the National Vice-President and due to be our leader the following year. At the forthcoming National Conference to be held in Bournemouth, he was to be the Chairman at what was called the Overflow Party on the final night. He approached me and asked if I would like to be the toastmaster. It was called the Overflow Party because the Pavilion Ballroom, Bournemouth, was not large enough to take everyone who wanted to attend, so they split the evening into two events, the President presiding over the main dinner and Peter over the other. What I did at that dinner must have been acceptable because I was invited to the main ball afterwards – my first of what would be over twenty national conferences.

Every final night at a Round Table conference is 100% fancy dress... if you are wearing anything formal, you don't get in. However, there is a simple expedient of removing your jacket, turning it inside-out and putting it back on; that way, you qualify!

That final night is indelibly imprinted on my memory and was the first of twenty or so such evenings I was to experience – but afterwards, always in charge! Peter Bush loved my work and told the convenors of his own conference in Aberdeen that I was to be the toastmaster at all social events.

The Beech Ballroom, Aberdeen, held around 1,500 diners and dancers. At conferences, there were invariably three main activities: the International Luncheon – always my favourite as I was given complete scope to 'ad lib'; the main conference banquet and ball; and the final night fancy dress ball with competing floats. Individual Tables, or 'areas' into which the whole of the UK had been divided, built floats which they would bring into the auditorium to be judged by the President and other officers. Huge fun, no one took them too seriously and many were extremely well and cleverly prepared and funny.

At the Aberdeen Conference, during the ball after the main banquet, I was given free rein as a dance Master of Ceremonies. I pulled out all the stops and received a five-minute standing ovation. My continuation at Round Table functions was assured and, as I was only 27 at the time, I knew I had a great future with that organisation which I loved. And so it proved. It also introduced me to great artistes and bands that I would otherwise not have met.

In Aberdeen I met and compèred onto the ballroom floor that wonderful and legendary Scottish artiste, Jimmy Logan, who tore them up. Years later we both became Water Rats and he never forgot my control of that crowd which enabled him to be so hugely successful. Jimmy Shand, one of the bands, was wonderful, and Chic Murray, the comic at the banquet, was brilliant. It was a lovely conference which set me well on the road to a highly enjoyable Round Table career.

All conferences were memorable for one thing or another and I clearly recall very nearly breaking the ballroom floor at *Butlins* holiday camp, Pwllheli, terrifying hundreds of Tablers drinking in the 'Car and Starter Bar' below. *The March of the Mods* was brand new to the dancing world. As an MC, I had learned it and asked the bandleader to get the music, which he did. *The March of the Mods* is in strict 4:4 time, with all the dancers jumping up and down to a very precise rhythm. The 3,000 or so Tablers loved it and I let it go on for several minutes. However, the sprung floor upon which they were dancing was rocking like waves and was immediately above a bar. As soon as the rhythm began, dozens of decorations in the Car and Starter Bar began to drop down from the ceiling to the revellers below! They fled! Nothing serious actually happened and at a post mortem weeks later with the bosses of *Butlins*, we were all reassured that everything was quite safe as their buildings were very strong. However, they did tell us that had the floor become rigid, then that really would be trouble as it would mean that the springiness had broken and it could have collapsed!

It was at that conference that I met my great idol as a comedian, a man I had heard many times on the wireless in *Ray's a Laugh* and whom I never thought I would meet. I refer to the legendary Ted Ray. His real name was Charlie Olden and in his early days he flirted with the idea of reversing his surname. Sadly, Charlie Nedlo proved disastrous so he dropped it. He was a keen golfer and eventually chose the name of one of the greatest golfers England produced back in the early 1900s, Ted Ray. Incidentally, Michael Nosnikrap did well not to follow Charlie's precedent, although he did consider it… briefly. You work it out!

Butlins holiday camps do not really lend themselves to banquets with dances to follow, but great endeavours were made to create a huge banqueting room for about 2,000 delegates and their wives. The remainder of the 5,000-6,000 chose not to attend the banquet but returned from dinner elsewhere in time for the cabaret. As usual, the banquet and speeches dragged on and the ten o'clock cabaret time drew ever closer.

As the time approached, I began receiving messages that a Mr Robert Butlin, son of the boss, was getting agitated in the dressing room and wanted 'The Toastmaster' to speed things up. Now, there are some things that are impossible even for toastmasters and interfering with formal speakers and Presidents of organisations is one of them, so I sent a rude message back to Bobby Butlin, whom I knew, telling him that we would be there when we were good and ready and to calm down! Eventually, the speeches ended and I instructed everyone to make for the appropriate ballroom as quickly as possible. Trying to seat several thousand men and women on a restricted number of chairs and benches, encouraging most of them to squat down on the floor, is not something that can be rushed, but I worked at it.

Ted Ray was in a real state of flux about how he would be received by such a vast audience: Would they listen? Would they talk? Could they hear? How well would he go down? were the thoughts crowding his mind. I reassured him that everything would be great and that I would get them ready, but it would take time. The earlier arrivals had become a bit restive and began their usual chant, *Oh Why are we Waiting?* – at which point I walked to the microphone and began conducting them, also singing along. When it eventually ended, I simply said to my Round Table mates, "You're waiting, 'coz I ain't bloody ready yet!" They roared their approval because they knew me. As a Tabler, I could get away with it.

At last everyone was settled and I managed to get total silence to introduce the inimitable Ted Ray. Within the first two minutes of his act, one of the clever-clog would-be hecklers shouted something at Ted. His reply was instant and absolutely brilliant, bringing a roar of approval from the audience. In one quick retort, he had totally silenced a stupid heckler and completely won over a vast Round Table crowd. Nobody could heckle Ted and get away with it; he was the king, the master. Ted Ray did an hour, after which he came down the slope from the stage with tears rolling down his cheeks. The audience had risen to their feet cheering him to the rooftops. He handed me his violin and said, "Do you mind if I go back and do some more?" What could I say? They were going mad for more and he gave it to them. One of my cherished moments.

There was a surprising sequel to this story. Many years later I was invited, as the guest celebrity, to go onto a popular radio programme called *Does the Team Think?* chaired by Macdonald, Hobley with Cyril Fletcher (later to become my agent for speaking engagements), Jimmy Edwards who did not know me, Tommy

Trinder who did, and Ted Ray, as the team. At the top of the show when I was introduced, Ted Ray told the studio audience, and the millions of radio listeners, of the first time we had met and he recounted that Round Table Conference many years before. He was effusive with his praise about my handling of that crowd and said that he could not remember a more stupendous evening in his career. I felt a million feet tall.

My question to 'The Team' was: "How would you stop a person speaking at a function who had been going on for too long and was boring people silly?" I knew that this would play into the hands of Tommy Trinder, as when he was King Rat he built a huge traffic-light box which he put on the top table. When each speaker began, the green light was on; when he had spoken for a while, the amber light went on and he knew that he only had one minute left in which to finish. When the red light went on, the audience could shout, whistle, boo, chuck rolls or serviettes, or do anything to make the blighter shut up. Of course, as the comics came on, he played around with the lights mercilessly and switched to red the second a comic started – it was great fun. There was one occasion when HRH Prince Philip was speaking and going on and on, but in deference to the royal guest, Tommy did not bother with the lights. After about ten minutes, the now disturbed Prince Philip said, "I wish Trinder would switch that bloody light on, I want to sit down." It brought a roar from the audience and an immediate red light.

Mac Hobley asked me if I had any ways of stopping speakers from droning on and on, so I recounted a story that had happened to me a day or so before. I was officiating at a luncheon and immediately before introducing a certain speaker, was handed a note. It said, "There is a *Ford* car outside, registration number ABC 123, which is illegally parked. Will the owner attend to it right away or the police will deal with it. Pause... Pray silence for Rabbi Cymberg." The Rabbi rose to his feet to declare, "This is going to be the shortest speech on record... that's *my* car he's just mentioned!"

There were many memorable occasions at the 24 or so National Conferences I did for both Round Table and Round Table International, later to become The World Council of Young Men's

Service Clubs, shortened to WoCo. Some great international acts were booked with varying degrees of success. As they were so huge, conferences had to be held in some strange places, including on the pitch at Blackpool United Football Club – they simply covered the entire area with a massive marquee.

I recall with some sorrow the only time I met the wonderful Billy Connolly, who was young and right at the peak of his fame with his own special brand of humour. Sadly, I have to report that on that occasion he died rather spectacularly, but it was not his fault. With the enormous stages, sometimes right in the centre of the dance floor, stand-up comics had virtually no chance of success. Of the thousands present, only a few hundred could actually see and hear the great man and noise from the others was loud enough to drown out his material. The vast crowd could not get close enough – Billy just 'died', and there was nothing anyone could do. I remember hearing him in a radio interview several years later when he mentioned the event; he was rather embarrassed that he had gone down so poorly. I could have told him it wasn't his fault; no comic would have stood a chance in those circumstances.

Now, Round Tablers are respectable businessmen aged between 18 and 40, not renowned for indulging in mass hysteria, or allowing their wives to scream and shout, trying to tear the pants off 'rock stars' like a bunch of teenage bobby-soxers. But Bill Hayley and the Comets didn't know this and in the contract of their booking it stated emphatically that, "When Mr Hayley and his musicians go onto the stage to perform, they are to be protected by a personal bodyguard of no fewer than ten armed men to escort them from the dressing room and off again after the show." When this was read in the committee, we all fell about laughing. Needless to say, they didn't get it, nor the mass adulation and I sensed they were disappointed that the crowd was so docile. Despite this, on the first night they were great and the crowd loved them. However, because of the massive cost, they were contracted to perform the following night, to more or less the same people. Expecting something different, we were disappointed that the act was identical in every way... including the 'impromptu' ad libs! Bill Hayley and the Comets were not the most popular act we saw.

For many years, the favourite band with Round Tablers was Kenny Ball and his Jazzmen; they adored them, not only Kenny, but his super clarinettist, Andy Cooper – he of *I'm the King of the Swingers* fame. They were always the second band to whichever other group had been engaged and I was in charge of production and timing. In my programme, it would be arranged that the main band play for an hour, after which Kenny played for about 1¼ hours when the bands changed back again for the rest of the night. However, the noisy, boisterous Round Table crowd never wanted Kenny to stop.

When they had been on for about an hour, I would appear on the stage, give them a big 'thank you' hinting that they had to stop and get off. The crowd would go barmy, wanting more, and Kenny would have none of it – he wanted to carry on and played to the crowd mercilessly, making me the spectre at the feast. Whenever I tried to get Kenny off, I would be booed like the pantomime 'baddy', and Kenny would say through the mic, "Would you like another one?" sending the crowd wild. So they played another number, after which we repeated the dose again, with the same electric effect on the crowd who, good-naturedly, made various suggestions as to where they would like me to go… the second word being 'off'!

What the noisy mob did not know, and never found out, was that it was all a big scam. Ken and I had carefully worked out how his slot would end as he was professional enough to know that timings had to be met. The fun and games about me trying to get him off began a good fifteen minutes before he was due to end, but it made for such good entertainment that we hammed it up every time. The crowd loved it and we both came out smelling of roses.

He went on for three encores, one of which was a tune called, *That was a beautiful song; sing us another one, do!* – the main verse being a limerick, which usually began with, 'There once was a xxxxx called xxxxx,' with the chorus being sung by all the band in between.

Each member of the band would sing a verse and get huge laughs from the crowd. Occasionally, Kenny would call me over and say, "Come on, Bryn. Have you got one you can sing for us? I bet you have!" whilst handing me the mic. I just loved it and actually remember the two that I sang.

> There once was a lady called Myrtle,
> Who went off to bed with a turtle.
> Come one sunny morn,
> She gave birth to a prawn,
> Which proved that the turtle was furtle.

That was a beautiful song… sing us another one, doooooo!

> I once knew a man from Darjeeling,
> Who rode on a bus bound for Ealing.
> It said on the door,
> 'Please don't spit on the floor',
> So he carefully spat on the ceiling.

That was a beautiful song… sing us another one, doooooo!

Exit stage left.

NCH Action for Children – later to become simply NCH – was a wonderful charity for which I did a great deal of work. One of its keenest supporters was the former Speaker of the House of Commons, the Rt Hon George Thomas, later to become Lord Tonypandy. Those with long memories will certainly recall his beautiful Welsh inflection when he intoned, "Order, order!" to bring the Members of Parliament under control. The hierarchy of the charity decided to honour him by creating an influential section called The George Thomas Society. To launch it, a banquet was held at The Guildhall in the City of London at which HRH Princess Alexandra was the guest of honour. George Thomas explained that the Society was to be limited to 100 men and women willing to donate £1,000, and it was hoped that they could be found at this banquet. I was so impressed with what was planned that I immediately became a Fellow – breaking the news, as gently as I could, of spending the thousand quid to Ann when I got home! George himself was number one, Prince Charles was the second and Prime Minister Maggie Thatcher was the third, and very soon £100,000 was raised to start it off.

Over the years, several functions were held by the Society at which I officiated. As a result I met Lord Tonypandy many times and we became firm friends. Indeed, I have a limited edition print of his portrait personally signed to me. It hangs in pride of place, on the wall in my office beside a photograph of my father – another great Welshman.

Prince Charles invited the Society to Highgrove for a tour of his estate and tea, to be followed by dinner in a local hostelry. Ann and I drove down but told the organisers that we could not stay for the dinner and would have to leave after the tea. This was helpful to them as George Thomas could not stay either and needed transport back to London. He had contracted cancer of the throat, for which he was undergoing treatment, and had been told to speak as little as possible and rest his voice.

Prince Charles was the perfect host, making us individually welcome in his home and proudly showing us all around his land; it was a very special afternoon. (There is an aphorism about hosts. It is said that the perfect host is one who makes you feel at home – when he wishes you were!)

On our way home, George Thomas sat in the passenger seat beside me. Ann and I confidently expected him to go to sleep, but not a bit of it. For the whole of the two-hour journey made through pouring rain, he alternated between holding us spellbound or laughing uproariously with stories of his life, his politics, his religion, his views, his term as Speaker of the House and so much more. We took him to The Reform Club and bade him farewell after one of the most memorable journeys we can remember.

One of the saddest occasions of my career was a night when we all thought that we had lost George through his illness. The Society had organised a large teaparty at the Guildhall where hundreds attended. It was to be followed by a banquet where, again, Princess Alexandra was the guest. Prime Minister Margaret Thatcher had been the guest of honour at the tea and Lord Tonypandy was obviously very ill, struggling to get around and speak to everyone. He was a strong-willed and gutsy Welshman and refused to stop, but sadly it became far too much for him.

Towards the end of the party, he nearly collapsed and Maggie Thatcher caught him, took him firmly by the arm and led him out. He was as ashen as grey flannel and could hardly walk. She called out to me, "Get an ambulance quickly. Lord Tonypandy is very ill and we must get him to hospital." The Lord Mayor of London heard this and ordered me to go and get his chauffeur so that George could be taken to St Thomas's Hospital in his *Rolls Royce*. We took him into the Sheriff's Room, where he laid down. Three men asked if they could go in to see him – they were his London doctors. I was relieved and let them in. One immediately came out and said, "Lord Tonypandy is very ill. He's dehydrating and must get to hospital as quickly as possible." I had the temerity to ask why he was dehydrating and was told that he had been prescribed medicine by a local doctor which was totally the opposite to what they had been prescribing. It was causing almost disastrous effects. He was whisked away to St Thomas's and all of us were convinced that the headlines the following morning would be his obituary. As I said, he was a gutsy old man and it wasn't his turn to go yet. He made a full recovery and was released from hospital after a couple of weeks.

Lord Tonypandy had a lovely head of grey hair, strong and thick. He told me a true story about his chemotherapy, which went something like this: "Bryn, I must tell you, the quacks all told me that when I started on the chemo, within seven weeks I would lose all my hair. But, you know, as time went by, I laughed at them because I didn't lose a single one. I was so pleased, and thought that I had beaten them. And then, one morning, exactly seven weeks to the day, I was taking a bath in my little house in Cardiff, and was astounded to find, swimming around in the water, a whole lot of hair – my hair – it had all come out in one go and there I was, as bald as a coot! Can you believe it? On the very day they forecast – it really made me laugh. So I prayed to my God that when it grew back again, it would be black and strong and curly! But He didn't answer my prayer as it grew back exactly as it always had been!"

George Thomas never forgot to send Ann and me a Christmas card from wherever he was in the world, mostly South Africa, as well as holiday postcards during the summer. He was a Methodist Lay Preacher and one of God's perfect gentlemen – the Welsh word for which would be 'Duwiol' or Godly. He told us that his greatest joy was to preach on Sunday mornings in Welsh chapels, to which people flocked when they knew he was coming. When I celebrated my fortieth anniversary as a toastmaster and held a large cocktail party at the Café Royal, which is detailed elsewhere in the book, I invited him to speak on my behalf. He told me that he was proud to do so. I was equally proud that such a great and wonderful man would so honour me. May God rest his soul.

Chapter 6

The Founding of Two Toastmasters' Organisations

"Ours is the second oldest profession, which, like the first
is being ruined by amateurs!"

Anon

History tells us that the wearing of the scarlet coat was started by William Knight-Smith in around 1892. His main claim to fame was that he was an official starter of the Olympic Games, and he became a very successful toastmaster. His portrait, owned by The National Association of Toastmasters, is currently in the Tudor Room of the Café Royal, having been presented to Lord Forte at one of our banquets. William Knight-Smith was something of a maverick, being the first toastmaster to wear a red coat rather than the traditional black, but he set a trend and the red-coated toastmaster became prominent during the mid-20th century.

A City Toastmaster and Beadle to the Worshipful Company of Innholders, Gordon Marsh had a different story which is rather more glamorous. The word 'Toast' actually derives from an ancient tradition of viniculture. For centuries the wine was none too palatable and the cellarmen who looked after the wines of the great houses needed to find a way of improving it. A simple solution to the problem was discovered. The Master of the Wine brought the wine up from the cellar and poured it in a very large bowl, around which were several smaller ones containing spices and other flavourings. He would take a piece of bread on the end of a toasting fork, heat it in a flame, toasting it, dip it into these spices and stir it into the bowl of wine. He became known as The Master of the Toast and was a most important and influential part of any large banquet, continuing well into the early part of the 20th century.

Way back in the middle of the 19th century, the then Earl of Derby was a shy, diffident man who hated the limelight. Protocol required that he give lavish parties, but he did not enjoy the formality of it. The shy Earl suggested that it would be a good idea to get his 'Master of the Toast' to introduce the various 'Toasts' he wished to drink, thus starting a trend which became fashionable. Embellishing the idea, and to ensure that this servant could be better seen, the Earl dressed his Master of the Toast in one of his old hunting-pink jackets for the occasion. Thus began the tradition of wearing a pink (not red!) tailcoat. You pays yer money and you takes yer pick.

It is often asked, how does one apply the word 'Toast' to a pledge or greeting over wine? There was an article in *The Tatler* in the mid-seventeen hundreds which states:

> There was, in the Pump Room in the City of Bath a Celebration on a Holy Day when two fellows, both half 'fuddled', discovered a lady taking to the waters. As she languished there, one of them expressed the desire to jump in but was prevented in his purpose by the other who, scooping some of the water into the glass he was holding and raising it said, "NAY, though I likest not the beverage, I will take the TOAST to this woman," and drank a long draught. Thereafter that has been the word used when pledging the Health of a Lady.

The Toast referred to was the sop or piece of bread left in the glass by the Master of the Toast. I tried to corroborate this story when I visited Bath but was told that it is apocryphal. I don't care – I like it, as it's somewhat romantic! What is undeniable is that the word 'toast' in my professional title definitely derives from that source.

About forty years ago, I decided to research the history of the profession and went to the library of the British Museum. I was surprised to discover a couple of small books on the subject, one of which gave a long list of names of 'Masters of the Toast' around the middle of the 17th century. There were many high-faluting titles and one I particularly recall was 'Witty Bald-Archie'. Their duties were precise and very important for the stimulation of fun, laughter and drunkenness at formal occasions; the incumbent was charged with 'inventing' amusing Toasts – or as they were also called, 'Huzzars and Pledges'.

At this time it was also traditional for the host to drink or pledge the health of many of his guests… and when each one was honoured, both the host and the guest were obliged to drink a full glass, then invert it to prove that it was empty – anything left in it was tantamount to an insult. There was, at some very special events, a tradition where they drank a glass of wine 'for every letter in your name'. Imagine if you were someone with a daft surname like Massingberd-Montefiore-Smythe! It's little wonder that they earned the reputation for being drunken, debauched Bacchanalian bashes! On these occasions, the Master of the Toast was also required to drain his 'own' glass, which begs the question, how did he stay sober and on top of the job? Anyone old enough will recall that wonderful record made by Michael Bentine of The Toastmaster: 'The Duke of Bessarabia will now drink with the…' Hilarious.

I possess a small collection of what are known as toastmasters' glasses or firing glasses. They are very small with a tiny bowl that holds no more than a thimbleful of wine. They are made of cheap, thick glass with a solid stem and a wide, flat-bottomed base. They had a dual purpose: the base was strong enough to allow the toastmaster to bang it on the table for silence – gavels not then being used for that purpose – and the small bowl meant that the content was little more than a sip, enabling him to drink it all without getting stoned out of his brains. So you can see, the Master of the Toast played a very important part in the junketings and jollities of yesteryear. Each was engaged for his wit, humour, inventiveness and ability to amuse the drinkers with his anecdotes.

During the period up to 1939, there were a number of highly successful toastmasters who dominated the profession. They were a stiff and starchy lot with, apparently, no sense of fun or humour, the veritable antithesis of their mediaeval counterparts, simply running the banquets in a deadpan, straightforward manner. They would condescend to compère the musical entertainment, which invariably followed the dinner, and go home. The words 'Master of Ceremonies' did not even enter their rather narrow minds. Even introducing acts was very formal, as every performer was called either 'Mister' or 'Mistress'. "We shall now be entertained by Mister Bryn Williams who will sing in a tenor voice and be accompanied at the pianoforte by Mistress Ann Williams." Stuffy, pompous twits!

In 1945, these toastmasters, many nearing their eighties, with the odd sixty-year-old, tried to pick up the cudgels (or gavels) where they left off six years earlier, before the war. Sadly, things were not the same and they began to feel that their lofty, self-imposed position of superiority was fading like their reputations. The names that I remember through a gap of fifty years are: John Humphries, Arthur Marsh, Gordon Marsh (no relation), Cyril Ivory, Harold Dean, Harold Davy, Sidney Creasey, John Mills, Arthur Whitehead, Harold Tinsley and Barney Woolf. Somehow, and it is not documented anywhere, they earned the soubriquet of 'The Guild'. They certainly didn't apply it to themselves but it became a general term for those 'ancient' toastmasters who survived the war.

These men found it extremely difficult to adjust to the modern trend and maybe there was a little of the green eye towards the dozens of younger men, straight out of HM Forces, who had bought themselves red coats and given themselves the title of 'toastmaster' with a small 'T'. The tide of new toastmasters became unstoppable, especially as many of them proved to be excellent Masters of Ceremonies at the dances which followed the dinner, even if their toastmaster talents left a lot to be desired.

In the 1950s, many of these newer toastmasters were beginning to make a name for themselves in the Masonic world, where 90% of the available work was to be found. 'The Guild' obviously felt the need to strengthen their position within the profession and collectively decided to form an organisation. It therefore came as something of a surprise to us lesser mortals that they didn't consolidate that name, but, in 1952, founded The Society of London Toastmasters (SLT), deliberately and carefully avoiding any reference to being Masters of Ceremonies (MCs), or working anywhere other than the metropolis.

My father, his friend Maurice Lewin and several other toastmasters not invited to join them at the outset, thought that a toastmaster organisation was a good idea and applied to join. Sadly, the intransigence of these older brethren restricted membership to any toastmaster who was not and did not profess to be an MC, singer, musician or theatrical agent. On those grounds, these men were precluded from joining – in other words, they shut the shop and tried to keep it exclusive. Likewise, when others applied to join, they were turned away dismissively – there was no way they were going to demean their Society by allowing MCs and singers to join. This was extremely petty and short-sighted as their professional life expectancy was limited due to their age and the whole ethos of the business was altering dramatically, but they failed, dismally, to spot it.

By the mid-1950s, I was a young, skinny upstart who was beginning to make a name for myself, but I had been told, in no uncertain terms, not even to bother to apply. I was too young, too good-looking (Ann's words, not mine), too popular as an MC and, horror of horrors, I was also a theatrical employer… the lowest of the low! After all, I booked bands, singers, artistes and all 'those' types of people! "We don't want the likes of *them* in the London Society… we are Toastmasters." And so, at end of 1955, an irate and, in his view, deeply insulted Maurice Lewin rallied seven of his colleagues who had suffered similar disfavour and said, "OK mates. If we can't join them, let's form our own association and let them take it out of that!"

This disparate crowd consisted of my father; Hugh Owens, whose traditional pre-war literature styled him as 'The Entertaining Baritone', and he really was; Maurice Lewin, formerly a London cabby; Johnny Fuller, a very good-looking singer-drummer, together with his friend and tutor Alfie Howard, a great but not very dignified little Master of Ceremonies later to become the Town Crier of Lambeth; Bert Burrows, a gentle giant of a man who was a retired bailiff; Charlie Semus, a thorough professional; Reginald Solomon, who suffered from alopecia and ran a laundry business; and Sam Gooud, a beadle from Wandsworth.

Maurice set this all up as a rival to The Society of London Toastmasters and, following several meetings, The Association of Toastmasters and Masters of Ceremonies was formed at a small, grubby pub called *The Champion* in the Goswell Road, Islington. Frankly, I was totally uninterested and thought it was a whole load of rubbish. However, after gentle persuasion by Dad (and threats of being left out of his will!), I reluctantly agreed to attend the meeting at which we would all become founder-members. They made him the first President; Maurice Lewin was Secretary and Alfie Howard the Treasurer; and so began a 'rivalry' to the only other toastmaster body in the UK.

It was a ridiculous situation! Why they could not have been more far-sighted, and accepted us at the beginning, will never be known. At a general meeting following our founding, it struck us as extremely odd and quite significant that the SLT 'opened their doors' to about six new members, many of whom were perfectly capable dance MCs… some of whom had been turned down by us as being not very good!

The one very sensible thing the SLT did was to 'appoint' Lord Mancroft as their Honorary Toastmaster, a position he was proud to hold until he died. It was a great idea; he was perfect for the job as he was one of the finest after-dinner speakers I have ever heard, and he took his responsibilities seriously. He was a charming and gentle man. One day he rang me, inviting me to visit him in his office. He expressed his strongly-held belief that to have two organisations within the UK in the same small profession was absolutely idiotic. He made me promise that I would do all in my power to try to arrange a merger. I tried and failed dismally. Those in control of the SLT, and our lot, Maurice Lewin in particular, were vehemently against the idea.

We did have a joint meeting about it at the Innholders' Hall but many reasons for not joining were put forward. The road to hell is paved with good intentions, which we all had, but with no great hope. It would certainly have been of benefit to us all had it happened, but feelings were running too high at that time as neither organisation wished to lose its identity. I tried hard to bring the two tribes together and smoke a pipe of peace with a number of joint activities, but alas! it was never followed up and we still have our individual organisations. I guess it will always remain so.

Through the years, our Association flourished and grew. We changed the name in 1974 to The National Association of Toastmasters (NAT) and included members from as far afield as Plymouth and Edinburgh. I was President in 1962. We took it in rotational order and I was the penultimate founder to take office. I held my big thrash in the Café Royal, at that time the largest that we had run, with over 400 attending. I became President again in 1990, my fortieth year in the business, but as I was putting all my energies into my fortieth anniversary banquet at The Grosvenor House, I had a smaller banquet as President. My two speakers at that function were the inimitable Roy Hudd and Peter Goodwright, two great and super Water Rats and good mates.

I must have been the most obnoxious and precocious kid because I have always wanted to 'organise' people, and throughout the years I applied that idiosyncrasy to the NAT. With my dear friend, Johnny Fuller – sadly no longer with us – we organised some car rallies, ending at The Bellhouse Hotel in Beaconsfield. In 1986, when the Queen celebrated her sixtieth birthday, I garnered together a committee from both organisations and proposed a nationwide competition to find the best 'Loyal Toast' to commemorate the occasion. We managed to get a spot on both ITV and BBC news and asked Mr and Mrs Public to write to us with their proposals for either a Toast or a poem, one for adults and another for children under 15. We were deluged with thousands of replies and sat for hour after hour reading through them.

The prize was an all-expenses-paid day out in London! We arranged first-class return rail fares, took the winners to a four-star hotel for morning coffee and rented a big red London bus which took them on a conducted tour of the capital. It stopped for half an hour at *Hamleys,* where they were given presents, and then carried on down to the River Thames for a boat trip luncheon. Afterwards, it was back on the bus again for a further tour until teatime when they were all dropped at the House of Commons. Following a formal tour, they were invited to tea in the House of Lords, hosted by Lord Forte. It was a huge success which received a great deal of publicity, as the Toasts, in the form of poems, were read on television by the winners. The winning entries were also sent to the Queen, who expressed her delight and appreciation... well, she would, wouldn't she!

Centuries ago, in the year 978, an act of treachery fiendishly devised by Queen Aelreda down in Corfe Castle led to the invention of the Loving Cup Ceremony, enacted to this day in the City of London. King Edward (The Martyr) was on the throne of England, but the jealous queen wanted her son Ethelred the Redeless (The Unready) to take over. The boys were friends and she invited Edward down for the weekend. Whilst he was still sitting on his horse slaking his thirst after his long journey, she had him killed; stabbed, I think, but some say he could have been shot with an arrow. He was, after all, only a youngster and so it seemed a bit harsh at the time. But, either way, he died and his cousin got the job. Having done this terrible deed, the queen was filled with remorse and, possibly, a load of wine as well and swore she would never leave Corfe as long as she lived, which she didn't. She also, in her remorsefulness, founded a hospital in that region, so she couldn't have been all bad! This terrible deed was then immortalised in a ceremony about which all toastmasters know everything. It is where drinkers are protected by two people, one back and one front, so that they are quite safe from any kind of attack whilst drinking the health of their neighbour.

In 1977, I noted that the millennium of this act would occur the following year and suggested that we do something about it. A committee was formed between the two organisations with my good and very longstanding friend and colleague Martin Nichols as secretary. He was a professional accountant, and a leading and active member of Round Table, missing out on the top job of

National President by a mere handful of votes. He was Round Table's convenor of a couple of National Conferences and at that time began doing toast-mastering, which he continued thereafter. He and I became Life Vice-Presidents of our Association, he having fulfilled the jobs of treasurer and secretary very successfully over many years.

(It is with great sadness and deep regret that I have to insert here, whilst editing this book for the umpteenth time, that Martin developed cancer of the oesophagus and died in July 2004. Not only did Ann and I lose a very close and much-loved friend, but I also lost a valued colleague and confidant. We went through Round Table together, sharing the running of several conferences until they eventually 'pensioned me off' and Martin took over. I always referred to him to Table audiences as 'my son', although he was only a year my junior. In his passing, our Association has been left with a void which can never be filled. He was friend, father, adviser, counsellor to individual members as well as the whole Association as he was so very wise and kind in all his deliberations. This is not intended as an obituary, but so close was our relationship in all professional matters (and many social ones) that I cannot let it pass without this very small tribute. It is my sad regret that he never lived to read this book. May his soul Rest in Peace.)

I contacted Alderman Peter Vanneck (his Sirship came later), who was designated as being the next Lord Mayor of London, and asked if he would consider hosting a banquet at the Mansion House celebrating one thousand years of the Loving Cup Ceremony. He immediately agreed, a date was fixed and we set about organising the thing. We also commissioned a new solid silver Loving Cup as our own, the small but exquisite cup being beautifully crafted by Brian Toye of *Toye, Kenning and Spencer*. Brian and I had known each other for years as we used to chase each other and a little rubber ball around a squash court at his club, the RAC in Pall Mall. We commissioned fifty cups, but actually only sold 33, of which I have numbers two and three. Number one was produced in gold and is the joint possession of the two organisations, NAT and SLT. It formally changes hands at a brief ceremony at each other's annual banquets, thus ceremonially cementing the friendship that really does exist between the two organisations.

Since we founded our own Association, loads of others have burgeoned. All over the UK there are heaps of them, proving that there must be hundreds of blokes who own red coats and go out at night to earn pennies (a quotation from my daughter, who was six at the time). I have no idea of the standards they boast, but I do know that ours are the highest attainable because of the detailed study and attention to protocol that we have diligently researched and imparted to our members. End of propaganda!

Martin and I had the task of virtually single- (or is it double-?) handedly organising everything. Eventually, just over 300 attended the Mansion House, with all toastmasters wearing their scarlet coats. The City of London is still entrenched in its traditions and has steadfastly refused to accept the red coat as our uniform. Any formal functions in the City require us to wear a black tailcoat with a red-and-white City of London sash – rather dashing really and no hardship to wear. However, we asked the Lord Mayor's permission on this occasion and I believe it was the first, if not the only, time that toastmasters have worn red at a City function in the Mansion House. Being in charge, I gave myself the privilege of proposing the Civic Toast – to speak in the Mansion House is a moment never to be forgotten. I tried to make it an amusing toast and I was grateful to receive a standing ovation, which really was a wonderful feeling. However, as half the room were mates of mine, they would have done that whether it had been funny or not!

The whole event was a resounding success, made all the more significant by the fact that a dozen or so of us were invited onto *Blue Peter* to demonstrate our ancient little ceremony. We all trooped off to the TV studio, dressed ourselves up in our finery, and I was interviewed by none other than John Noakes ('Down, Shep!'). I told the audience of children all about the history of an act of treachery 1,000 years before. The response from that programme was terrific and we received many plaudits… except for a couple of moaning minnies who complained to the producer that we were encouraging children to become alcoholics! You can't win 'em all!

As 2002 approached, when the Queen would be celebrating her Golden Jubilee, my organising instinct reared its ugly head again and I went to my Association with the idea that we should, somehow, commemorate it. The enthusiasm was underwhelmingly lukewarm, perhaps because I made it clear that I was genuinely not prepared to undertake the task of organising it. After fifty years, I felt I had done my bit for the Association and it was high time for some of the younger blood to take over. I could have p****d into the wind for all the reaction I received. So I weakened and said that I would 'look into it'!

I'm told that it is printed in her recipe for jugged hare, that Mrs Beaton states, 'First catch your hare.' I sent a circular to my members, 'First catch your Royal.' If you are going to celebrate on a big scale, you must have a Royal at the party or you won't sell tickets; nobody will come just because a few guys who like to dress in red coats ask you to – you need something special. So I dropped a line to HRH Prince Philip, telling him that all members of The National Association of Toastmasters wished to celebrate and commemorate the Queen's Golden Jubilee by organising a luncheon for charity and would he do us the great honour of accepting an invitation to attend, at the same time suggesting a charity to which the proceeds could be directed? I offered him a choice of five or six luncheon dates from which to choose and was thrilled with his reply that he would be delighted to accept on Thursday 5th November. As it happened, it was a lousy day for me as I already had a lunch booked which I had to farm out, but if you want a Royal, then tough! I notified my membership with glee and set about giving a whole load of instructions and requests as to what was needed.

As his personal tribute to the Queen's celebrations, Prince Philip chose the Commonwealth Veterans Association as his charity. Some of the smaller Commonwealth countries were finding difficulty in looking after their veterans, many of whom were nearly

100 years old and were desperately in need of support of every kind.

Where do you begin to organise a Royal Luncheon, hoping to raise a few grand for a wonderful charity? What do you need? Where do you get it? What venue? What entertainment? What price? What advertising? What paperwork? What would be the 'theme'? Who would be the speakers? And very many more questions that had to be addressed. Well, at least we had begun. We had a Royal. We had a date. We had a charity. We had the blessing of all the membership (well, nearly all!) of the Association and a willingness to support it, and a capable if reluctant organiser: me! The biggest question of all was, how much were we hoping to raise for charity? We had absolutely no clue and just hoped that it would be good.

For a venue we chose The Royal Lancaster Hotel, where the Banqueting Executive, Andrew Bachelor, was marvellous and helped us with everything. We had several members who were happy to give a great deal of time and effort into organising parts of it. At the beginning, the most important item was printing, as we required headed notepaper, advertising blurb and ticket order forms – all of which would have been expensive to produce as we needed thousands. A reasonably new member from Yorkshire was Sue Johansson who ran her own promotional business. She immediately volunteered her services and those of her staff to design and produce all the paperwork – a saving of thousands. She was absolutely great and the quality of her work was supreme. We contacted the charity and they promised as much support as possible, being delighted to be a beneficiary.

The knotty problem of ticket price had to be discussed. How much can you charge the clients for a Royal Luncheon? We eventually settled on a price which terrified most of the members, £120 per ticket. £1,200 per table of ten with all the members coming for free – it's the only way you'll get some of the b*****s there!

Having established that, what about the speakers and entertainment? It had long been a dream of mine to do what the Yanks call 'A Roast'. I had seen it done on a pilot TV show on which I had appeared with Ken Dodd many years before. It was a great concept, but he screwed it all up by going on too long and the idea crashed. I decided to make this our theme, so we needed someone well-known and with a sense of fun to be the butt of our humour. There was only one choice, Jim Davidson, and knowing his love of British and Commonwealth Forces, his reply to my request to attend and speak was immediate. He was thrilled to be asked.

Having got the target of our roast, we needed to find a few speakers who could roast him... it was time for me to pull in a few favours from mates. Thanks to their kindness and generosity, this was not a problem. I asked Barry Cryer, Bob 'The Cat' Bevan, and Roger de Courcey and Nookie Bear to join the top table as speakers and take the mickey out of Jim Davidson. They jumped at it, so that part of the event fell into place.

I also wanted a surprise musical act to perform during the luncheon. A few years ago, the legendary Howard Keel had become a Water Rat, and I knew that he occasionally visited these shores, especially as he had his own golf classic over here. Through his lifelong friend and brother Rat, Clive Stock, I called him in California. He was out and I left a message with his wife. One afternoon, Ann was reading the newspaper when the telephone rang. She picked it up and said, "Hello!... Who? Who? Er... Who did you say you were? Oh, OH! Er... Yes, Er... He is here. Er... Bryn... It's Howard Keel for you," and handed over the phone. We chatted for over half an hour about the business and life in general. Sadly, he said he could not make our lunch on that day due to work on a new show, but he sent everyone his love and it was a purely magical thirty minutes. He really is one of the loveliest men in the business and, when he was made a Rat, I had a very long chat with him and his wife about my favourite musical, *Seven Brides for Seven Brothers*. He told me it took only six weeks to make and was very low-budget. It don't matter a jot, I still think it's sensational.

So, it was back to the musical drawing board. Years ago I had been invited to work at a wedding of a girl I simply adore, Anita Harris, and her charismatic husband Mike Margolis. We've known and loved each other for over thirty years and she was my next obvious choice and readily agreed. She would sing her heart out for me, so that little problem bit the dust.

Sponsorship was my next target. I knew I wouldn't make any appreciable figure without scrounging some generous sponsorship from somewhere. Over many years, I was delighted to do several functions for Companion Rat, Sir Donald Gosling. He virtually ran the White Ensign Club with a whole bunch of events. He was also deeply enmeshed with the Kelly Association, the former, below-decks crew of *HMS Kelly* whose captain was The Earl Mountbatten of Burma. The patron was Countess Mountbatten and the president was HRH The Prince of Wales, and alternate years Sir Donald ran a lunch for all the survivors at which Prince Charles presided. Every other year, Prince Charles invited them to dinner at Highgrove, which demonstrated his love and respect for them all. Sadly, they have nearly all gone to that great ocean above and the Kelly Association has gone with it.

I recall one particular Kelly Luncheon at which I organised my usual raffle; Don provided a case of wine as prizes and I set it all up. At the lunch, Grace was said by the Reverend Canon Roger Royle. When it came to the draw, his name came out of the hat and I said, "The problem with this lunch is that we've got too many 'Royals' in the room." Which made them all sit up and grin. I continued, "… 'Cos one of them has just won a prize. It's Roger Royle." Lots of applause. The next ticket that was drawn had the letters PoW on it and so I said, "Do we have any Prisoners of War here? I've got a ticket which simply says PoW, so it must mean Prisoner of War." Prince Charles looked up at me with a broad grin on his face and said, "It's Prince of Wales, you idiot!" "OH! sorry, Sir. Didn't think of that. You've won a bottle of booze!" He said to me, "I don't drink; would you like it?" I said, "No thanks. Let's give it to one of the lads!" The Prince agreed. The youngest 'lad' there was over 90.

For years Don Gosling had been telling me how kind I've been to him, so the time was ripe for me to call in another favour. I contacted him through his wonderful secretary Anne Yussof and he agreed, without any hesitation, to give £10,000 to the event.

Ticket sales were going well, but I now had to address the matter of advertising to raise more cash. Most charity events I've attended have printed brochures, which undoubtedly raise a great deal of money, but in my view they are a virtual waste of the advertisers' money. If the punters look at them at all, it is only a cursory glance and then they get chucked on the floor and forgotten. It is doubtful whether one in ten is actually retained by anyone, and I vowed that this would not be the case at my lunch. At my fortieth anniversary dinner, I produced a diary, which many have kept as souvenirs, and I decided to have one again this time. But where to go to obtain them? I contacted several publishers and was given ridiculous prices.

One of our Past Presidents was Ken Tappenden, MBE, formerly Commander of the Kent Constabulary. His son works for a national newspaper, is a brilliant artist and designer and is very skilled in print production. Ken happened to know a bloke in his area of Rochester who worked for a publishing company called *Allen and Bertram*. It was a mighty coincidence that their premises are in Cuffley, literally at the end of my road. To slash a lengthy diatribe to pieces, they agreed to produce a diary for me and at the keenest price imaginable. All the employees there are Plymouth Brethren and are the loveliest people in the world with whom to deal. In these IT-controlled times, it came as a real surprise to learn that not only do they not own a computer, but neither do they have a facsimile machine. They simply run their very successful business with snail mail and telephones and are blissfully happy. They produced 1,000 of the most exquisite and magnificent diaries, which we gave to every guest. We sold over thirty pages of advertising which added substantially to the pot. We were up and running.

We had a venue, a Royal, a charity, a date, speakers, advertisers, over 35 toastmasters in their red coats, ticket sales were booming (even at 120 quid a throw), and we had musical entertainment in abundance – in addition to Anita Harris, some musical friends of mine, Bob Bates' Souzophonia, a trad-jazz trio, agreed to give their services. So we were flying high. We just needed a bit more sponsorship – if poss!

I had never actually met Mr Philip Green. His wealth and generosity were legendary, but he had not flown into my spider's web until one very special evening. I was invited to do the Breast Cancer Care evening at the London Hilton Hotel at which Cherie Blair was to be the guest of honour. Mr Green's company, *BHS*, were the main and extremely generous sponsors of the whole evening and all was going like a dream. There were about 700, mainly ladies, attending a banquet and fashion show, and it really was a glitzy and delightful do. Mr Green was thrilled to be with Cherie and tried to persuade her and one of the artistes to join him in singing *Maybe it's because I'm a Londoner!* on the catwalk. He pledged £20,000 if she would agree, and sought my help in arranging it. I tried my hardest, to no avail, but he was grateful for my support.

In a quiet moment I had the temerity (or as my Jewish friends would call it, *chutzpah* – my old headmaster would have called it 'b****y cheek') to mention my Royal do. Philip Green said, "Have a word with my secretary and tell her what you need." She was super and told me to call her the following day. This I did and she said, "Well, how much would you like him to give you?" Gently suppressing the urge to say, "What about a million?" I said, "Well, we are producing a very high-quality diary which is costing ten grand. Anything he can give towards that would be wonderful." She said, "Leave it to me. I'll wait till he's in a good mood and ask him!" Two days later she called and said, "You've got your ten grand. He's agreed to sponsor the diaries." My God was smiling down upon me, and the charity too.

In between times, Martin, his wife Sally, together with Ann and I, had been invited to a Buckingham Palace Garden Party. It was a great day, and anyone who has been to one of these events will know that when The Royal Party comes out of the Palace into the grounds, they divide up and go in different directions. We decided to stay with Prince Philip's group and eventually he saw us. He recognised my Water Rats emblem – he is a Companion Rat – and came over to talk to us. I said, "You've very kindly agreed to come to our lunch in November for the Commonwealth Veterans Association!" "Have I?" he said, and in the course of conversation asked, "Well, how much do you think you will be able to raise? Have you any idea?" I said, "No, Sir. Not really. I suppose we are hoping for around £20,000. Will that be OK?" "Well, I should think so," he said. "But do your best and good luck." And he moved on. We genuinely had no idea of what we might raise and just prayed that we would hit that figure.

The lunch was a riot. Thirty-six scarlet-coated toastmasters formed a guard of honour. The President of the Association, Martin, who was in charge of the money, and I met Prince Philip at the door and conducted him to an enclosure where he met sponsors and representatives of the charity. We had a group photograph of all the toastmasters, with him sitting in the centre, and then went into lunch. During the meal, Anita sang her heart out, singing a song especially written for the occasion by husband Mike, and I introduced her to Prince Philip. Jim Davidson sat one side of him, our President Steve Warwick on the other, and all went swimmingly. I had managed to scrounge about ninety raffle prizes and placed three on each table for fund-raising, and the speeches began.

I pinched Tommy Trinder's idea and produced three traffic lights for all to see, giving each speaker a maximum of eight minutes, before switching the green light to amber… and then to red when they had to get off! The King Rat at the time was Keith Simmons, a lovely entertainer and writer of pantomimes and shows. I put him wholly in charge of the speakers and the lights and I asked him to introduce the show. I was to be the first, with a speech full of thanks and congratulations for all those who had made the event possible, ending with a formal introduction to Prince Philip. He had agreed to speak for exactly five minutes on the charity, and stuck religiously to that time. We then came to Jim Davidson's Roast, which began with Water Rat Barry Cryer. Seeing all those red coats around him, he began by saying, "Welcome to the Royal Lancaster Hunt Ball!" He went on to talk about Jim's ex-wives and said, "Looking for Jim Davidson's wives is like looking for hay in a haystack!"

He was followed by another Rat, Bob 'The Cat' Bevan, who was just as great. He started by saying, "Jim and I have just been abroad entertaining the troops and, if you'll forgive the lack of modesty, I went down rather well. In fact, there was a cutting in the local newspaper, which read, 'Bob the Cat Bevan was the best thing to hit this town for many months...' and that was from the *Kabul Evening Telegraph*!" He continued, "Recently, Jim and I were together at a function – not quite as posh as this one – which wasn't really a great success. It was the annual dinner of the Gay Agoraphobic Society... every time one of them came out, they all went back in again!"

Then came Past King Rat (PKR) Roger de Courcey and Nookie Bear who began with: "Talking about the Forces, my father was in the army and when it came to rifle practice prior to going to the front, he was the worst shot – one bullet up there, another round the back, the third one on the ground, and so on. The instructor said, 'You're the worst shot I've ever seen.' Optimistically, my father replied, 'Does that mean I ain't going?' 'No,' the Sergeant replied, 'It means you ain't coming back!' Actually, Jim's dad was very clever. He was an Elvis impersonator... There wasn't a lot of call for that in 1938!"

It was then Jim Davidson's turn to defend himself. Being the great pro he is, he rose to the occasion and recounted a story about the (late) Queen Mother. He had met her at a Garden Party and one of the corgis was driving him mad sniffing round his ankles. He didn't know what to do and said to the Queen Mother, "One of your corgis, Ma'am, is sniffing around and nipping my ankles. What shall I do?" The Queen Mum said, "Kick his balls," ...which I did. ...And pointing, she then said, "...they're over there on the lawn!" Prince Philip loved it, which removed any worry from Jim that it might cause offence.

The very last item in the programme was the presentation of the cheques; I had promised the Rats 10% of everything raised, with 90% going to the Commonwealth Veterans. Martin Nicholls was thrilled to announce that the total raised was just a few pounds short of £60,000. The crowd went wild and were absolutely bowled over by the result. Prince Philip was equally delighted and thanked us all profusely. Sir Donald Gosling, who had had one of the best lunches he could remember, added yet another £10,000 to his first donation, really putting the cherry on the icing.

Among the dozens of letters I received after the event was a personal one from HRH Prince Philip, Duke of Edinburgh, expressing not only delight but great amazement at such a huge sum raised at a luncheon.

* * * * *

"When I retire, I'm going to become a toastmaster and do your job – it's easy," is a statement I have heard hundreds of times. It is similar to another, "When I retire, I'm going to run a nice little pub in the country!" Most men who utter the second statement haven't got the faintest idea of what they are talking about… they are living in a fantasy world. Anyone who knows the slightest thing about it will tell you that running a pub is extremely hard work with long hours, no holidays, and that you're at the beck and call of any old bore who comes into your pub. A sinecure it certainly ain't, but you can't tell them.

Similarly, men who are bored with their lifestyle think, when they see a professional toastmaster easing his way through a function, that it is the simplest job in the world and just money for old rope. There is an oft-used simile, which I have heard quoted many times – "A good toastmaster is rather like a swan: calm and serene on the surface, but paddling like hell underneath." And so it is with every performer.

To become a toastmaster *is* the easiest thing in the world. Simply go to *Moss Bros*, hire a red tailcoat, white evening dress shirt, waistcoat and bow tie, black dress trousers, patent leather shoes, put a few ads in magazines and newspapers and sit back and wait for the telephone to ring. That's all you need to do. If you have been to events and watched toastmasters work, simply jot down what they do and just read it aloud – it really is as easy as that. The four-letter word I left out of this paragraph was 'good'. If you want to become a 'good' toastmaster then it is very much harder.

117

In The National Association of Toastmasters, we became concerned that there were dozens of men – and, lately, women – all over the UK taking the easy route and doing a very poor job. They were bringing the whole profession into disrepute with depressingly poor standards, taking money from unsuspecting clients, ruining weddings and other milestones just because they thought it was easy. We became concerned about this and learned that a number of our members had been approached to provide lessons. After much debate, it was agreed that we form a training arm of The National Association. This was strongly resisted by some who pointed out, quite correctly, that in training others we were bringing new blood into an already overcrowded but small profession. Others pointed out that since many of these would-be toastmasters were determined to do the job anyway, would it not be sensible to ensure that they were properly trained?

Toastmaster Training Limited (or *TMT*) was duly formed. I was appointed chairman, Martin Nicholls was company secretary, with Douglas Hill and Malcolm Clayton being directors – it was to our deep sorrow that they both died suddenly, leaving a void. Sadly, Martin is now also up there with them.

We planned a programme for educating toastmasters and discovered that, despite a profession dating back to the Middle Ages, there was nothing written down as to how the job was to be done. Over the centuries, the craft has been passed down from one toastmaster to another, and while there are books covering every area of protocol and procedure, none actually explain what to do in any given situation. So we set about making enquiries from every conceivable source about what was right and what was wrong. For example, anyone who has been honoured with an MBE by the Queen knows precisely that it means Member of the Most Excellent Order of the British Empire, and that they are entitled to that formal address whenever they rise to speak. They may know nothing about any other part of chivalry, but that's their little bit and they're proud of it – so if any announcer makes a mistake, they are, quite rightly, upset. That is one infinitesimal part of a toastmaster's knowledge, but it is amazing how many amateurs get it wrong.

Our work involved a great deal of research, and we even surprised ourselves as to the breadth of canvas to be covered if we were to train candidates in the full panoply of the profession. It transpired that the lectures came under many headings, all of which had to be accurate and reliable. That was not as easy as it appeared as ours is not a precise science – protocols and traditions varying from company to company, county to county, City livery company to City livery company, borough to borough and religion to religion, but we had to prepare our students for every eventuality. It was a fascinating and absorbing study – it was astounding how little we really knew and yet we were setting ourselves up as experts. Of the fifteen or so lectures we created, I actually wrote about twelve of them. The subjects were:

> Christian Weddings
> Jewish Celebrations
> Royalty
> The Peerage
> Parliamentary Procedure
> Titles and Forms of Address
> Right Honourables
> The Church
> The City of London
> County, Borough and other Civic Procedure
> The Legal Profession
> The Diplomatic Corps
> The Licensed Trade
> Freemasonry, Rotary, Round Table, etc
> Cocktail Parties and Birthday Parties

Over a period of twelve years, *TMT* courses were held in various places, but most regularly at Birmingham University, consisting of six days of lectures and participation skills. When the lectures were over, the course administrator took the delegates through difficult scenarios, requiring them to put into practice what had been taught. It was tough and gruelling but, for many, highly rewarding.

Around 100 candidates from all walks of life attended our courses – people who thought that the duties of a red-coated toastmaster were simple, glamorous and fun, and with the chance of having a good time with the guests. Oh, how wrong they were! Certainly, standing out in a crowd dressed in a colourful uniform has its advantages. What it does *not* show is the enormous amount of background work and knowledge, the behind-the-scenes activities and the hard-earned skill of the professional practitioner which, when put together, result in a smooth, seamless function enjoyed by all. As Ann always says, to appreciate a good toastmaster, you have to experience a bad one! It is reassuring that almost half of NAT members are *TMT* graduates.

In 2003, it was decided to wind up *TMT* and train would-be toastmasters in a different form. I enjoyed my twelve years, imparting as much of my knowledge as the students could absorb. I also found it a learning curve for myself, making me wiser and more competent. It is very easy to spout lectures, but a different matter completely to train technique – something which only comes from actually going out and doing the job. I am often asked what percentage of my success is knowledge and what is experience. My answer is, I doubt if I use more than about 5% of my knowledge – the remaining 95% is technique and experience.

There is one other important facet within the toastmaster's armoury, and that is personality. It requires a certain conceit and strength of personality to go before a body of complete strangers and make one's presence felt, but it is vital. It is equally important to establish a happy rapport, not only with the client, but also, as soon as possible, with the audience. The statement, "You never get a second opportunity to make a good first impression!" applies totally to toastmasters and they would do well to remember it.

However, there is one rule that we ram down their throats. When people ask me what is the most important function at which I have worked, my answer is simple, "All of them!" And it's true. At every function, it is vital to someone that things go well. They are not interested in any personal problems you may have. It is their occasion – that is all they care about and we have to ensure that it goes well. We tell the students to remember that above all else, and if they do, then they will succeed.

I'm reminded of a wonderful story about one of the funniest men in British show business. The occasion was a pro-am/celebrity charity golf tournament in Portugal. During the morning round, the heavens opened – thunder, lightning, flooding, the lot – and they all scurried back to the clubhouse to dry out. Several of the 'stars', Bruce Forsyth, Roger de Courcey, Henry Cooper and others decided to go for a sauna, and having sat there for several minutes, through the little window in the door Jimmy Tarbuck spotted Eric Sykes about to come in.

As a gag, Jimmy said to the lads, "Listen fellas, here comes Sykesy; let's have a bit of fun! When he comes in don't say a word. Schtoom! Nothing! Just keep quiet and see what happens." Eric walks in, sees all his mates and chatters away... "'Ello lads"...(no replies)... "Rotten weather"...(nothing)... "Wasn't it terrible this morning?" (Silence, all heads down looking at their feet... pause.) "D'you think we'll get out this afternoon?"... (Absolutely nowt. Wiping of sweaty brows). Silence, as Eric potters around, puts his towel on the wooden slats and sits down. Total silence from everyone, now sweating like fury. After what seemed an eternity, Eric came out with the classic line to the mob now trembling with suppressed laughter... "Does this train stop at Calcutta?"

Chapter 7

Grand Order of Water Rats

"A jolly lot of fellows are the Water Rats."

As a child, I listened for hour upon hour, night after night to the wireless (the word 'radio' was not used in those days) and I learned all the signature tunes and clichés verbatim. I would save all my pocket money to go to the Wood Green *Empire*, sitting in the Gods for sixpence (2.5p) to see great entertainers. Occasionally, Dad would know someone doing a week there and take me backstage to meet them. Bliss!

Many of the variety shows on the wireless had great entertainers doing 10-12 minute slots, and the word 'Variety' was paramount. I sometimes heard mentioned the mysterious words, 'Water Rats'. Water Rats! Grand Order of Water Rats! King Rat! Prince Rat! What was all this business about rats? I had heard about it and was well aware that it was the most influential and prestigious fraternity within the world of variety and entertainment. But who were they? What did they do? How did you get to know more about them?

In 1889, five of the finest entertainers in the world of Vaudeville owned a trotting pony which they used to race against tradesmen's ponies from Streatham to Brixton. The pony was won in a deal by one of them working in Newcastle; he did not get paid for a job so the promoter gave him the pony instead, which he brought down to London in the carriage of a train – records do not describe the condition of the carriage when it got there... just use your own imagination. The intrepid five met at a pub in Sunbury-on-Thames called *The Magpie*, the name by which the pony duly became known.

(There are still many photographs on display at the pub today.) The pony won them a great deal of money – the trick being to give the poor beast half a bag of food at the beginning of the race, taking the bag away and giving it the rest at the end! It was so hungry that it ran like hell just to get fed – and won them pots of money.

One wet and miserable day, our heroes, soaked to the skin, were walking the pony back home after another successful race. A bus driver saw these famous guys and hollered, "What you got there, lads? Call it a 'n'orse! Looks more like a bleeding water rat." And instantly the name was changed to 'The Water Rat'. Being successful and well-paid performers, they all agreed that, as they did not need it themselves, it would be a good idea to donate all winnings and prize money to the poor and needy. When the Sally Army set up soup kitchens in the East End of London, they funded that cause.

These pros formed a small body called 'The Friends of the Water Rat' and attracted more to join them. Eventually, they changed the name, and in 1890 The Grand Order of Water Rats was formed. They were soon known simply as Water Rats and based the various offices within the Order on that theme; for example, Chief Trap Guard, Trap Guards, Bait Rat, Test Rat, etc. Rats are the lowest form of animal life, but a rat is also a vole, which is an anagram of 'love' upon which the order is based. Also, spell 'Rats' backwards and the word 'Star' appears, and it is from this lowly position that all Rats aspire to the highest attainment in their profession. It is also strictly non-hierarchical, and no matter how great or small your fame, once a Rat, you are all equal in the Order. It is only when you graduate to various offices on Grand Council that you become more senior, and then only for a year.

From their very beginnings, the Rats have been proud to admit many of the greatest names in the world of entertainment from both sides of the Atlantic. The little gold Rat worn in the lapel is called an emblem and not a badge, and only 850 have been admitted to the Order. A list of the famous and good of our profession would fill this book, so I will mention but a few: film stars like Peter Lorre, Jack Buchanan, Maurice Chevalier, Charlie Chaplin, Laurel and Hardy, Danny Kaye, Ben Lyon, Howard Keel and Bob Hope have all taken the initiation ceremony. Others include George Robey, Teddy Brown, Bud Flanagan and Chesney Allen, Charlie Chester, Ted Ray, Ben Warris, David Nixon, Danny la Rue, Roy Hudd, Roger de Courcey and, more recently, Sir John Mills and Engelbert Humperdinck. They have all been proud to be admitted to a very special Order and display the emblem.

Throughout the 20th century, the Order was very high-profile indeed and renowned for its philanthropy. It was also in at the birth of the 'wireless', gaining much publicity through that medium and regularly taking over the London Palladium for what were called Rats' Revels. These were always a remarkable sell-out and raised thousands of 'coins' (Rats do not refer to it as money) for many charitable causes. The Entertainment Artistes Benevolent Fund (EABF), which organises the annual Royal Variety Performance, has been one of the main beneficiaries.

As I progressed as a toastmaster and master of ceremonies, I did more and more Masonic, Rotary, Round Table and various social organisations, Ladies' Festivals and Dinner Dances and found myself working with wonderful, professional entertainers – the same people I had seen onstage at the Wood Green *Empire*. On very rare occasions (because their fees were greater if they had worked on 'the wireless') I met some of the variety artistes I had listened to and loved.

Without being obviously aware of it, my father's training, professional expertise and skill as a concert performer had had a material effect on me and I discovered that I had a flair for the entertainment side of our business. He was a true genius at handling social audiences. I don't think he had a nervous bone in his body; he was supremely confident, and had a lovely amiable way about him, which endeared him to 99% of the audiences he entertained. He was simply adored by the people at his work, which he loved passionately; the fact that he had a beautiful singing voice was a bonus.

My ability to entertain a crowd, warm them up, make them hot, sweaty and happy with lively and novelty dances was finely tuned. I was the son of my father and had developed his knack of how to 'handle' a social crowd. It is certainly a gift and cannot be trained. If you have the flair the world's your oyster, if you haven't, then you can almost forget it so far as being a successful master of ceremonies.

When an artist appears before an audience, the atmosphere in the room, the general ambience, the warmth and genuine feeling of 'having a great time' is immensely important to the success or failure of their performance. Dad had that talent in abundance. All his fellow-pros knew it and they acknowledged Dad as a master of his craft. He had the best reputation in the banqueting world and acts used to love seeing him 'on the job'; their confidence grew appreciably as they knew they would be 'put on' at the best and most suitable time for them and, what is even more important, properly introduced. A bad introduction can destroy a performance and many artistes are very sensitive about it.

Ann tells me, and many pros have also mentioned it, that there have been some guys who own red coats and purport to be toastmasters, who, where cabaret is concerned, are an absolute disaster. They have no 'feel' for the occasion, do not create a rapport with the crowd, screw up the announcements, get the names wrong, announce acts when the people are just leaving the floor to sit down and listen, make announcements before the 'props' are set, and a whole raft of ill-considered and damaging actions which can destroy a performance. There are many today who are ill-equipped to handle entertainment competently... it cannot be taught!

Dad had pushed me to this period in my career. He gave me every possible tip in what was to become my lifelong profession. I played the piano for him at dozens of concerts and Ladies' Festivals and it was his proudest moment, at the end of each performance, to say to the audience, "... and may I introduce my accompanist this evening... my son Bryn!" He revelled in it! However, the money for an accompanist, two and a half guineas at the most, was not as good as that of a toastmaster at three guineas, and was less productive. So my musical career came to a quiet and uncelebrated end. Also, as he was such a good toastmaster himself and the money was better 'in the red coat', Dad's singing work became less as the toastmaster work grew. He had shown me the way in the world of banqueting; I was now on my own.

It was at one of these Ladies' Festivals that I was seen by a couple who were to change my life and set me off in a new, exciting and lucrative direction at the very heart of entertainment. Johnny and Vie Riscoe must have realised that, in the rather small world of banquets and balls, I had something to offer. I knew neither them nor their connections with the profession and they certainly did not come to me with the old cliché, '… we've seen you work, like what you do and want to use you!' but use me they did.

Johnny and Vie eventually adopted me as their own sort of personal toastmaster. At that time, he was King Rat of the Grand Order of Water Rats over whom I had drooled as a kid. Vie was a member of the sister-organisation, the Grand Order of Lady Ratlings, ultimately to hold their highest office as Queen Ratling and very much later a Dame of that Order.

As well as the Water Rats, there was, and indeed still is, a parallel organisation called The Vaudeville Golfing Society, with many who are members of both. The VGS Stag Dinner at that time was legendary. It had been held at the Park Lane Hotel, Piccadilly, since the years following the war. Tickets were harder to get than for the FA Cup Final. It was packed solid with the greatest names in variety and vaudeville and was renowned for its humour, its fun and near-the-knuckle comedy from the funniest men in the business. Names like Ben Warris, Donald Peers, Albert Stevenson, Ted Ray, Charlie Chester, Tommy Trinder, Leslie Sarony and many more appeared every year. It was, to my young and ambitious dreams, the ultimate event at which to appear.

Older readers will just remember the Crazy Gang who, year after year, filled the Victoria Palace for weeks at a time with their own very funny, oddball, zany comedy. They were Naughton and Gold, Nervo and Knox and Flanagan and Allen and, although not actually a member of the Crazy Gang, 'Monsewer' Eddie Gray was frequently in their show and they pulled every comedy gag possible. One year at the VGS Stag Dinner they put a microphone in the gent's loo relaying the sounds and conversations to the dining guests. Another year, after the hors d'oeuvres and soup, there were no knives or forks on the table. Eventually, the waiters came out with newspaper packets and dumped fish and chips in front of everyone – they had to eat with their fingers.

At one dinner, when Albert Stevenson, producer of *Juke Box Jury*, was Captain, he began the meal by saying, "Gentlemen, for the first time ever, the hotel has had to use waitresses to serve the meal rather than just waiters. In deference to these ladies, we will cut out all the blue comedy during the meal and save it for later!" Whereupon a waitress, who had been standing beside me holding a large dish of hors d'oeuvres, shoved past me and Albert, grabbed the mic and shouted through it, "Well, if that's the case, you can stuff your dinner – I'm gonna f*** off 'ome," and she tipped the food all over the Captain's head. It brought the house down. Of course, she was a plant and the 'food' was fake, causing no damage.

Yet another was when Ted Ray said Grace at the beginning of the meal. He began, very quietly, "Dear God, Bless our food and..." when he was interrupted by one of the comics in the room who yelled, "Speak up! Carn't 'ear yer!" To which Ted replied, "I'm not talking to you!" Wonderful. Another time I simply said, "Pray silence for Grace." Pause. Then through the PA came, "Salleee, Salleee, pride of..."

I received a telephone call one day; it was Johnny Riscoe asking if I was free on Armistice Sunday (traditionally since 1945, the day of their dinner), and would I like to 'do' the VGS Stag Dinner? I was almost speechless and incoherent in my reply. Was I free? Would I like to do it? Would I like the job? Oh boy! Would I? As far as show business was concerned, this was it – the acme, the Alpha and Omega, the prime job in the banqueting world, and it was being offered to *me*... and I was still only in my twenties.

At that time, the doyen of the profession was a certain John Mills; a dignified, serious, highly professional and hugely respected toastmaster, who had been successful since before the war and was at the very top of the tree of our calling. As far as I was concerned, the Stag Dinner was his sole preserve. When I mentioned this to

Johnny, he informed me that they were looking for a change and that John Mills was happy to be released from a job he had done for years... or words to that effect! And so, I was in. My introduction to the greatest names in British variety, cabaret and vaudeville began there.

Guests used to book their places for the next year the day following the last one. They all came to the dinner with notebook and pen to write down the gags and comedy routines which abounded. It was very blue, but it was unquestionably the funniest night of the year.

Over the years, the Crazy Gang had been quite incorrigible and it was at one of these events that I met the legendary Bud Flanagan. By the time we met, I had 'done' the VGS Stag for a few years. It was an extremely difficult job as they managed to squeeze over 700 into the ballroom of the Park Lane Hotel, which now has a top limit of about 400. There was a very long top table from which eight or nine sprigs extended into the vast room – all were packed solid. On the balcony were half a dozen more tables filled to capacity; guests simply did not care where they sat so long as they could attend.

One of the features of the dinner was what became known as the 'I Say, I Say, I Say' gags, or the 'Knock, Knock' routines which they bounced off the Captain, all of whom over the years were top names in entertainment. The routine was that a Water Rat called Lew Lane, for over thirty years the producer and director of cabaret at the Astor Club and Churchills, the leading nightspots in London at the time, would go around the tables with a microphone. He would hand it to a well-known comic like Leslie Sarony, who would stand and announce in a loud voice, "I Say, I Say, I Say, Mr Captain."
"Yes, Mr Sarony. What do you say?"
"What is the difference between a street-trader and a Dachshund?"
"I don't know, Mr Sarony. What is the difference between a street-trader and a Dachshund?"
"The street-trader bawls out his wares on the pavement..."

One evening when I arrived at the hotel, I was told by the then Secretary, Len Barry, that I was only to look after the more formal part of the event, like announcing dinner, saying Grace and the speeches after the meal. He then told me that the 'I Says' and 'Knock-Knocks' during the meal were to be handled by Bud Flanagan, simply the greatest and most loved man in the business at that time. After Grace, I made a grand announcement that I was proud to be handing over my red coat, divested myself of it and 'dressed' Bud. The crowd loved it and were thrilled that they were to see the master at work again.

What Bud Flanagan had not appreciated and, indeed, what nobody really knew, was that this part of the dinner was, unquestionably, the most difficult to handle. There are so many facets to it. You have to work in conjunction with the banqueting staff, the guy taking the microphone around, the Captain, the noise of the guests and a whole lot more. It is very tough indeed and, frankly, it was the part of the evening I dreaded. I was delighted to hand it over to anyone!

Bud Flanagan soldiered on, flogging his nearly eighty-year-old self along manfully. The crowd adored him and cheered him to the rooftops when he had finished and, at the end of the meal, standing behind the Captain, he took off my redcoat, soaking with perspiration. I re-dressed him with his dinner jacket and he sat down – nay, collapsed into his chair. As he handed me back my coat, he thanked me and said something I will treasure for the rest of my life. "Bryn, mate! I wouldn't do your f*****g job for all the money in the bleedin' world! You're welcome to it!" My mind instantly flew back to the days in my small bedroom where I listened for hours to all the great broadcasting names and marvelled that, here was one of those, wearing MY jacket, doing MY job and being kind and generous to me. On such things are dreams made!

It was shortly after that that my 'guru' Johnny Riscoe rang again and this time said to me, "How would you like to do the Rats' Ball? It's on the last Sunday in November at the Dorchester? It's yours if you want it, 'coz many Rats saw you at the VGS Stag and thought you would be great!"

And so it was, on the last Sunday in November 1962, that I arrived at The Dorchester Hotel to officiate at my first Ball of the Grand Order of Water Rats. It was jam-packed with famous names and I was 'in charge'. The list was a *Who's Who* in show business, but, to

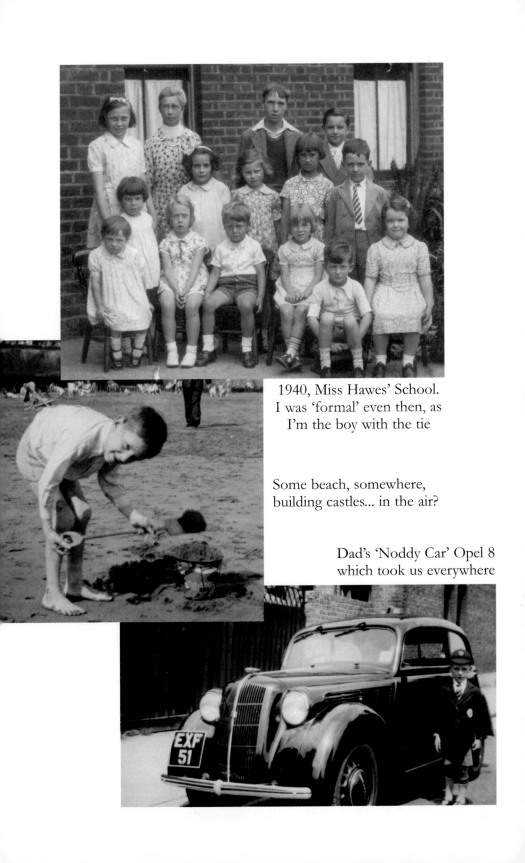

1940, Miss Hawes' School.
I was 'formal' even then, as
I'm the boy with the tie

Some beach, somewhere,
building castles... in the air?

Dad's 'Noddy Car' Opel 8
which took us everywhere

The early 'Clippies'
Mum 2nd from left
back row

Dad and Mum,
Hugh & Billie Owens

HUGH OWENS

THE ENTERTAINING BARITONE
TOASTMASTER AND COMPERE
BOWes Park 2398

Dad's brochure

Billie Owens, Ivy Williams,
Miss Brown, or Grandma - pick a name

Lock up your daughters...
...I wish!

Dad's gas-guzzling 'Olds', but 5 bobs'
worth of petrol went a long way

Mum and me
'Strictly Come-Dancing', 1951

MY
LORD
LADIES
& GENTLEMEN

"THE
BABY
TOASTMASTER"!

BRYN
WILLIAMS
BY
Pol.
1951

Master of Ceremonies

Proud father, nervous son, c. 1953

1962, President (NAT) Bryn and Ann,
pleased to meet you... Mum and Dad

I did manage to get
into single figures!
D'you like the hat?

1957, 'Guard of Honour' with raised gavels

Love's young dream, 1956

The Harmony Hi-Lites, 10 very happy and successful years
5 beautiful girls, 9 lovely legs! Clockwise from far left:
Wenna, Glenys, Hedydd, Anne (Knight) and my Ann

Dad and me with our band, 'The Gaythorn Orchestra', named
after a street in Wood Green! Uncle Alf Hedges at the piano

Tim and Tracy join
us in their glad rags

Me und mein
Austrian Frau
in Dirndl und
Lederhosen

Lady Sheila Butlin,
Companion Rat
Prince Philip,
King Rat Davy Kaye

King Rat Bert Weedon
presenting me with
the King Rat's Award

3 would-be toastmasters
PKR Ted Ray, PKR Ben
Warriss and mate?

PKR Frank and
Stella Vaughan

With Pam Ayres and
Tracy, c. 1975

A brief 'snog' with
the gorgeous Anita
Harris whose
wedding to Mike
Margolis I did;
daughter Tracy
enjoying the fun

Enjoying a joke
with Jilly Cooper

Nelson Mandela - a remarkable man

1960, Archbishop
Makarios, Cyprus

Chief Rabbi Lord Jacobovitz,
a wise, kind and gentle man

President Ronald Reagan.
A great wit, a great guy!

President Bill Clinton at a charity
extravaganza in St Petersburg 2005

A Plethora of Prime Ministers

Edward Heath at my
40th anniversary
cocktail party, 1990

The lady's not for turning,
but nonetheless very special

John Major

Me and my mate 'Tone'

My 40th Anniversary

Card showing a
portrait of our dear
friend George
'Tonypandy', with
his Christmas
greeting inside

*With greetings for Christmas
and the New Year*

Bless you both.
May 1990 bring you
health & happiness.

George.

Princess Anne who is quite brilliant and a joy to meet at any time

The two sexiest ladies in my life

Prince Charles at a reunion of the Kelly Association

Initiation of Prince Charles as a Companion Rat,
with Companion Rat Andrew Neatrour

'Who's taking you home tonight?
He is

my enormous delight and surprise, they were not the hard-nosed, unapproachable, stand-offish, aloof crowd that I half expected in my ignorance of their private lives. They were all kind, warm, friendly, helpful and, in many cases, terrified and nervous of performing. Yes, it is quite amazing that so many artistes everyone sees entertaining – confident, brash, exuding power and personality – are frequently, when they are in a different scenario, nervous and apprehensive. It makes them human after all.

At the ball the following year, I bumped up against one of the rare ones who was obnoxious and who tried to give me a hard time. I refer to Past King Rat Wee Georgie Wood, a comedic legend during his lifetime with a sharp, rapier-like wit which was both very funny, but frequently caustic. He had a brilliant brain, but because of his stature and his unhappy love life, he was somewhat embittered.

During the banquet, Bebe Daniels was to reply to the Toast to the Ladies. Bebe Daniels, a famous comedienne, actress and broadcaster, was married to another Water Rat, Ben Lyon. Their radio show, *Life with the Lyons*, ran very successfully for many years and included within it another Rat, Vic Oliver, the Austrian-born comedian and violinist who married Sarah Churchill.

It was, and still is, my personal method of putting people at their ease by talking to them quietly before I introduce them just to see how I can make their life easier; believe me, if you have not spoken in public yourself, it is a very nerve-racking business. In fact, it is said by the pundits that the four most stressful activities that one can experience in life are: moving house, getting a divorce, dying, and making an after-dinner speech – and the last one is the most horrifying of the lot and the one most feared!

PKR Wee Georgie Wood was to be the first speaker; he was to propose the Toast to the Ladies, to which Bebe Daniels was to reply. There happened to be an empty chair at the top table and, as she was seated elsewhere, I thought she might like to move to it before she started. I went and put this to her and was astounded to see that she was absolutely terrified and dreading making the speech. She welcomed the idea, but as I was escorting her to the top table, that vicious little man got up onto his soap box – yes, he was only about four feet tall – grabbed the microphone, and said, in squeaky, but rather stentorian tones, "MY name is Past King Rat Georgie Wood and I am the next speaker. Your toastmaster has made a mistake by bringing Miss Daniels to the top table too soon!"

Imagine my horror at such a public lambasting. The looks, which shot over to me from the good and the great in vaudeville, could have killed. He was, as expected, extremely funny and made a wonderful speech, but it gave me time to think of an appropriate reply in my defence. When I came to introduce Bebe Daniels, I said words to the effect, "I do apologise most sincerely to PKR Georgie Wood for failing to introduce him. However, I knew that Miss Daniels would prefer to sit at the top table before he began his toast as she would feel more comfortable, hence the apparent mistake. Indeed, I meant no discourtesy to one so great and entertaining as Mr Wood and hope he accepts my apology." It brought the house down as he was not the most loved man in show business and I had gently and firmly, but politely, put him in his place. I learned later that this episode was mentioned at the next Lodge meeting of the GOWR and it had gone down very well indeed!

In 1965, Tommy Trinder was King Rat for the second time. By then I had done the Rats' Ball for many years and become established; they knew me, liked me and trusted me and I was able to steer many of the Past Kings through the difficulties of 'their' ball. Believe me, it really is a tough job at the top table. During the cabaret, Dad arrived to see me work as he had been working elsewhere. Backstage, I introduced him to Tommy and they chatted. Out of the blue, Dad then said, "Well, Tommy, why don't you make Bryn a Water Rat? He'd be very good for the Order and, after all, he is a pro." I was embarrassed and furious and said, "Dad, for God's sake shut up! I'm not a performer in the theatrical sense and there's absolutely no way they would take me in. So, please! Shut up!" At which Tommy just laughed.

Tommy was compèring the cabaret and went out onto the floor to introduce the next act. Whilst he was out there, he said in his gruff cockney accent, "Ladies and Gentlemen, Brother Water Rats, I want to introduce you to a really great bloke who never gets any recognition at all. Believe me, at that top table, it's b****y hard and he makes it all so easy for us. I mean our toastmaster Bryn Williams! Come out here Bryn and meet the crowd." What could I do? So, out I went amid roars of applause and cheers. Tommy praised me, with his hand around my shoulder. His final words were, "And if Bryn ever wanted to become a Water Rat, I would be the first to propose him. He's great!" It is impossible to describe my emotions and feelings at that moment. I walked off as if I was on a cloud.

Immediately after the cabaret, Johnny Riscoe, grinning all over his face, said to me, "Well, mate. It looks as though you've scored. Well done. For various reasons, Tommy cannot propose you this year, but your mate Harry Morris (the then Scribe of the Order) will, and I will second you – we'll get it moving." (Harry was one half of a lovely old-fashioned act called 'Morris and Cowley' – two delightful little brothers who were then well into their seventies. He was also Val Doonican's manager.) The following year I heard that I had passed the ballot and had been accepted. In those days, that required 99% acceptance of all voting members, who were required to know you personally. It was a huge fillip to know that so many great names were rooting for me.

Harry Morris rang and told me that I would be 'made' in November and would be the Baby Rat at the next ball. The King Rat was Arthur Haynes and I would attend his last meeting before the ball. The morning of that meeting, Arthur died and everything was turned topsy-turvy. I was made a member of the Grand Order of Water Rats in the January of 1967 when the King Rat was Terry 'Toby Jug' Cantor.

My impossible dream had become a reality and words cannot describe the immense pride I felt when that little gold emblem was pinned on my lapel by Harry Morris. I know, too, that Mum and Dad were equally happy and proud – as far as they were concerned, their little boy had arrived in the world of entertainment. Tommy and I became firm friends, and when Fulham reached the FA Cup Final, as Chairman, Tommy invited me to Wembley as one of his guests; I ran the banquet for the team and their wives. I won't bother to mention the result of the match!

I have now officiated at 41 Rats' Balls and, in recognition of that service and the many other events I have run for them, they gave me a special Tribute Luncheon at The Savoy Hotel in 2003, which was a huge honour.

There are hundreds of stories I could tell about Rats' events. Indeed, if I put my mind to it, I could possibly fill another book. Like when Eartha Kitt was in cabaret and I had the pleasure of introducing her whilst she sat at the top table. As soon as I said the words, "Please welcome the legendary Eartha Kitt," she rose from her chair and made towards the ballroom floor. Her intro music was playing, but as she oozed her way through the tables, she 'seduced' with her eyes every man she passed, sending their temperatures soaring. I swear, it took her nearly five minutes to make it to the mic, but, oh boy, what an entrance!

Or the wonderful occasion when that sensational mouth organ player (he never called it a harmonica) Larry Adler was to reply to the Toast. He rose and said, "Years ago, I was very friendly with the late George Gershwin and we played together his composition, *Summertime*. Well, I am proud that I have a record of him playing the accompaniment of that great song and I would like to play it for you now." And with that we were all transported on a cloud of nostalgia as Larry Adler played that classic number accompanied by the composer – a unique experience.

Another story is perhaps best told in the words of PKR Roy Hudd, as it appears in one of his own books:

> Bryn is the doyen of toastmasters. Enough said. He always officiates at the Annual Water Rats Ball and here's his version of a very special night when Water Rat Danny Kaye attended.
>
> It was quite a palaver getting a huge international star like Kaye to the ball, and the agent who arranged it said, 'In return for the favour, the Order must have another of my acts in the cabaret.' This was agreed and the act

134

duly appeared. They were a family flamenco team consisting of a very ancient mother and father and their seven middle-aged and not terribly attractive offspring.

On the large raised stage they arranged themselves in a semi-circle of chairs on which they sat when they were not actually dancing. At the end of each dance, they all stood and took a bow. After the seventh, or it may have been the seventeenth of those feet-clattering, handclapping, castanet-clicking marathons, which all sounded exactly the same, the mainly show business audience started to get restless. Backstage we were sweating. We knew there were loads more dances to come; we HAD to get them off or face a riot.

Lew Lane, producer of the event, and our compère, a great little comic called Jimmy Jacobs, saved the day. Gathering a posse of Rats around them, Lew said, "Follow me. When they stand up to take their bow – we'll run on and pinch their chairs… they can't carry on then."

We did as instructed, to the uproarious delight of the crowd and the unbelievable fury of the act. That night we learnt every swear word in the Spanish language. They threatened to go to the Embassy, sue us – the lot. We didn't care; we'd got 'em off.

Later on in the cabaret, the audience became restless again, but Jimmy stopped the noise and the show when he advised them, "Shut up and listen, or I'll bring back the bleedin' Spaniards."

Bryn has a story which has stayed with him for forty years, concerning a very popular act in the cabarets of the 1950s and '60s, namely, Roy Dexter. The roller-skating act was called variously The Skating Dexters or the Skating Royals, in which Roy and his lady partner would perform all sorts of fancy skating tricks on a specially prepared mat.

Audience participation is always good in cabaret and Roy had an excellent gimmick. He would invite any of the punters to 'Go for a spin with Roy.' He would hold them from behind, lift them gently and give them a few revolutions before letting them stagger back to their tables. The audience loved it. He would take on all-comers, but one night at the Connaught Rooms he met his match.

The volunteer was a tiny little old lady. A sensational 'spin' looked in the offing and it certainly turned out that way. Neither Roy nor Bryn knew that the volunteer had imbibed rather too unwisely. She was as light as a feather, so Roy gave her the works. Faster and faster she spun until her legs were horizontal. Spurred on by the shouts of the crowd he 'waved' her up and down. It was at this moment that her liquid intake became out-take!

Suddenly there was the most almighty stampede from the people sitting at the tables nearest the floor to the back of the room. Pandemonium reigned. The poor lady was spraying everyone within quite a considerable range. There was total uproar and Roy, totally unaware of the waltzing water, was inspired by the roars of laughter to even greater efforts. Round and round and up and down she went. The floor was now drenched and the crowd were in hysterics.

Roy finally stopped to discover all the tables deserted and nearly the entire room crowded together against the walls crying with laughter. The little old lady star, unable to stand, crawled back to her table. She had no idea what had happened! As Bryn says, "I don't think the Skating Dexters ever went down so well."

This chapter on the Water Rats would not be complete without a reference to a very special Companion Rat, HRH Prince Charles. Companion Rats are not performers or entertainers, but men who have given freely of their professional services, or donated large sums of money to the Order and are important supporters. HRH Prince Philip was the first Royal Companion and he loves to attend our meetings and formal events. It was he who suggested that we invite Prince Charles to be a Companion, which duly happened in 1975. More recently, HRH Prince Michael of Kent has honoured us by accepting the Rat emblem and even invited his son, Lord Frederick Windsor, to one of our in-house dinners while he was still at school.

A luncheon was arranged by Companion Rat Andrew Neatrour, the man who looked after our PR and who had the ear of most members of the Royal Family. It was held at The Press Centre, a large banqueting room on the second floor of the building in Holborn and was attended by over 400 Rats and guests. King Rat Joe Church (nickname 'Jossel Schule'), a delightful and naturally funny comedian, was in the Chair. Speeches were given by Ted Ray, Ben Warriss and, of course, The King Rat who presented a cheque to Prince Charles for The Prince's Trust, which he accepted with dignity and spoke with his usual warmth and charm. It was the final act of the luncheon, after which came the formal departure of the King Rat, The Prince and other guests. The comedy trio, The Goodies, were also at the top table and jokes about their recently published book had been bandied about. Prince Charles said that he would love to buy one… only he didn't have a fiver on him! So, as he passed by them to leave, I pulled out a five-pound note and thrust it into his hand so that he could pay as he left. This caused much laughing and banter which everyone enjoyed.

As we were going down the first of two escalators to the ground floor, Andy Neatrour came roaring up to me in a fury – I've never seen him so angry. He said, "Bryn, gimme your instruction sheet. Now! I must have it." "Andy," I said, "I've left it on my table and it's too crowded to go back in and get it." At which he exploded. Alongside him, in an equal state of fury, and metaphorically spitting blood, screaming at Andy, was Group Captain David Checketts, Prince Charles's Equerry. This row continued down the escalators behind the Prince. They were going at each other like fishwives saying things like, "Oh yes, you did!"
"No, I did NOT! You've got it all wrong!"

"No, I haven't. It's in the programme – go and look."

"It's not in the programme; I would never have allowed it!" and on and on it went.

When they had all reached the lobby, Prince Charles saw them still bickering and turned on them both. He was as angry as they were and, almost shouting, spat, "Shut up, you two! Be quiet and behave yourselves. We will sort this out when we get back to the Palace. Now, calm down, both of you!" Suitably chastened, they shut up and Prince Charles and David Checketts drove away.

Andy eventually grabbed my order paper and looked for the paragraph which had caused the furore. Whenever a member of the Royal Family attends a function, every item of activity concerning it is covered in minute detail from the moment they leave their residence: the time of arrival, which door is to be used, who they are to meet both at the entrance and in the formal reception, the precise timings, the formalities such as Grace before meal, Loyal Toasts, speeches, presentations, auctions, raffles and any other items to take place whilst they are present. Any errors or indiscretions are carefully ironed out long before the date so that when they arrive, the plan of the event is known to everyone participating. This programme of events is given to the hotel management, photographers, the toastmaster, the speakers and anyone concerned and, earthquakes excepted, it has to be adhered to unequivocally.

It is also a little-known fact that it is an offence in law to present the Monarch or the Monarch Presumptive with either a cheque or money in public; they simply are forbidden to accept them and any breach of that protocol is an embarrassment to them and the organisers. As I mentioned above, the King Rat handed a large cheque to the Prince for his charity – a serious breach of etiquette which made David Checketts so mad and why he singled out Andy Neatrour for his anger. The reason why Andy wanted my programme of events was to prove that it said, quite clearly: "…In his speech, the King Rat will present a cheque for £15,000 to HRH for The Prince's Trust." This should NOT have got through and should have been picked up by Checketts well in advance. It was this very sentence over which they were arguing so vehemently.

That evening I telephoned to speak to Andy who had not returned home. His delightful wife Pat said that Buckingham Palace had telephoned her a dozen times to speak to him but she had no idea where he was. We learned later that he was so terrified of the wrath of the officials at Buckingham Palace that he was scared to go home and even more frightened to call them. Eventually, he did and was immediately put through to David Checketts who said, "Andy, I have been ordered by Prince Charles to apologise to you most sincerely and profusely. The mistake was wholly mine. It is clearly written that he was to receive a cheque, which I should have spotted. It should, of course, have been removed. I am personally very sorry!"

The two of them had been close personal friends for years and Andy was so deeply relieved to learn that the mistake had not been his that he simply accepted it and poured himself a large scotch and soda. It was an event I shall never forget. Not only was it one of the funniest luncheons I had ever attended, but it ended on a note of high drama and anger, and – thank heavens, harmoniously. What's more, it was just as well that I wasn't castigated for handing the prince that fiver... I might still be in The Tower now!

* * * * *

Towards the end of her life, HRH the Princess of Wales became the highest profile royal name. Even after her sad departure I was asked more questions about her than anyone else, especially in the United States.

I was privileged to meet the Princess many times, to such an extent that she was pleased to call me Bryn – an honour of which I was proud. I have steadfastly refused to take sides in the endless discussions about that lady who was always kind, charming, thoughtful and co-operative to me and we had many laughs together. Yes, I was deeply saddened by her divorce and everything that led to it as I have always held the Prince of Wales in the highest regard and felt so sorry that it all went pear-shaped. On the many occasions when I met them, either together or individually, they seemed to be a happy, care-free young couple who were a delight to meet. OK, so maybe I was wrong! You can't win 'em all!

In 'Princess Di's' very early days, she was terrified by the prospect of making public appearances and having to make speeches to which she was so patently unaccustomed. She was young, callow and frightfully nervous. She had the same problem as my daughter Tracy that whenever she was worried or embarrassed by having to become high profile or appear before an audience, she developed a bright red rash around her neck and throat, about which she could do nothing. It was very revealing!

The first time I met 'Charles and Di' together was following a gala concert at the Royal Opera House, Covent Garden, followed by a dinner for about 50 special guests in the River Restaurant at the Savoy. Luciano Pavarotti was the soloist. Prince Charles was placed on one side of a very large table seating everyone and the Princess opposite. *Il Maestro*, having freshened up after the performance, made a grand entry into the dining room, and amid tumultuous applause went and sat beside the Princess. International language barriers made conversation between them virtually impossible, but she struggled gamely on throughout the meal. Standing behind them I 'ear-wigged' as they tried to converse and actually heard her say, with a bright smile on her face and a twinkle in her eye, "Do you sing *Just One Cornetto?*" and she giggled with him. He hadn't a clue as to what she meant, but she teased him and actually sang quietly to him the opening notes. I never heard his reply.

That evening as they were leaving, bidding them farewell, I said to the Prince of Wales, "I'll see you Friday, Sir, at the Kelly Association Dinner!" which he acknowledged. Princes Di then chipped in, in mock frustration, "Oh dear! Where's he going on Friday? And am I coming too?" and she gave him a kind of reproachful look that any 'hard-done-by' wife might have done. It was all in good humour.

Possibly our most memorable meeting was at a huge family conference in Brighton one very sunny afternoon. Together with the Roman Catholic Archbishop of Westminster Cardinal Heanon and three members of the organising committee, the Princess was to sit on a raised platform, later giving an address. In the room prior to following me out I could see that she was absolutely petrified, the revealing rash being there in all its unpleasant glory. Describing what was to happen and preparing to lead them out I said, as I have done so often in other places, "Right team! Follow me – to the ends of the earth – or the stage… whichever is the nearest!" This silly little joke brought a gentle giggle from the others but from the Princess a mock rebuke: "I'll make the jokes, if you don't mind!", as she lowered those gorgeous blue eyes and gave me a very worried smile.

As I was introducing the Archbishop, I noticed four or five young people coming up a short flight of steps on to the stage – totally unscheduled – heading toward the table where the principals were gathered. I stopped my announcement and gently ushered them off. Carrying on as though nothing had happened, my reaction to this small demonstration brought a roar of approval from the 6,000 delegates. At the end of the afternoon, as the Princess was leaving, she came across and thanked me profusely for all I had done for her that day and helping her through some extremely difficult moments. The 'protest,' for that is what it was, hit the headlines the next day and I came out of it to great critical acclaim.

Our infrequent meetings were always a joy and personally I have only happy memories of that very beautiful young lady.

Sir Billy Butlin was the founder of holiday camps, opening Skegness between the wars. After the Second World War, a young upstart named Fred Pontin got on the scene and opened several of his own in competition with *Butlins*. Time and their joint success eventually brought the two men together and, superficially, they became friends. Indeed, such was their generosity to charities that they both became Companion Rats. Fred Pontin (later to be Sir-ed) was generous enough to admit, in public, that Sir Bill "… taught me all I know about the business". In private, Bill's rather perspicacious response was, "Yes, I agree. I taught him all *he* knows… I didn't teach him all *I* know!"

Wood Green Round Table was running a big bash at The Grosvenor House for the NSPCC which had agreed to match whatever we made pound-for-pound to build a baby unit in Leeds to be opened by their patron, Princess Margaret. I contacted Fred Pontin asking him for a prize for our fund-raising. He happily gave us a Pontinental Holiday, worth at that time about £400, and said to me, "I don't mind giving as many of these as you like on condition that you raise at least double its value for your charity. I get annoyed when I give something worth four hundred quid and they only make two!" We were targeting at least £1,000.

It was to be a prize in a game of Bingo, for which I had asked Harry H Corbett ('arold of *Steptoe and Son*) to be the caller. All was going well: heads down, looking in and everyone quiet as he intoned, "… all the sevens, seventy-seven. Clickety Click, sixty six," and all the usual rhymes. Suddenly, from the middle of the room came this shrill, loud voice. "It's me! It's me! It's me. HOUSE! HOUSE! HOUSE!" and a tall, slim, blonde and beautiful, vociferous young lady leapt to her feet, waving her bingo card in the air, obviously having filled in all the numbers. She was delirious with joy as though she had won the crown jewels, and rushed up to Harry to have her card checked. And who do you think was the winner of this Pontinental Holiday? It was Billy Butlin's daughter, Cherrie!

Cherrie, in her high heels, stood well over six feet tall – Harry H Corbett was much shorter, but they knew each other well and, as she approached him at the table, they both had their arms outstretched which they wrapped around each other in a warm cuddle. Cherrie was wearing a luscious, white, full-length, halter-neck dress, clasped at the throat with a neckband. Her entire back was bare, with the skirt hooked at the lower back just above her bum! As his arms encircled her, Harry's cufflink got caught in the clasp of the neckband at the back and stuck there! He couldn't move it, and it somehow became locked with his other arm, causing Cherrie to continue to hug him. I heard him mutter to her, "F*** it. I'm stuck!" The farce increased as it became obvious that neither could disentangle themselves. She being quite 'well endowed' at the front, Harry's face was buried deep into her bosom – which nearly suffocated him! (He not only couldn't see, he couldn't hear the band!) Both tried to retain their dignity, but fickle fate stepped in and they tripped on the skirt and fell with a plonk onto the ballroom floor with Harry on top. I heard her whisper in his ear as they fell. "For Chrissake, don't pull or I'll lose the bleeding lot!" By now the crowd was in hysterics as it was just like a scene out of a Mack Senett film.

Order was restored when, very carefully, I unhooked the erring cufflink and they got up off the floor, undignified but intact. It made what was, up to then, a rather pedestrian evening into a bumper one. I later learned that Cherrie actually went on that Pontinental Holiday. She's that kind of girl!

Chapter 8

Daft Doubles

"Distance lends enchantment…
except when you want to get somewhere in a hurry!"

Anon

In the world of cabaret and entertainment at dinners, dances, banquets and balls, one of the most common phrases to be heard from singers, comedians, conjurors and other artistes was, "I've got a double tonight. I have a 9.30 at the Connaught Rooms and have to be at the Park Lane for 10.30. Doing 'doubles' was part of the game. The business was very fragmented and erratic, and work had to be taken whenever and wherever it was offered. Consequently, we all had to take huge risks, hoping to get away from one job to be at another in time simply to earn extra fees. I've had more than my fair share of these over the years, some more hair-raising than others. It is to my eternal credit and humungous luck with traffic that I have never missed the second – or in some cases a third one. I have actually had four functions on the same day, and that really is pressing your luck. One particularly mind-blowing day will live in my memory, more of which later. 'God Save our Gracious Queen' – she needed saving that day!

Companion Rat Andrew Neatrour was formerly the 'Press Guy' at the Variety Club of Great Britain and latterly the man in charge of publicity and press for the Grand Order of Water Rats. Andy was a Canadian businessman who, through the two offices I mentioned earlier, had almost complete freedom of entry into Buckingham Palace and was on as near first-name terms to most of the Royal

Family as protocol and politeness would allow. HRH Princess Margaret, Countess of Snowdon, used to telephone him personally and ask him to be her escort on certain occasions. He was a good deal older and so there would be no silly talk of a 'liaison' or relationship; he was simply her escort. In return for this privilege, he was frequently asked by the royals to organise gala functions for their favourite charities.

Andy founded a small organisation called the Combined Charities Committee (CCC) which ran dozens of events all over the UK. This was where I came in as he relied upon me to organise the formal side of things at whatever venue he selected. It was all for free – just hotel and travel expenses were provided. He had an unlimited supply of names of great celebrities and artistes, and when he called them and said that Princess Margaret, or Prince Charles or one of the others had asked them to appear to help raise money, most of them leapt at it and programmes were soon put together.

I recall a CCC event with Andy and Princess Margaret – whom I fancied like mad. She was absolutely gorgeous; she had beautiful clear blue eyes that bore into you, and frequently she would wear very low-cut, off-the-shoulder gowns revealing a most beguiling bosom. When she spoke to you, she almost defiFed you to look down and, as she was tiny, this became extremely difficult. She and I met on many occasions and I was told by a number of people close to her that I was her favourite and that she loved to see me at functions. Sadly, my wife, and Royal Protocol, meant that I had to admire from afar; but, at times, she really was a stunner!

Actually, Princess Margaret and I shared a bed on one occasion. It was at Skindles, a now defunct nightclub in Maidenhead where there had been a rather odd party to raise funds for one of her charities. Nightclubs were not the easiest places to work as they mainly consisted of a discotheque, a revolving stage and no focal point. Anyway, Andy got us all there and after the party we were invited to the private quarters of the owner for a late-night noggin. Margaret was very partial to the odd G & T (go easy on the tonic!), and there were about twenty of us packed into this small room which was lounge and bedroom – it really was very cramped. Noticing a large bed covered with a tacky leopard-skin bedspread, Her Royal Highness said to me, "What kind of a bed is that?"

"It's a waterbed, Ma'am," I replied.

"Oh really? I wonder what it's like. Shall we try it?"

What a question!

So we both sat on the edge and bounced up and down for a few minutes. "I don't think I'd like one of these, do you?" she said.

My reply was lost in the noise, atmosphere and my dream of sharing a bed with a very fanciable young princess!

One daft double concerned an evening with a very young Prince Charles. Andy had booked the *Adelphi Theatre*, Liverpool, for a huge charity show. The top of the bill was the inimitable Ken Dodd: "... Give me the keys. I'll lock up and put the lights out when I leave!" He was, and still is, notorious about never stopping, just going on and on interminably. He has to be one of our greatest living comics, and one with whom I have had the pleasure of working dozens of times.

I remember the very first time I met Ken. It was at a Round Table Conference at *Butlins* Holiday Camp in Pwllheli, North Wales. He did well over an hour and absolutely stormed a very tough but good-natured audience of several thousand. In the dressing room afterwards, we had a chat during which I noticed that his hands were filthy – they were literally covered in ink. When I managed to get a closer look, I could see that single word 'memory ticklers' were written on every available space: his palms, the pads of his fingers and thumbs, the back of his hands, his wrists... everywhere he could write something. It was his script. I learned that when he was doing all the funny bits with his hair and his 'tickling stick', he was really prompting himself for the next gag.

A dear friend of mine, comedian Peter Hudson, has become a very close friend of Doddy. He had been with Tommy Cooper as a 'warm-up' comic for over 25 years and discovered that Doddy is a passionate admirer of Cooper, wanting to know everything about him. Peter told me why Ken Dodd goes on and on when performing. His answer is rather poignant. Ken Dodd has no family, he is not married but does have a lady friend. He says that most of us go home to family or friends with whom we can talk about our work and the jobs we have done. He goes home to an empty house. All of his audiences are his 'family' and he just wants to hang on to them for as long as possible, for, when he comes off-stage, it is back to solitude.

But I digress. On the day in question, I had a luncheon in London ending at around 3.00 pm. I then had to catch a plane to Liverpool where I would be met by a driver to take me to the *Adelphi*. Arriving at Speke Airport, I was in a lounge suit, but black tie and dinner jacket were required for my evening engagement. Prince Charles was due to arrive at 7.00 pm to meet the VIPs and be in the Royal Box by 7.30. I had to get there before him to organise the Royal line-up and generally sort out the reception bit. My plane was due to land at around 5.30 and the onward journey was at least one hour. Even if it was dead on time, it was going to be tough, especially as I had to change.

My flight was late, landing nearer to six o'clock, and then I discovered to my absolute horror that I was being collected in a two-seater sports car. Very fast indeed, but where do I change? Picture the scene: I squeezed into the front seat of this very small car, shoved my case on what purported to be the back seat and we sped off. Speed limits? Forget it! I had to be at the *Adelphi Theatre* before 7.00 pm and to hell with driving laws.

I managed to open my case, take out my dress trousers and 'moon' to any passing pedestrian or cyclist as I removed my other trousers, hoiking on the black ones at close on 100 miles per hour. I ripped off my shirt and struggled and juggled into my dress shirt, fighting with the studs as I did so. I grappled with my black tie as we entered − nay, tore − around the environs of Liverpool, knowing what it must be like to drive in the 'Le Mans'.

My own personal 'Juan Fangio' raced through the police cordon and ground to a halt, bang slap in front of the *Adelphi* just as I was dragging on my DJ. The crowd of thousands behind the barriers waiting to see our Royal guest thought it was he who had arrived in an odd car. With all the dignity my frazzled brain and sweaty body could command, I alighted from the car to the beginnings of a tumultuous roar from the crowd… which died like a damp squib when they realised that I was not the Royal He! I entered the Theatre at 6.55 pm.

His Royal Highness Prince Charles arrived at 7.00 to a perfectly organised reception committee and line. Ken Dodd went on at 9.45 pm, having been told to 'come off' at 10.25. Much to everyone's astonishment, he complied to the minute, and our Royal guest went on stage at 10.30 for a brief speech and some presentations. He never knew of my 'Paul Revere' type journey in a small two-seater.

For many years I was friendly with Charles Forte and his family; I have known him since the early days when he bought the Café Royal and many of the Piccadilly Circus banqueting houses. Our friendship grew and I was delighted to attend many of his private and personal celebrations, one in particular being his eightieth birthday party in the Great Room of The Grosvenor House at which both HRH Princess Anne and Prime Minister Margaret Thatcher were guests of honour.

Trusthouse Forte built a beautiful hotel near Famagusta, in Northern Cyprus, and I was invited to attend the formal opening. The Golden Sands Hotel had a beachfront of over one kilometre and was quite superb. The guest of honour, Archbishop Makarios, was a great personal friend of Charles Forte and agreed to perform the opening ceremony. Security was unbelievable; armoured cars and motorcyclists driving up and down the road outside the hotel, helicopters flying around all day overhead and an armed guard of huge thug-like gentlemen who spoke no English – there were even armoured boats at sea keeping watch and escorting away any would-be spotters on the water. The adoring crowds of admirers and supporters of the Archbishop filled the streets just to get a glimpse of their hero.

When Archbishop Makarios arrived, we were taken on a tour of the hotel and I somehow ended up in a private bedroom with him, Charles Forte, two other priests and a security guard! I learned that, despite speaking Greek in public, the Archbishop spoke fluent

English, having been educated in England. When I returned home, I told my friends that he very strongly resembled the great comedian and actor Alfred Marks!

My duties for the opening of the hotel were not too onerous, except that on the last day I had to attend a formal working breakfast and then fly back to London for 5.30 pm as I was due at a Round Table National Conference with 5,000 delegates in Bournemouth. Impossible? Not quite... even though it involved catching a connecting flight in Frankfurt!

When I got to Heathrow, all the miracles fell into place. My suitcase was the first up the carousel – unheard of! Next, my wife had driven the *Jag* right up to the door of the terminal – utterly impossible today – and actually had the engine running. I kissed her hello/goodbye, jumped into the car and went, while Ann caught the tube home. I arrived at the hotel in Bournemouth at 5.15 pm, whereupon the convenor casually greeted me, "Oh hello, Bryn... had a good trip from London?"

"Not really," I replied. "I was in Cyprus this morning and only landed a couple of hours ago at Heathrow!"

"Thank Christ you didn't tell me you were going to do that. I would have died!"

But I suppose the most dramatic of all my daft doubles was when I did four functions in one day, the third of which contained all the Royal Family. For many years, the Royal Horticultural Society, organisers of the Chelsea Flower Show, hosted many events throughout the week. A tradition going back dozens of years was that on the first or Royal Day, HM The Queen and as many members of the Royal Family who were both interested and able within their busy schedules, had their own private viewing. They would arrive around 4.00 pm and tour the show, meeting exhibitors and officials. It would culminate in the Royal Marquee at about five o'clock where they would take tea and chat for about one hour. The newly-inducted Mayor of the Royal Borough of Kensington and Chelsea was always with the Queen, and it was usually so close to the Mayor-Making that it was virtually his first official engagement; and there he is, 'taking tea' with Her Majesty.

On that never-to-be-forgotten day I was to attend two parts of a daylong function for a foreign delegation – a working breakfast at Lancaster House which ended at 9.30 am, and a presentation cocktail party at the Victoria and Albert Museum starting at 6.30 pm. Even with the Chelsea Flower Show at 3.45 pm, this gave me time to slip in a formal luncheon between noon and 3.00 pm for another client.

The first two functions went like clockwork and I was feeling quite content as I made my way to Chelsea Hospital to await the royal party at 3.45. My duties here were quite simple, merely indicating to each 'Royal' their particular table. As the Queen usually left Chelsea no later than 6.00 pm, this would leave me enough time to scamper across to the V & A.

Not this time! Firstly, Her Majesty was a bit late in arriving. Secondly, she loved the show and spent much longer talking to exhibitors. Thirdly, instead of reaching the Royal tent by 5.00 pm, she didn't arrive until nearly 5.30. Fourthly, she was enjoying her tea and was in no apparent hurry to leave. Now protocol dictates that members of the Royal Family arrive in very strict order: The Queen, Prince Philip (when he came, which was not often), Princess Margaret, Princess Anne (who sometimes walked straight through and out the other side without stopping for tea), The Duchesses of Kent and Gloucester, Princess Alexandra and Princess Michael of Kent, all of whom had their own groups of friends with them. They had specially designated tables in strict order and knew their places perfectly. It was not difficult.

Departure was in the same order and their cars were parked inside the hospital grounds at the back of the marquee – as was mine. I was now in a desperate state of panic, knowing that I was 'on duty' at the V & A at 6.30 pm and there was our beloved Queen having a great time at 6.15... 6.20... 6.25... Would the Lady never go? I then spotted the 'sign' which seemed to telegraph itself to all the other royals – she picked up her handbag and tucked it under her arm, followed by her gloves, and I began to breathe again. She rose and, telepathically, so did everyone else. Then she began her farewells... which are never quick! Eventually, she reached her car, followed by the rest of the royals, but oh so very slowly. The last was chatterbox Princess Michael of Kent, whom I like enormously. As she left the marquee, I rushed around to my car, hanging on the tail of the last royal car as it nosed out of the grounds.

To say I belted to the V & A would not be true because of the traffic. But when I arrived, I drove onto the pavement, leapt out of the car and, seeing an attendant by the door, threw him my keys and hollered, "Please move it! Park the b****y thing anywhere you like!" to which I heard the horrific reply, "I don't drive!"
"WELL FIND SOMEONE WOT DOES!" I yelled back.

The walk from the front door to the gardens of that great museum goes on forever and, when you're in a hurry, it seems like miles. I ran like blazes into the garden and there met my mentor and organiser who greeted me with the comforting words, "Don't worry, Bryn, you've still got another five minutes and I have your written script and details all set out for you." He really was a friend in need. I went up to the microphone and made the announcements as though I had been there all the time. Nobody knew!

No, it doesn't really pay to double up to such an extent that you get ulcers. I have many more doubles stories I could tell – but maybe another time.

For as long as I can remember, Ann and I have been collectors of autographed first edition books and we have dozens with such names as Sir Archibald McIndoe, the surgeon who founded the Guinea Pig Club in East Grinstead, for giving plastic surgery to airmen burnt in their aircraft; Lord Thompson of Fleet, who owned *The Times* and 363 other newspapers and whose ambition had been to own one for every day of the year; Ronald Reagan and many others.

Many years ago, the Entertainment Artistes Benevolent Fund (EABF), with which I am closely connected, ran a concert at the Whitehall Banqueting House. The guest of honour was Princess Michael of Kent, and the guest artiste was that fabulous violinist Nigel Kennedy, a delightful chap but a complete maverick. Every time I met him he used to put his arm around my shoulder and call me 'Dad'. His concert was to be an hour of jazz with a rhythm quartet. During part of the performance, the quartet played on their own while Nigel came and sat in the front. He actually sat next to me, and I was thrilled to look after his priceless Guaneri violin. I asked him why he had dropped classical music and he showed me an allergic rash on his neck caused by the varnish from the fiddle. He said that classical music required a much tighter hold under the chin, so until he was better he would be playing jazz which needed less stringent control and which he loved anyway.

Nigel had recently completed his autobiography, of which I had a copy. Coincidentally, Princess Michael of Kent had just published one of her books as well. Being smart, Ann suggested that I take both books to the function to be autographed and, whilst there, I was inspired. Before going down to the Undercroft for dinner with about 100 special guests, I drew people's attention to these two books and, when we were at table, I asked both of them if they would be willing to give a copy as a prize for that dinner. I said to Peter Elliott, the Director of the EABF that, if they agreed, I would auction them, but only on condition that they both signed both books. They agreed.

When I began the auction, Princess Michael said to me, "How much do you hope to raise? Don't forget, mine costs £29 to buy. So whatever you do, don't undersell it, will you? How much does your book cost, Nigel?" "No idea, mate!" was his laconic and almost disrespectful reply. "Abaht fifteen quid, I fink!" (Yes, he does talk like that despite coming from a respectable middle class family and having had a public school education.)

I began the auction and rapidly reached £1,000, at which Princess Michael expostulated, "A thousand pounds? *A thousand pounds!* My book's not worth a thousand pounds!" I whispered to her – equally disrespectfully, "Shut up, woman! Leave it to me," receiving a lovely warm glance in return. She then said, "For a thousand pounds, I'll autograph every page. That's wonderful!" The books eventually sold for £1,100 to the delight of everyone, especially the two authors and the EABF.

Chapter 9

Name Dropping!

"What's in a name? That which we call a rose
By any other name would smell as sweet."

William Shakespeare

I swore that were I ever to write my autobiography, it would not be a 'name-dropping' exercise. I have read many and find those with a catalogue of famous, infamous, well-known, less well-known, unknown and never-will-be-knowns become boring and unreadable, and resolved that mine would not be like that. As I said to Prince Charles at dinner the other evening at Highgrove, "Charles, my Dear Chap. I simply cannot abide name-droppers!" Old and hackneyed, but it expresses my views entirely.

Having said all that, I must now, in part, break my own pledge and mention a few names of friends, acquaintances and colleagues who, throughout my long and varied career have meant a great deal to me and given me countless hours of pleasure by their talents. Unless my readers are over the age of 50, it is highly unlikely that they will have heard of most of them, but for those of a more mature vintage the names I mention will hopefully raise a smile. But few of these acts – if any – would admit to being famous or 'celebrity'; they were just great performers in their own field.

Throughout this book, I record anecdotes and incidences with famous men and women from all walks of life – it is inevitable in a career spanning 55 years. Any toastmaster of similar longevity will have met just as many as it goes with the job. It doesn't make us special – it is simply that the nature of our work means that we will encounter people in the limelight, especially entertainers of every kind. I have therefore decided to dedicate one chapter to some of these great artistes. I make no apology for it because they have enriched my working life more than they can ever know, and I am grateful to them all.

I am only familiar with my side of their varied professions, the cabaret and the ballroom floor; I know nothing about the variety stage, vaudeville, summer season, pantomime, radio broadcasting or the many other branches of their profession. I only ever met them in possibly the most difficult and demanding corners of their lives, the open ballroom with audiences 'in the round'. The cabaret floor is probably the most difficult forum for any artiste, compared with a theatre stage built purely for the purpose of entertainment. Every ballroom floor is different; bands are often in the wrong place, special effect lighting is non-existent, the rooms are an odd shape with twenty people immediately in front but with tables seating 100 or more either side. There may be wine waiters wandering around, lousy and badly maintained microphones and a multitude of problems not otherwise seen in theatres. And yet many of those I met preferred doing cabaret because, when 'you've gone well' and had the crowd roaring for more, the feeling of elation and achievement is indescribable, especially as the audience is so much closer and more personal. I recently took Barry Cryer and wife Terry home from a gig and we discussed this point. His perspicacious reply was that when an act is working in a theatre, the punters have chosen to go especially to see him work. At a banquet, the act is 'thrust' upon them by the organisers whether they like the act or not. Psychologically, there is a world of difference. But where to begin?

One of the funniest little men of yesteryear was a chap called Sid Marx. He was a blond-haired comedian, about five-foot tall, who played several odd instruments. I heard him dozens of times over the years and could probably do his act verbatim. Indeed, many of these artistes really only had one act which lasted their entire careers and the prospect or thought of going on the wireless – television was very much in its infancy in those days – was anathema to them

156

as their material was limited to about 60-70 minutes. Sid played an ordinary everyday carpenter's saw which produced a delightful, very mellow sound, as well as a specially adapted stirrup-pump. He told a wonderful gag about two fellows who each had a terrible stutter. One went into a pet shop and said to the bloke behind the counter, "Err... Excuse me M...mer...mer...Mister, b...b...but, her... her...er...how mer...mer...much is the per...per...per... per...parrot in the wer...wer...window?" The bloke behind the counter had a worse stammer said. "Tw...tw..tw...twwennnnty p...p...per... per...ounds, mer...mer...mer...mer...mate!" "Tw...tw...tw...tw...twwennnnty p...p...per... per...ounds?" repeated the first bloke incredulously. "That's a l...l...l...l...ot of m...m...mer...money! C...c...c...c...can heee sper...sper... sper...speak?" And the parrot looked down and said, "A bloody sight better than either of you two!"

Sid was working with me on two consecutive evenings at a small, undistinguished hotel in Hendon, where I worked dozens of times. They were both Masonic Ladies' Festivals, on a Monday and Tuesday – different audiences of course, but otherwise identical situations. On each occasion he went on at around 10.30 pm but on the first of these he 'died on his arse'! (Forgive the vernacular, but it's part of the business.) He came off feeling utterly depressed, to the sound of his own footsteps. The audience did not seem to want to know and there was no apparent reason. The following night, as you would imagine, he was anxious. The situation was identical and from the moment he appeared, they loved him. He wowed them, they fell about at all his gags and antics – in short, he tore them apart. No one could or can explain why these things happen, they just do. Over the years I have studied audience reactions and why artistes go well sometimes but fail at others and put it down to the word 'chemistry'! There is unquestionably an indefinable 'something' which links a performer to an audience; if the chemistry between the two does not work, then the artiste will have a tough time. There is no act or artiste in the history of entertainment that has not tasted the bitter flavour of failure before an audience; it is the most horrible and daunting of experiences and is like eating charcoal. When it happens, you just pick yourself up, put the failure behind you and make sure that you do better next time.

Another act I loved to watch was a wonderful Chinese pickpocket conjuror called Ming Chow. His real name was Bertram Otto and he would arrive, fully dressed in a long Chinese robe, with slanty eyes and false pigtail. I would set up his props and he would do 35 minutes of magic and skilful pickpocketing – he was a genius. He would go around the audience, grab the men very roughly and drag them onto the ballroom floor. He would then do a few conjuring tricks with flags, cards and rings before sending them back to their places. I loved to hear him counting the flags in a pseudo-Chinese accent: Onnnnne, Twoooooo, Flllleeee…, Flooooourr, Flllive. As the stooges went back to their seats, he would pull out of his flowing gown a wallet, wrist-watch, badge or brooch, and hold them up and saying, "And preeese, who is the owner of this pllitty rittle fling?" and return all the stuff he'd pinched… especially the braces he'd removed. In the height of the season, he would be doing two or three functions every night.

Bertie Otto had the softest and most gentle hands I ever held. He also had a talent for making small models, especially model railways and, for many years in the Winter Garden at Eastbourne, he ran one of the largest model railway exhibitions in the country, with lights, sound and hundreds of moving passenger and goods trains, buses, trucks and cars covering a colossal display area; all this long before the days of electronics. This was exhibited for year after year at Lord Montagu's stately home in Beaulieu where it was run by Bertie's wife Lilly – it was seen by millions of people. Sadly, he died at the age of fifty playing tennis.

Gordon Turner and Linda Mason were a husband-and-wife duo; he was a pianist and comedian and Linda was basically a lovely singer with a huge personality. Pianos were always a problem and frequently set well back into the middle of the stage. In the days when he had to play that instrument, after being introduced he would sit down and play some ghastly discords which made the piano sound tinny, flat and horribly out of tune, slam down the lid and say to the audience. "*Bechsteins* have asked me to announce that

that piano is a *Blüthner!*" Eventually, he got so fed up with the lousy equipment that he had a small white piano constructed with its own in-built PA system. This gimmick took off to the extent that he became known as 'The man with the White Piano'. He had dozens of gags which he put to music. One I clearly remember was,

> "Georgie Porgie pudding and pie,
> Kissed the girls and made them cry.
> When the boys came out to play,
> He kissed them too... He was funny that way!"

I even told him one, which duly appeared in his act, for which he gave me a quid:

> "Oh! The Grand Old Duke of York;
> He had ten thousand men...
> ... And his case comes up next week!"

Another regular was Sandy Sandford, a cockney comedian married to a pretty soubrette and multi-instrumentalist named Mary Buddell. Both artistes were a big hit at Masonic functions. Another very special lady from London's Old Kent Road who was always in great demand was Florence Raynor. In the twenty or so years she was on the circuit, she was a legend and known to everyone as 'Our Flo'. She had a true Cockney accent when she spoke, but a lovely singing voice, and she always appeared with her hair tightly combed back. I will never forget being backstage at a restaurant ballroom when she was showing off her very expensive, brand-spanking new dress. She went on and as she reached the centre of the ballroom floor there, at a table right in front of her, was a lady with the identical dress! She was horrified. But was she lost for words? Not Our Flo. She 'teetered' across the floor and said to the lady wearing it, "Cor Bloody Blimey! I spend a fortune on a bleedin' dress and then go an' 'ave to bump into someone else wot's got the same one.

Just my bloody luck… (Pause for effect)… But, darlin'," she grinned, "Ain't we got good taste?" They loved her, as did all her audiences.

One of the funniest double acts was Ted Durante and Hilda – he was a 'strong man' and she was very glam. He would be pretending to do strong acrobatics and Hilda would come on, try to join in and walk literally all over him – up his legs to his knees, on his chest, on his shoulders, tread all over his face and then down his back and walk off again. She never said a word and did this several times, sometimes carrying a tray with a drink on it. With a deadpan expression all the time, she was excruciatingly funny.

Conjurors were among the more popular acts and I recall with much affection a diminutive man called Jimmie Rogers. He came on in a long flowing cape, didn't say a single word and produced about twenty doves and masses and masses of artificial flowers from 'nowhere'. For well over twenty years Francis White was the very popular and much loved President of the Magic Circle. In a thirty-minute act, he only used three tricks, the rest was very elegant, funny and sophisticated patter. He told me a fascinating story about another great illusionist named Robert Harben who invented the now well-known illusion, 'Cutting the lady into three'. A very slim, small girl – vital for the trick – stands in an upright box with three doors, hands protruding from two holes at the top, and feet likewise at the bottom. After twirling it around a few times, he moves the middle section out sideways, creating three separate boxes – the top one above the bottom one, but with a big gap in the centre – where the belly ought to be!

Frank White told me that one night he and his wife Ann were asleep in bed when the telephone rang. He answered it and the voice said, "Frank, it's Bob here. I've just invented the greatest illusion you've ever seen. You must come over at once and see it." Francis looked at the clock and said, "But Bob. It's three o'clock in the morning. You must be barmy. I can't come now, I'm in bed." Robert Harben, being a typical genius, was rather vague said, "Oh, is it really? Well, it doesn't matter; just throw something on and come over. You MUST see it first." He did, and was proud that what is now one of the most used illusions performed throughout the world of magic, was first seen in Bob Harben's lounge at four in the morning. That original equipment is now owned by Alan Shaxon, the current President of the Magic Circle. I worked with Alan and his wife Ann hundreds of times and am pleased to count them among my friends; they too are both great entertainers.

When it comes to 'close-hand-magic', the universally acknowledged doyen of the world of prestidigitation was a lovely little guy named Ken Brooke. He did not have a strong personality but was a brilliant magician who also ran a magic shop in London. Paul Daniels, Frank White, David Nixon, Tommy Cooper, David Berglas, Ali Bongo and all the greats in magic bow their heads in homage to that wonderful little man who sadly developed arthritis which prevented him working. He died prematurely, but left a legacy of tricks and skills coveted by magicians worldwide. His bottles-and-glass-in-the-tube trick was simply astonishing, so fast and slick.

Harold Taylor, yet another magician on the circuit, was noted for his rather flamboyant dress. He was a member of the Grand Order of Water Rats, where tradition dictates that any late arrivals at their meetings must stand before all present and apologise in a prescribed manner. At the time, the Prince Rat was Bob Pearson – one half of that great double act, Bob and Alf Pearson, whose signature tune was 'We bring you melodies, from out of the sky, my brother and I.' (Bob and Alf Pearson were virtually the very first variety act to appear on the radio. In the 1920s they did daily performances on 2L0, the precursor of the BBC. Alfie Pearson, a Past King Rat, is still going strong at 95.) Upon arriving late, Harold Taylor stood before the Lodge dressed in blue and white shoes, green check trousers, a striped blazer, multi-coloured shirt, red cravat and with a flower in his buttonhole – a veritable kaleidoscope of colour. He delivered his apology for being late and was welcomed back by the King Rat. As he went over to take his seat, Bob Pearson, in little more than a *sotto voce*, uttered the immortal words… "Were there many at the funeral, Harold?" He was awarded our coveted Jester's Medal for a great impromptu gag.

Many years ago, a famous comedian decided that when a Rat delivered a great gag, or impromptu funny line, he be rewarded. He therefore had a star-shaped medal specially made and hung it on a satin rope as the gift. If it is thought by those attending and approved by the King Rat that the gag really was 'a belter', then it is formally presented and, as a 'penalty', all are asked to put 'a coin' in the collecting box to swell the funds. This award is very highly prized and many comics try to win it at Lodge Meetings.

However, there is another type of pun, or gag or 'groaner', as they are called. These frequently die and don't get a laugh, but only a series of moans and groans by the members. In short, the joke 'lays an egg'! We are proud of the fact that two of our more famous Rats were Laurel and Hardy. They were active and enthusiastic members and were frequently seen wearing their emblems when making public appearances in the States. They decided that these 'groaners' should also be rewarded and so presented the Lodge with a large golden egg on a chain. So, now, when anyone cracks a gag that is just rubbish, cries of, "Egg, Egg, Egg," echo around the Lodge and it is duly presented. On that occasion, the miscreant has to put a few coins in the pot himself. One of the greatest tellers of these so-called gags was the late Cardew Robinson, known during his career as Cardew the Cad of the School. He specialised in them and loved getting the Egg. (A fellow went into a pet shop and said to the man behind the counter, "I want to buy a wasp!" "A wasp? We don't sell wasps!" "Well you've got one in the window!")

Rod Taylor was, for thirty years, a producer/director of radio and TV shows in the north east of England. He is now a super after-dinner speaker recounting many tales of the dozens of famous performers with whom he worked. He tells a true story about when he was driving Tommy Cooper between two studios either side of Manchester. He did not know the large gentleman very well (Tommy took size 14 shoes!), but they were chatting as he drove. Suddenly, Tommy said, "STOP! Stop here. Now. Just pull up!" So, rather bewildered, Rod did; when he had stopped, Tommy wound down his window and said to a little old lady walking along, "Er... Excuse me! Excuse me!" She stopped and looked in amazement

162

at the great Tommy sitting there and said, "Yes. How can I help you?"

"Do you know how to get to Acacia Avenue?" asked Tommy.

"Acacia Avenue? Acacia Avenue?" she mused. "No, I'm sorry, I don't know Acacia Avenue?"

"Well," said Tommy, leaning out of the window, pointing, "You go up the road there, take the first turning on the left and then..."

And Rod just drove off leaving the poor, bewildered lady standing there. Tommy was that kind of guy.

Of the many double acts around, some of those I loved working with were: Martin Gluth & Helen James; Gwen Overton & Clive Stock (the latter of whom has written his own very interesting autobiography); Norman Lumsden (who found late fame and fortune as 'JR Hartley' in the *Yellow Pages* advertisement) & Irene Palmer, and Raimund Herincx & Jean Waugh. All were lovely singers, performing great songs and pleasing countless audiences. Tommy Wallis and Beryl were brilliant xylophonists who are now called 'The Plummers' as their father, Sid Plummer, was an even greater exponent of that instrument. I consider myself lucky to have been friends with them all.

I am thankful that my career started at a time when ballroom dancing was immensely popular. This elegant, social activity made my work both highly pleasurable and very easy... it was never a problem getting an audience up onto a dance floor. Many of the functions at which I presided engaged professional ballroom dancers for cabaret, most of whom had been world champions. Wally Fryer and Violet Barnes, Bill and Bobby Irving, Harry Smith-Hampshire and Doreen Casey, were among just a few of the many ballroom dancers I met, while Wally Laird and Loraine Reynolds were the absolute stars of Latin-American dance. I used to think that Loraine Reynolds was one of the sexiest and most fanciable women I had ever seen... she just oozed sex in her every movement. (Casting her eye over this drivel, my wife Ann contends that I would not have given Loraine a second glance had she been dressed in a sack! Baloney!)

There are so many dear friends whose friendship I cherish that I really do not want to leave anyone out or forget all the wonderful moments they gave me. Gate Eastly was an elegant, sophisticated comedian who actually DID come from Purley. He was one of the 'Purley Gates'. Ouch! And yes, Gate really was his name. Les Henning was a gentle, smooth-talking London comedian with a very relaxed style. The gag I always loved to hear him tell was, "A fellow takes his dog into a cosy pub with a lovely log fire and asks for a drink. The barman says, "That's a nice dog you have there. Anything special about him?" The fellow replies, "This is the best-trained dog in the world. I trained him and he will only take orders from me and no one else. Most obedient!"

"Nobody else, eh?" said the barman.

"Yep! Nobody, and I'll bet anything you like that he'll ignore everyone!" At which the barman said, "OK. I bet you a fiver he'll obey me!"

"Done," said the fellow and they put their fivers on the bar. Whereupon the barman comes around to the front of the bar, picks up the dog, chucks it on the fire and says, "GET OFF!"

For many years, Peter Hudson was Tommy Cooper's warm-up comic, priming audiences in that quiet, gentle patter of his. Jimmy Tarbuck tells the story that Tommy Cooper telephoned him one day and said, "Jim – just thought I'd give you a call. I'm doing a TV show tonight from the Palladium." As they chatted about the show, Tommy confided, "The problem is, I haven't got a finish. I can't work out how to get off, what to end the show with; it's all a blank!" Jimmy's answer was, "Well, Tom, you're the greatest ad libber in the business, you'll think of something." Tommy went on and stormed them. Just as he was about to finish, right at the end of the show, in front of millions, he collapsed on the stage and died. Weird, ain't it?

Having mentioned Jimmy Tarbuck, I feel I must tell another anecdote about that legendary comic-cum-semi-professional golfer; he works for fun, but plays golf for a living – he's that good! He and a dear friend of mine, Michael Silver, were due to meet at Grayshott Health Club in Surrey. Jimmy had been there a week, and on his last day decided to play golf with Mike at Liphook, just down the road. They arranged to meet in the car park of the health club, because Mike was just arriving for a week's stay. Just before they drove off together, Mike handed Jimmy a suit and said, "Will you take it into reception and ask them to hang it in my wardrobe? It's brand new and I don't want to get it creased in the back of the car." Which Jimmy duly did and off they went to play golf. At the end of the week, Michael went to take his suit out of the wardrobe only to find that it was missing. He rushed downstairs and said to the receptionist, "Someone's pinched my suit. It's not there where I asked you to put it. In fact, I asked Mr Tarbuck to bring it in when I arrived. What's happened? Where is it?" The girl looked rather sheepish and said, "Well, Mr Silver, I was on duty when Mr Tarbuck brought it in and I remember exactly what happened. He said, 'I've lost so much weight this week, I won't be needing this suit any more; would you like to give it to charity'... and we did!" Mike was horrified and said, "Well where did you take it? Where's it gone? I must get it back. It's brand new and never been worn." She replied, "We took it to the Oxfam Shop in Haslemere." "OXFAM?" he hollered. "My suit went to the Oxfam shop? I don't believe it!" Without further ado, he leapt into his car, belted down to Haslemere and found the shop. There in the window was his £300 Savile Row suit marked up for £20. It hadn't even been sold, which slightly miffed him, but what was worse was that he had to pay twenty quid to get it back! I would love to have been a fly on the wall when Mike and Jimmy met again!

Another memorable act was The Minitones, two midgets who were fantastic – they stood about three feet tall, played musical instruments and were just lovely. The slightly larger one was always 'nagging' the smaller one – Kenny Baker, who later played R2D2 in Star Wars – and used to say to him, "If you don't behave yourself, I'll put your dinner in the middle of the table and you'll die of starvation!" Then there was petite and agile Eva May Wong, a most beautiful oriental contortionist. Her movements were slow, lithe, sexy and extremely difficult – she would contort herself into some of the most amazing positions and ended the act by drinking a glass of wine held between her feet over the back of her neck, whilst lying flat on the floor. Extraordinary! This delightful lady lived just around the corner from us and is still a very active Lady Ratling.

Johnny and Suma Lamont were two exotic dancers who enjoyed a long, active and successful career, and Beryl and Bobo were another unique act. Despite the fact that there was only one Beryl, there were many 'Bobos' over the years. Usually introduced as 'Bobo and his Trampoline', the gymnast would perform various athletic antics, bouncing, twisting and turning, before inviting anyone from the audience to come and join him on the trampoline. Several guests would come up and do a couple of gentle jumps and then return to their seats. The last one was always Beryl, who would have hidden herself in the audience before the act began. She was absolutely hilarious in the way she got things wrong. Nobody suspected that it was a 'plant' and Bobo would ask her to perform some ridiculously difficult tricks which she messed up and fell about. The whole charade was stupendous and very funny. She then took off her 'evening dress', revealing her costume and demonstrating her talents as a supreme trampolinist.

I was particularly fond of a comedy double act consisting of a broad Scot named Charlie Stewart and his English wife Anne Matthew. The first time I met them, I was a young toastmaster eager to learn and I asked Charlie how he wanted to be introduced. He said, "Tell them the last time you met Charlie Stewart and Anne Matthew, they were just leaving to seek fame and fortune in the States, and that if they were any good, they would never return... I now have much pleasure in introducing Charlie Stewart and Anne Matthew." Charlie and I played a lot of golf together; he was such great company, but sadly died in his fifties. Anne subsequently married Peter Saunders who bought The Mousetrap, which must have made him many fortunes. One day I played golf against Anne in a match for the Concert Golfing Society versus the Highgate Ladies. In those days, I was a long hitter and this particular day I was really on song and hitting the ball 'out of sight'! I could do no wrong at the first four holes and, as we approached the next tee, a very long par five, I was just about to drive when Anne said, in a deadpan voice, "Would you like me to go and hold the flag?" It cracked me up so much that I missed the damned thing! Smart gamesmanship and great memories of a super lady.

Accordionists were always very popular and I remember five in particular. The first two are ladies, Adele French and Phyllis Gillingham, wonderful performers who always got the crowd singing. Both are today very active Lady Ratlings. Then there was Carlo (Charlie to his friends), a short, quiet man who played on a huge accordion that almost dwarfed him. He would stroll gently around the ballroom floor just playing beautiful melodies. He would take requests and his memory was such that he never failed to respond with their chosen number. Gerald Delmonde was one of the finest accordionists of his day, possibly second only to the sensational Norwegian player Tollefsen. Gerald was a tall, quiet man with a gentle personality, so that whereas he was a fabulous player, he did not possess great showmanship. He briefly teamed up with a lady violinist, Frances Taylor, and together they thrilled the audiences. The final accordionist I must mention is the Scot, Steve Merrick. He also sang and, for many years, he plied his trade most successfully in Spain... no doubt the excellent golf courses there were part of the attraction. It is to my great regret that one never sees accordion acts nowadays; they really were lovely entertainment.

Despite all the above, the *crème de la crème* of the cabaret world were the floorshows. From the early 1950s well into the early 1980s, they were very special indeed. All glitz and glamour, or as Ann used to call them, 'all Tits and Tinsel,' these thirty-minute sparkling shows usually featured eight or nine lovely, scantily clad highly talented girls and a 'speciality act'. The whole bunch would arrive, dump their cases all over the place and spread themselves out and start to strip. Modesty? In show business? Forget it!

The pianist, for they all carried their own Musical Director, would make his way to the toastmaster to see how things were getting on. He needed to know such things as who the band was, were they willing to play for the girls, what time they were going on, and whether there had been a break yet. Sometimes a buffet of tea and pastries was laid on for the audience and no act liked going on during the tea as people were more interested in pouring a cuppa than watching the show. I cannot count the number of times an MD has rushed up to me and said, "Bryn, can you do us a favour and get us on a bit earlier? We've got this one at 9.30, but we've got to be at the Connaught Rooms at 10.30 and then at Slough for midnight. If we can pinch a few minutes here, it'll help!" It happened all the time and, if I was on the ball, I could usually help. Sadly, I gather, not all of my colleagues were so accommodating!

Eric Ross's 'Dazzle', run by his daughter Brenda, was possibly the greatest floorshow of them all – Eric more or less started the genre. He chose the best girls and acts, had the most spectacular costumes and was by far the slickest of them all. Another great was Wilby Lunn and his show 'Cavalcade'. All these floorshows were famed for their pretty girls, ten rapid costume changes, bright dancing and singing and strictly timed to thirty minutes.

George and Bert Bernard were legends of mime between and just after the wars – their miming of The Ride of The Valkyries was just amazing. Another super miming act was Phil Burn, a big blustery guy who simply came on, played various records and mimed to them – it sounds simple, but he was brilliant. His *pièce de résistance* was hilarious mime to Mozart's Largo al Factotum. He teamed up with, and eventually married, another lovely artiste Pamela Moon and they called their show 'Glam'. Phil used to recount a true story about when Glam was appearing at Lyons Corner House, Coventry Street – otherwise known as The Coventry Street Corner House – where incidentally I did my very first and utterly disastrous professional engagement. Glam had torn the crowd apart; they were receiving a standing ovation from the 400 or so guests in this very glitzy, rather gaudy room – the dancers and singers were taking their bows beneath brilliant spotlights and everyone was going wild. Phil was loving it all and drinking in the applause when a bloke walked right across the middle of the floor and straight up to him. In front of the whole show, the band and the audience, he said to Phil, "OK, Mate. 'Ow much do I owe yer? And will yer take a bit less for Nelsons?" (Nelson Eddys, readies, cash!) He then proceeded to take a wad of white fivers out of his pocket, licked his thumb and began counting. That's show business for you!

Jean Belmont was a great dancer and was in the Four Jays, before producing a floorshow named The Gayetimers. (You couldn't use that name now! Oh, how times have changed.) Her partner at that time was a chap called Don Rico (later known as Don Belmont), a smooth, flash, glib-talking, swarthy but very good-looking agent who charmed the birds off the trees. He was a great friend of Frankie Howerd and helped him enormously during his depression. Another sensational dancer was Barry Manning who had a solo act entitled 'Dancing Round the World'. He would dance solidly for 25 minutes, stripping off one costume after another. Each would have a theme and the music altered accordingly. When he went onto the floor, he was wearing twenty different costumes, so he began the act looking rather thick-set and ended with just a shirt and very tight trousers. He too flirted with floorshows and eventually found work on the continent.

Skating acts, singers, impressionists, belly dancers, knife-throwers, slack wire acts, unicyclists, trumpeters, pianists, violinists, cartoonists, formation ballroom dance display teams with eight couples, military bands and clowns are just a few of the eclectic types of entertainment who regularly appeared on the Masonic circuit all over London and the Home Counties… and, of course, there were also strippers. Unquestionably, every toastmaster with more than 25 years' experience will have run a stag night with strippers, snake charmers and blue comics. They are still very popular in many quarters.

Sheila Sands was possibly the most sophisticated stripper around London at the time. She was very nice-looking, had a gorgeous body, and had developed a brilliant technique of removing her clothes which was titillating, sexy and clever but done in the very best of taste. Off-stage she was a charming, modest girl, happily married and, with her husband, ran a marketing business from home. As she moved around amongst the men, she would take off one garment after another, dropping it casually on the floor. However, over the years, she'd had many items pinched by leering, lager louts (although that expression had not been invented then, it describes them well). One night she asked me if I would help her by picking up each item of clothing before others got there. This

169

is not as enjoyable as it may sound in a roomful of lecherous, semi-drunk men, whose only interest was seeing this girl's naked body and hoping that she would come over and wiggle her boobs in their faces! For them, watching a young, not very good-looking toastmaster in a formal red jacket sneaking around behind her snatching up the odd bra, stocking, dress or knickers, was not too popular.

On this particular occasion, *The Harmony Hi-Lites* were to follow Sheila's act. Ann tells me that she and the girls – and Morris – were in stitches watching me creep around the floor trying to look invisible, whilst the erotic Sheila cavorted her nubile body all over the place. They were beside themselves with laughter at me, almost totally ignoring the act. She told me that as I picked up each frippery I stuffed it in my pocket like a guilty husband, and when Sheila was wearing nothing but a smile I apparently ducked down and scampered off the floor. The *Hi-Lites* were convulsed at my embarrassment and never let me forget it.

Fortunately, they did not emerge entirely unscathed either. Sheila Sands ended amid tumultuous applause, wrapped her large cape around herself, took her bows and came off. I then went back to introduce *The Harmony Hi-Lites* who simply came on and sang to the carefully rehearsed and choreographed movements. They were fully clothed, with dresses covering all the way up to their necks. The men, by now really randy, were not interested in such cultured fare and just shouted, "Get 'em off… Go on, girls, show us yer tits!" and other less refined suggestions. It was now my turn to sit back and giggle while they soldiered on. The likelihood of five, religious young mothers, raised in the small, close-knit, narrow-minded communities of the Welsh valleys taking anything off was as remote as Cuffley Academicals winning the Football League. Indeed, my wife was reluctant to take all her clothes off when we were first married; she always came to bed wearing at least one garment. I said to her one evening, "Why don't you strip off and come to bed?" to which she replied, "My mum always told me to keep the mystery in our married life and never take all my clothes off. That's why I always keep one bit on. So there!" "That's fine," I said, "But a hat?"

In 1995, the son of Their Majesties King Constantine and Queen Sophia of The Helenes was married. They are extremely popular with their fellow-expatriate countrymen and women, and the following day decided to invite virtually the whole community to a cocktail reception in the Great Room of The Grosvenor House. It needed three toastmasters simply to control the numbers and we arrived to take instructions.

The format was simple. At that time, the entrance to the Great Room was along a corridor with a row of glass doors opening onto the balcony. It is now open-plan and what took place then could not now be so easily controlled. The guests would be directed along that corridor, through two open doors to meet Their Majesties in a recess just at the top of a flight of stairs leading down into the main ballroom. When they were in position, we opened the doors – it would be easier to say we opened the floodgates – to allow in this heaving, laughing, boisterous and extremely happy throng of very excited Greeks. Indeed, as we arrived, we had noticed that there were already hundreds waiting outside in Park Lane several hours before they could be let in. It was instant pandemonium as they all wanted to be first! We managed to get them under control just to funnel them through the correct door, but it nearly all went pear-shaped because of their euphoria. The actual receiving lasted for about ninety minutes, but such was the pressure that my two colleagues were literally standing in the doorway, their arms outstretched pressing against the door jambs just to hold the crowd back, getting battered and bruised on their backs and arms. We managed and let them through one family at a time. We really had never seen such love and adulation for their deposed Monarch and had we not been there, they would certainly have been mobbed uncontrollably. Eventually, the queue ended and about 1,700 or so Greek men, women and children were downstairs enjoying refreshments.

The plan was that the King and Queen would go to a large stage to address them, before which there was to be some entertainment by a Greek band and some very colourful and pretty dancers. This proved very difficult to stage-manage, as the crowds had crushed around the platform to await the speeches. Eventually, we managed to force our way through the throng and it was a fight all the way, as no one wanted to let them pass. Once there, the stampede continued with hundreds of them wanting to come onto the stage to be photographed with their King and Queen; it almost became necessary to throw them off physically. At last peace was established, silence was called for and His Majesty King Constantine spoke, kindly but passionately, to his fellow-countrymen, thanking them for their love, support and genuine good wishes for his son and new bride.

One problem remained: how do you get a King and Queen off a stage and out of the Great Room without them being mobbed again? The King had already told me that he needed to be away by a certain time for other pressing business, and because of the huge numbers and general atmosphere, his departure time was rapidly approaching. To step down from the stage and try to go back through the mob would have taken forever! Fortunately, I was able to suggest a little-known service passage at the back of the stage, and when he ended his remarks I spirited them off the platform, through a curtain into the passage and up the stairs. It was all done so very quickly that none of the guests noticed that they were not there until they had gone completely. The route took us along the Great Room balcony overlooking the main area. As they departed, they were able to look down to see nearly 2,000 of their devoted countrymen celebrating the wedding of their son. My colleagues and I agreed that it was unquestionably one of the more unusual functions we had attended, and they both had bruises on their arms and backs to prove it!

Chapter 10

The Licensed Trade

"Come landlord, fill the flowing bowl."

Anon

'In the beginning God created the heavens and the earth...' In the beginning God created Masonic Ladies' Festivals by the dozen, weddings by the bucket-load and very little else. The occasional Chamber of Horrors (sorry, Commerce!), Round Table, Royal and Antediluvian Order of Buffalos (RAOB), Rotary Club, and 21st Birthday Parties were among his later creations and became reasonable money-spinners – that was about the lot. I had heard about the Licensed Victuallers Association (LVA) Dinners which were being held at various venues all over the UK, but none fell by me.

In 1951, I was offered a gig at The Bellhouse Hotel, on the main road into Beaconsfield, which had not long been doing functions. I was still too young to own a driving licence and telephoned the hotel to ask if I could stay over. I spoke to a Mr Maurice Cedar, the owner, who said that whereas it was not yet a hotel with bedrooms, I could stay overnight in his staff room and get a *Greenline* bus home in the morning. This I did and began a lifelong friendship (his life, because he died way back in the 1980s) with this charismatic and fascinating little man. Yes, 'little', because despite being very rotund, he was only five feet tall – a small, round, very jolly, roly-poly Jewish gentleman who, with his three brothers, had been in the *schmutter* business. When he became very successful, he drove a *Rolls Royce* with the number plate MC 1961, but he was too small to see over the top of the steering wheel and drove looking through it. Local Gerrards Cross residents used to say, "Whenever we saw a *Rolls* coming along with no driver, we knew it was Maurice!"

Maurice knew absolutely nothing about catering, but in 1945 purchased a roadhouse with a swimming pool and restaurant sitting in over five acres of Buckinghamshire pastureland. It cost him £1,500 and everyone said he was absolutely barmy. Anybody with long memories will remember the old-fashioned swimming 'lidos' all over the UK, outside which were great fountains in blue stone advertising their existence. Behind the fountain at The Bellhouse Hotel was one such lido surrounded by the usual changing rooms and other facilities. The 'hotel' had a small banqueting room holding about 150, ideal for small weddings and dinner dances, and it became very popular.

Maurice employed a Polish head waiter named Emil, with whom I worked on hundreds of occasions and who outlived Maurice by many years. The banqueting business was booming, yet the pool was becoming redundant and utilised a large area which could be put to better use. So, he removed the pool and built a ballroom for 300 people. He extended the reception area and bar, on the other side of which he built a further small restaurant and grill room. Use of the ballroom proliferated and in the season was working six nights a week; at the same time the grill room was doing great business. Maurice engaged a young lady by the name of Grace Coppen. She proved as smart as he and soon ran the business side of the hotel, later becoming his wife.

Since buying the place in 1945, Maurice had never had a holiday, but in 1960 he went away for a couple of weeks. Sadly, one Saturday evening, a chef turned his back for a few moments on something being grilled and the whole lot went up in flames. Not only did it destroy the grill room, but the fire spread through the bar and into the ballroom devastating the lot. Maurice, languishing in the sun somewhere on his first holiday for years, suddenly received an urgent call, "Come home quickly, your hotel has burnt down!" The destruction was not quite total as Maurice managed to resurrect the ballroom to some extent to keep things going, but eventually it all had to be completely redeveloped.

One evening after a function had ended at about 2.00 am, Grace was counting the takings and Maurice and I were sitting chatting. He was grinning all over his face, so I said to him, "What are you smiling about, you've just lost your hotel, your income, you've got to rebuild and put it back together again, and here you are laughing about it!" He replied, "Bryn, I'll let you into a little secret." He chuckled, "Just before I left for my holiday, I signed an insurance policy for loss of profits for any damage caused. It's going to take six months to put this lot right and I get paid for every week I don't use it!" He really did smile all the way to the bank.

The Bellhouse Hotel was eventually rebuilt to very high standards – the penthouse alone cost £220,000. In 1961 it was formally reopened and in the heavy wrought iron doors and windows at the entrance can be seen 'MC 1961' to commemorate the rebirth of The Bellhouse Hotel – hence the *Rolls Royce* number plate.

Back to 1951. I did my first job there travelling by *Greenline* bus both ways – actually the last time in my career that I went to work on a bus! The function went well and in the morning Maurice gave me breakfast and sent me on my way with the promise of more work, a promise which he steadfastly kept. He offered me every job he could when he was asked to provide a toastmaster, and the car I eventually bought could almost drive there by itself.

One of these occasions was a local LVA function at which licensees and pub owners could invite customers – it was all heavily sponsored by the distilleries, breweries and allied trades companies. Funds would be raised for local and trade charities and, as these were very specialised functions with complicated protocol, a toastmaster was essential – the various presidents, chairmen, visiting chairmen, representatives of one or other of the trade charities, and a whole raft of invited guests, expected a great deal of formality. I found them extremely difficult to master as the hierarchy of the 'Chain Gang', as it came to be known, had to be precise, any errors being quickly picked up by the cognoscenti.

175

In the years following the end of the war, the Licensed Trade was huge, vibrant, exciting and very active. Its participants were charismatic, boisterous and delightful people whose success and fortune was made over the bar talking and dealing with 'Joe Public'. Many of them made great fortunes in their premises, some of whom owned several, and enjoyed the fruits of their labours giving generously to their own licensed trade charities. They consisted of the Society of Licensed Victuallers and Licensed Victuallers Schools, of which they originally had two, a boarding school for boys and one for girls. In due time they added a preparatory school to the list – these schools were regarded as among the best of their type in the country.

Within the Licensed Victuallers National Homes (LVNH) there were 32 'Edinburgh Homes', named after their patron, HRH the Duke of Edinburgh. These extended from Cornwall to Scotland, with the showcase site being a huge estate in Denham with over 200 dwelling houses and bungalows, a hospital and nursing home, and even its own pub called *The Owl Bar*. I have spent many happy social and working hours at Denham and know it well. I became deeply involved with that charity, ending up as a President of one of its sections, following HRH Duke of Kent in that office.

Way back in the 1950s and '60s this charity incurred a huge debt by buying the freehold of Denham, borrowing the money on a bank overdraft. Their target for many years was delineated by the letters 'POO' – Pay Off the Overdraft – and anyone who gave money or supported was given a triangular blue and gold-coloured POO Badge which all wore with pride. Every June they held a massive garden party in the grounds, with ladies' committees coming from all over the UK. There were military bands, food tents, free-tasting bars set up by trade companies, and all manner of things to attract people to attend and spend money. The main event was a formal luncheon in their banqueting hall at which I was invited to officiate.

George Ives, a charismatic, charming but extremely punctilious gentleman, was the undisputed boss of the Edinburgh Homes. He offered me all their work, resulting in many jobs throughout the year. These included the Annual Convention held alternate years in the north and south of the country. I officiated at many, all of which were over a three-day period. In addition to the functions for the Homes, I would be 'out-on-loan' to many of the distilleries and breweries which ran small cocktail parties or luncheons. It was fascinating to meet so many people in that line of work.

It is impossible to count the dozens of individual companies that existed in the trade in those days, all of which were invited to give sponsorship. Among the more generous were distilleries like, *Arthur Bell & Son, White & McKay, Black & White, Famous Grouse, Dewars, Grants, Jameson's* and far too many more to list here. They were all independent, and rivals to each other. Likewise on the beer side were *Watneys, Charringtons, Whitbread, Guinness* and so very many more, all of which were heavily involved in sponsoring Licensed Trade activities. The soft drinks section was not to be forgotten either, and *Britvic, Coca Cola, Schweppes, Corona, Bulmers* and others became involved, as did what was euphemistically known as 'allied trades', providers of cigarettes, crisps, nuts and various nibbles.

At one time or another, all of these companies were invited to 'Take the Presidency' of the charities, which required a senior executive becoming totally involved on a daily basis and spending large sums of money during their year. It was here that toastmasters found themselves in great demand, and I travelled the length and breadth of the UK to their different events.

All senior officers of every charity were given a gold chain of office to wear on formal occasions. These spectacular chains were usually provided by one of the companies and were very expensive. It is a sad reflection on the way the trade has declined that all of what I have just described has virtually disappeared. So many of the individual distilleries, breweries, soft-drinks manufacturers and allied trades companies have either sunk without trace or been swallowed up by huge multiples – the competition between them has gone as well; they simply do not exist. Neither does the true traditional licensee – pubs are now owned outright by the few breweries that are left. The people running them are managers who receive a salary and have no knowledge of the charities, nor are they interested in them. The LVNH has, by law, become a housing estate allowing any person who is homeless to be considered, whereas beforehand the Edinburgh Homes were specifically for the use of people in or connected to the licensed trade, many of whom had paid vast sums of money over the years to be given a quality retirement home. Similarly, the banqueting, junketing and fund-raising functions have almost completely died out.

The LVNH elected a Chairman each year who invited one of the trade companies to become President. At the end of their year they became Past Chairmen but as they still wished to be active for the charity, formed themselves into The Society of Past Chairmen of the LVNH and each year needed a 'hands-on' President to help them raise funds. Over many years several companies agreed to take office, but one year HRH The Duke of Kent became President and attended a few formal functions.

The other day I received a letter to say that the Committee of which I was proud to be President in the 1980s had now held its last meeting. I understand that the only major trade charity left is the Society of Licensed Victuallers, which would seem to have absorbed all the others along the way – so sad for a once vibrant and worthy institution.

The Licensed Victuallers National Homes convention was being held in Bournemouth, and *White Horse Whisky* had played host to the Monday night celebration attended by about 900 people. Their star for the evening was the legendary and so very popular Vera Lynn (later to become Dame). She absolutely stormed them. They really would not let her go and she did encore after encore which were sensational. She ended with *We'll Meet Again,* which became the theme for the convention.

The following night the host company was *Guinness Brewery*. Their senior representative was Mr Edward Guinness, a gentle, charming and quite delightful man, with his wife Elizabeth. We became friends and I was fortunate enough to do quite a lot of work for *Guinness*. For entertainment on their evening, someone had engaged a husband-and-wife double act, he accompanying her on an electric organ whilst she took centre floor as a singer. In true theatrical manner, she swept, regally, onto the floor wearing an incredibly long, flowing, flame-coloured cape with an enormous train, which she dramatically divested and handed to me as she began singing. Beneath it, she was wearing the most extraordinary dress. Made from a kind of silver *Lurex*, it was full-length, but for some reason known only to her and her dressmaker, there was a very large hole in the midriff out through which her belly protruded – rather like a melon! I have never seen anything quite so weird. It was as though the thing had been too tight, and to fit her into it, they had cut this great hole!

In a banquet full of people luxuriating in the memory of Vera Lynn, this lady began to sing. From the very first note, we all knew that disaster was looming. She was ghastly – the wrong songs, badly sung, out of tune, poorly presented and quite awful… and she had been booked to do fifty minutes! What to do? After the second number, Edward Guinness, a man usually slow to anger, said to me. "Bryn, if you ever want to work for my company again you'll get that woman off. I don't care how you do it, but please do it, *now*!"

She was using her own microphone system linked through the electronic organ being played by her husband and, as I had access to the house PA, I said to the electrician, "Give me as much volume as you can without feedback. When she has finished this number, switch off the power to her old man's keyboard and her mic and I'll go out there and somehow get her off!" His timing was perfect and, as I stepped boldly out onto the floor, he pulled the plug on their keyboard killing it completely. Applauding as I walked, I lied to the now deliriously laughing audience, "Wasn't she wonderful, Ladies and Gentlemen? Thank you – thank you (whatever her name was), that was great, superb, well done!" I bellowed. Whilst out of the side of my mouth and away from the mic, I was saying in stage whispers, "GERRROFF! Go on. GO! That's it. They don't want any more. Finish. You've done enough!" "But," she tried to protest, "I've not finished yet. I've got four more..." My reply was much ruder and the second word was OFF! At the same time, smiling and trying to look as nonchalant as possible, I was urging the crowd to applaud the lady who, in the knowledge that she was 'on her bike', were whistling, cat calling and going wild at my and *Guinness'* discomfiture. The memory of Vera was strong, and this lady had failed dismally to deliver the goods.

The corollary to this embarrassing saga astonished me and many others. One would have thought that with such a humiliating dismissal from centre stage, the lady and her husband would have slunk out and buried their heads in the sand. Not her! She wheedled her way back into the room and spent the rest of the evening at the top table drinking hospitality champagne with her little pot belly still sticking out of that amazing dress!

Chapter 11

The London Palladium

"There's no business like show business..."

Irving Berlin

Companion Rat Billy Marsh was a highly successful, tough, very professional theatrical manager and agent. Together with Lord (Bernie) Delfont, Lew and Leslie Grade's brother, he was the boss of *London Management*, the most influential but terrifying show business management agency ever. He was small, around 5' 3", very shy and, deep down, a kind and thoughtful man, although there are hundreds of pros who would find that almost impossible to believe. He became a Companion Rat in 1968, the year Frankie Vaughan became King Rat as he was his manager and was as feared as he was respected. He smoked – no, sorry, he lit – about 100 cigarettes every day, took two or three drags and stubbed them out; he was never without a fag in his mouth but rarely smoked it through.

Ann and I held a garden party at our home when David Berglas was King Rat. It was always the custom to try to raise a few coins on these occasions and Billy Marsh came along with a pile of goodies from the business – records, tapes and a whole heap of memorabilia, and just flooded the little raffle we ran. He was married to Mary, a lovely lady whom he rarely saw as she lived much of the time in their house in the country. He and Mary took Ann and me to dinner at *Gennaros* in Soho where the service, to put it mildly, was dreadful. It was very hot and we had asked for some water, but none came. We were getting a bit cross so I simply called

181

over to the Maitre d' and said in my most authoritative tone, "May we have some water now, please? We have been waiting a very long time." "Yessir. At once, Sir!" and the water came immediately. Billy Marsh said to me, "How do you do that? I have always wanted to command such authority." After that, the waiters danced attendance on us all evening and we had a lovely time. This great leviathan in the show business world, this tough, little businessman was so very shy, but, boy oh boy, what an agent! He was also brusque, which added to his mystique.

One day the telephone rang; the conversation went thus:
"That Bryn? Billy Marsh here!" He didn't wait for the reply.
"You doing anything this Sunday?"
"No, Bill," I said, "Why?"
"Tribute to the late Eric Morecambe. London Palladium. Need a toastmaster. Interested? No money, just be there!"
"Yes, Bill. I am free and would be thrilled to do it. What's it all about?"

"Turn up at the Palladium around 3.00 pm and you'll be given a script. Gotta go. Thanks." And that was it. I was to appear on the London Palladium stage that Sunday in a Royal Tribute in memory of the late Eric Morecambe whom I, like everyone, revered.

I had met Eric many times and found him to be the most naturally funny man I had ever known and vividly recall a big charity thrash at The Grosvenor House Great Room where he was one of the guests. I asked him if he would draw the raffle, to which he replied, "Certainly Bryn. Any time. Just call me."

The raffle began and Eric took over the microphone. The first prize went to a lady in a skin-tight, bright red, extremely low-cut dress in which she sashayed across the floor to collect her prize and a kiss from Eric. As she walked away, all giggly and tottery in her very high heels, he said through the microphone, "I wish my watch had a movement like that!" But he topped it when the next winner came forward, another lady wearing a tight, silver *Lurex*, long, slim dress going from just under her chin down to her ankles. As she walked away, Eric came out with the line, "You remind me of a

Brillo pad!" I have scores of similar one-liners from that great and much-loved man.

There is always something of a tingle at the back of the neck, an indefinable thrill – especially to someone as stage-struck as I – to enter a theatre by the stage door. It is rather like an 'us and them' situation: we enter that portal to entertain, they enter others to be entertained – and there is a world of difference. At that point there is only one governor, the stage-door keeper. They've seen it all, met everyone, know the business inside out, upside-down and every whichway. They are unshockable and completely in charge in their area – a fount of all knowledge, a guide, confessor, trustee, looker-after-of things, indeed, anything that any performer from the lowliest back-line-of-the-chorus girl to the Danny Kayes, Shirley Basseys and Judy Garlands of this world. If they don't want you to 'pop in to see a mate who's performing in the show', then you don't get in and that's that.

At around 3.00 pm on the Sunday I timidly approached 'The Keeper of the Gate to Heaven', gave him my name and, after a long look down his list, he said, "Bryn Williams, Toastmaster. Yep. Dressing room on the top floor with your name on the door. You're sharing with Kenny Ball and the Jazzmen. Don't take a shower, it leaks into the dressing room below and we ain't had it repaired yet." (Kenny Ball did have a shower and, oh boy, what ructions!) I was delighted to be sharing with Ken and the boys.

The producer for the theatre audience and for BBC TV, which was covering the whole evening, was Robert Nesbitt, a legend in the business and one of the most frightening men I have ever met. I honestly do not think that I ever saw him smile. He was even more terrifying than Billy Marsh and, what was worse, he was in charge of the production microphone. I have never seen so many pros in such total awe of a man. "Yes, Mr Nesbitt. No, Mr Nesbitt. If you say so, Mr Nesbitt. Yessir. Will do, Sir." And this from the likes of Jimmy Tarbuck, Benny Hill, Bruce Forsyth and a whole raft of top-class comics.

It was then my turn and he then called me to the stage and gave me my instructions. "Ah! Er... Mr Er... Williams (at least a little respect from the great man), you are second spot in the second half after Bertice Redding. Mr Wise (Ernie of that ilk) will be downstage centre. The scene will be a kind of drawing room and he will explain to the audience that in the Morecambe and Wise Shows there were many great actors and actresses who are not variety performers, but they are all keen to pay their respects to Eric and agreed to appear on this show. As Toastmaster, you will stand towards the back, left of the stage and introduce them to Ernie downstage. Is that clear?"

"Yes, Mr Nesbitt."

"Right then, when you're ready. Just a brief run through for timings and with the names you are to announce."

All went well and he seemed pleased with my little part in the show, or at least as far as we could tell. Fired with unaccustomed confidence, I had the temerity to suggest to him that in the finale, when all the stars come back on stage to take their final curtain, I announce their names as they appeared. He seemed happy with the idea and so it was agreed.

Backstage was a hive of activity and we were falling over 'names' all day long. Ernie had been given the star dressing room and all of us popped in for a chat and a cup of tea. He was a lovely guy, but despite every effort to the contrary, he always appeared to live in Eric's shadow. This was certainly not of Eric's doing; he was far too nice and indeed too modest for that – it was just their totally different personalities that caused it.

Benny Hill was a complete bundle of nerves; he was terrified of, and loathed, live public performances of any kind. Take him away from a TV camera and small studio audience and he was petrified. It was impossible to talk to him as he was almost paralysed with terror. I said to him one day, "Benny, I believe you know my father, Hugh Owens?" Putting his hand into his jacket pocket, he immediately pulled out a business card and showed it to me. "Do you mean him?" It was my father's business card. "He taught me to sing. He's a lovely man and I am very fond of him!" In all the years of Benny's fame, Dad had never mentioned the connection. Mike Yarwood, the impressionist, is another pro who craves privacy before any performance, but on this occasion, no chance. He, too,

184

was sharing a dressing room and just had to put up with it. It was wonderful to be backstage, rubbing shoulders with the great and the good of British variety, paying tribute to a man they all loved and respected – and, what's more, all doing it for free!

Rehearsals over, we sat back, relaxed and did what we needed to do to get ourselves ready for the big moment. I should point out to the uninitiated, that during a TV rehearsal the auditorium is an unbelievable mess of wires, microphones, tables, lighting rigs, actors, actresses, comedians, singers, conjurors and others sprawled over the seats, drinking coffee, chatting, reminiscing and waiting to be called. You would never think that out of all this mega-chaos, order would ensue, but it always does.

Peering through the vast front of stage curtain just before the overture, I drank in the breathtaking splendour of the greatest variety theatre in the world in all its gilt, maroon, plush velvet seats, drape curtains, its magnificence and glory, with not a single thing out of place. It was a moment to treasure.

A day or two before the show, Billy Marsh offered me a couple of complimentary tickets for Ann – our daughter Tracy went with her. Just before the show, they came to the stage door to see me; they met a few performers and then took their seats in the stalls, the best in the house, and sat back ready to enjoy themselves.

HRH Prince Philip and Mrs Joan Morecambe arrived and took their seats in the Royal Box. Overture and beginners, curtain up and this wonderful tribute to the late Eric Morecambe began. The first half was a sensation; the atmosphere was of genuine warmth, love and affection for that master comic. Ernie Wise was given a standing ovation when he made his appearance on stage, and we all felt a buzz that this was something very special – as indeed it was.

Up in our dressing room the call came for everyone to stand by for the second half. Just off-stage were the dozen or so actors and actresses waiting for me to introduce them to Ernie. When Bertice Redding had taken her curtain-call, Ernie went to the front of the stage and chatted to the audience. He told them that in the dozens of Morecambe and Wise Shows there were many who appeared in

185

the 'Plays wot I rote', and that they had all been invited to pay their tributes to Eric. He added, "And so, ladies and gentlemen, in true British style, I am delighted that our very good friend, Toastmaster Bryn Williams, is here to introduce them to us. Bryn, who are my first guests?"

From my raised position at the back of the stage, in my best stentorian tones, I formally introduced the 'names' in pairs, and they descended a grand stairway to chat to Ernie, each of them receiving great plaudits from the audience. For me, it was a moment of sheer joy.

Our part of the show over, the stage was set for Wayne Sleep, who had choreographed a special dance with a partner. Fast, furious, energetic, balletic, acrobatic and in every way perfect, he and the girl jumped, twirled and whizzed all over the stage in a seven-minute routine – it was breathtaking. The finale saw Wayne and the girl flying all over the stage, and in the last seconds she laid flat on her back just looking up at the lights. Wayne did a couple of aerial pirouettes and landed, feet astride her, facing the audience. But the devil was there that night, and as he finished his last leap, standing with his hands high in the air as if in supplication to the Almighty, it became apparent that his zip-flies had split and his frilly shirt was sticking prominently out of his very tight trousers for all the world to see. He did not notice this immediately, but the crowd did and they roared, cheered, clapped, laughed and yelled, not stopping for several minutes. Wayne realised that something was not quite right! By now the girl, sitting up, had spotted the problem and pointed to his private area, simply crying with laughter.

Wayne's hands immediately went to the affected area where, actually, the zip in his trousers had given up the ghost. Covered in glory and embarrassment, the two stood back and the curtain came down on what really was a show-stopper. It was the talk of backstage and everyone agreed that Eric would have adored it as it really would have tickled his zany sense of humour. It was also generally hoped that it could be 'left in' the subsequent television broadcast because of Eric's oddball sense of fun. Sadly, this was not to be. The programme was scheduled to go out on a Sunday night, and it was felt by the powers-that-be to be too provocative for that family slot. The result was that, when everyone had left and the London Palladium was empty, Wayne and the girl had to do the whole routine again, with a new pair of trousers, but with no audience reaction. As expected, it was another magical performance demonstrating thorough professionalism.

The final curtain-call loomed and I took up my original position, this time armed with the list of the full cast. As they appeared downstage, I re-introduced them. Ernie Wise gave the final thanks to everyone, drew attention to Prince Philip and Joan Morecambe, called for three cheers and the National Anthem, and the curtain fell on one of the greatest nights of my life. I was, and guess I still am, stage-struck.

We all stayed put as Joan and Prince Philip came onto the stage to meet all the cast – actually an impossibility as, with bands, dancers, performers, actors and everyone else, there were about 200 people on stage. After that, it was time to go home.

I had arranged to meet Ann and Tracy in a bar in the Cinderella Bar, and when I eventually found them, my first question was, "Well, did you enjoy it? Have you had a great evening? What did you think of the show?" Expecting exuberance and excitement, all I was got was, "No! It's been horrible! Well, at least until you'd done your bit!"
"What do you mean?" I asked.
"Well," Ann said, "We were almost beside ourselves with nerves during the first half, worrying that you might make a mistake and screw everything up in front of this audience. My knees were literally knocking; we were so scared for you, we couldn't enjoy any of it until you'd finished!" Such confidence from the two ladies in my life!

That was the first of two occasions I appeared on the stage at the London Palladium. In 1992, the centenary of the Grand Order of Water Rats, the King was Roy Hudd. His ambition was to put 100 Rats on the Palladium stage, thus repeating a concert that had been held many times during the hundred years of the Order. This he managed to do, and exactly 100 Water Rats took to the stage in another memorable concert. I was as thrilled to be involved in that as the first one.

I cannot deny a deep feeling of pride in these two appearances, being the only toastmaster in our entire history to have worked on the stage of the world's greatest variety theatre, a stage which has witnessed the talents of so many of the most famous names in entertainment. That same year I had also worked at the most influential function in the UK, the Lord Mayor's Banquet at the Guildhall – quite a rare double.

* * * * *

No book so closely linked to the world of entertainment would be complete without reference to the greatest show business charity, possibly in the world. The Variety Artistes Federation (VAF) was founded many years ago purely for the benefit and assistance of sick, infirm and otherwise distressed performers – performers from every branch of entertainment be they singers, dancers, comedians, magicians, musicians, actors, writers or indeed any who throughout their lives have entertained multitudes. The name was changed in more recent years to The Entertainment Artistes Benevolent Fund with their headquarters based in Twickenham.

They purchased Brinsworth way back in the 1900s and have made it one of the finest retirement nursing homes in the country. It houses around 40-50 residents who are looked after and cared for by a dedicated and devoted team of professionals. The catalogue of names who have been thrilled to end their days in this lovely home is quite spectacular. Hundreds of the great and the good in show business who have aged, or whose health has become frail and delicate, have resided there enjoying the company of fellow entertainers in their twilight years.

The Royal Variety Show – it has not been called the Royal Command Performance for very many years – is held annually to raise funds for its upkeep. They are deeply proud of their relationship with all members of the Royal Family who attend each concert. These magnificent shows, now held in cities throughout the United Kingdom, are brilliant spectacles of variety and attract the greatest names from all over the world. For about ten years now they have held an 'After Show Party' at a nearby hotel. It has been my great joy to help run these super parties and welcome the guests so royally entertained that evening at the theatre. Members of both the Grand Order of Water Rats and the Grand Order of Lady Ratlings have strong connections with the charity and are frequently called upon to give their services to that most deserving cause.

The EABF is now under the superb leadership of Life President Laurie Mansfield, together with Past Prince Rat Peter Elliott and Peter Prichard OBE. Their work for the charity and all its residents is tireless and totally dedicated and I am proud to be just a very small part of their wonderful empire.

As well as fraternities and societies mentioned elsewhere I feel I cannot leave out others which I joined or with which I became closely involved.

The CAA or Concert Artistes Association (as it was then known) has had its headquarters in Bedford Street, Covent Garden for more years than I can remember. I became an 'A' member very early on in my career and am still there. It is an eclectic club with a super little bar and a hundred-seater ballroom/club-room, and everyone mentioned below either is or was a member. The CAA has boasted some of the really great names in the world of variety, vaudeville, cabaret and theatre as President and is still thriving and flourishing. My infrequent visits to Bedford Street are always exciting as the walls are covered with theatre bills going back hundreds of years. In the bar are displayed dozens of photographs (including one of me!) bringing back countless memories to older members of the greater days of entertainment – sadly now a thing of the past – but new and enthusiastic entertainers from every branch of the business are joining, ensuring an exciting and lively future.

In the mid 1950s two other great charity organisations were founded, SPARKS and The Lord's Taverners and I was actively involved in the functions of both. SPARKS was a kind of mnemonic for Sportsmen Pledged to Aid Research into Crippling, two of its founders being the footballer Jimmy Hill, still an enthusiastic member, and a gentleman, Buzzer Hadingham, sadly no longer with us. Buzzer was the boss of *Slazengers* and was, for many years, the Chairman of the All England Lawn Tennis and Croquet Club at Wimbledon, one of whose duties was to play host to the Royal Patrons, Their Royal Highnesses the Duke and Duchess of Kent. Buzzer and his wife Lois were one of the loveliest couples it has been my privilege to know and were both great supporters of mine. We enjoyed a warm friendship for over 40 years.

Buzzer told me a wonderful story of his first appearance in the Royal Box at Wimbledon from which he learned a singular lesson. The Royal Guests arrived at around lunchtime, receiving hospitality and refreshment before taking their seats. Unwisely he drank several cups of coffee and maybe a glass or two of champagne before escorting them to the box. Etiquette and protocol demand that at no time whatsoever is the chairman permitted to leave the Royal Guests unattended. It is also a well-known fact that many Royals seem to possess camel-like bladders enabling them to go for extremely long periods without having to spend even a farthing – let alone a penny. Buzzer's first year in the hallowed seat was one of complete horror as his needs manifested themselves early in the tennis proceedings and he literally had to sit there – legs crossed – until his Royal Guests decided to get up and go. It taught him a great lesson, and on future occasions he drank nothing and made many trips to the 'men's room' in advance. He is sadly missed.

Arden Camm, an old Etonian, was the founding secretary of both The Lord's Taverners and SPARKS, running them from home in the early days. One of life's genuine characters, Arden had an extraordinary telephone technique. At the end of any call he would simply say "...Byyyeeeey," which would fade into nothingness as he put down the receiver. Both organisations grew rapidly under his direction and he eventually handed over to other secretaries.

In those early days SPARKS owned 'SPARKLE', a boat specially converted to take wheelchairs and people with disabilities; it was their pride that invalids and sufferers could spend many happy hours taking short trips. An energetic and enthusiastic supporter was a lady with whom I became very friendly, she and I working together on several functions linked to the Annual Boat Show and having some great times. Her name is Lynda Chalker and when, in idle conversation over a cup of coffee, I quizzed her on what she intended to do with her life, she quite seriously replied, "Oh. I'm going into politics as a Tory MP." I teased her mercilessly about this, but she had the last laugh as she eventually became a Minister and is now The Rt Hon Baroness Chalker of Wallasey. We don't often meet, but when we do we wallow in nostalgia for those golden olden days.

The Lord's Taverners was founded by a brilliant English actor named Martin Boddey, with whom I occasionally worked at events. He called together ten other like-minded men whose passion was English Cricket and named them after the Tavern at Lord's Cricket Ground. They were obviously men of importance and substance as they had the temerity to write to HRH The Duke of Edinburgh and ask him to become their patron. He immediately accepted and is the permanent 'Patron and Twelfth Man' whose Loyal Toast is honoured at every Lord's Taverners' event.

I became member 875 and was actively involved in dozens of events in their earlier years, helping them raise hundreds of thousands of pounds for all the wonderful charitable causes they support. Although no longer a member of either, I warmly applaud the superb work that both of these great organisations do and I congratulate them on their achievements.

Companion Rat Andy Neatrour rang and offered me another 'freebie' date for the Combined Charities Committee at Wembley Arena. "Can you come?" he asked, "Prince Charles, Morecambe and Wise and Shirley Bassey there! Need you. Please say yes!" I duly arrived at this mausoleum, checked all the production arrangements beforehand, dinner arrangements afterwards, fund-raising and all the usual paraphernalia which accompany these glitzy royal events and prepared for a splendid evening. It was not a particularly difficult job. All I had to do was to get everyone into their seats, welcome them from the huge, open stage, introduce Eric Morecambe (Ha!), sit back and enjoy the show. I only had to appear at the finale and look after the dinner, which was very straightforward with no speeches and much fund-raising.

Guests were being funnelled into their soft seats and I was backstage with Mr Morecambe working out the preliminaries of the opening. I suggested that I simply go out front, introduce him to do the welcome and get off, leaving him to open the show. He had other ideas – and you do not argue with such a pro, especially one whom you revere. He said, "Why don't I just go out front, and just talk to them to get the show on the road? I don't think I really need to be introduced. Then, I'll leave it to you; when you think I've done enough, simply come onto the stage and stand there and we'll see what happens," and that was that – that was our entire rehearsal and I had to trust him. After about five minutes, knowing that we had to stick to schedule, I did as he asked and just walked centre stage and stood there, like a stuffed prune. He prattled on for a few minutes totally ignoring me. He then said, "A drunk's just come on stage!" which brought a roar from the crowd. He then proceeded, in the nicest possible way, to take the mickey out of me, getting loads more laughs. He then turned to me and said, "Is that it then? Have I finished? Do you want me to get off?" To which I humbly nodded and whispered, "Yes please, Eric!"

On either side of this open stage were two flights of about seven steps down into the auditorium where Eric Morecambe had a seat next to Prince Charles. I directed him stage right, and politeness decreed that I stood back to let him go down first. I bowed and extended my left hand, inviting him to go first. He bowed opposite me, extended his right hand inviting *me* to go first. I bowed again, and so did he – we both bowed at each other about six times. By this time the crowd was going potty at this stupid situation. In the end I just had to go down the steps, and spot on cue he too had made up his mind that he was going. We hit the top step at the identical moment, collapsed into each other's arms and together fell down the steps, landing in a heap on the floor. Unhurt, we got up, shook hands, had a laugh together and split. It brought the house down and was typical of the great man's perfect sense of theatre and stage – and boy, what a wonderful opening to a show!

The top of the bill was the legendary Shirley Bassey. Whenever she appeared on a charity bill, it guaranteed a full house and the charities benefited by thousands of pounds. The show was a massive success, with the star receiving a standing ovation. At the end, I had to arrange a formal walk-out of Prince Charles and the official party to a private reception. Dinner had been arranged for a couple of hundred sponsors with the stars in the show, and Prince Charles attended the party for about half an hour. Miss Bassey seemed to be a long time in changing out of her cabaret dress – very low-cut and revealing – into something a little more practical. I had to make several trips to her dressing room urging her to hurry as The Prince had to leave and wished to meet her and she was holding him up.

She eventually appeared, wearing a long, black, flowing evening gown fixed at the neck, with a black sequined collar: she looked stunning. However, closer inspection revealed that the entire top of the dress was made of black chiffon and was totally transparent showing quite clearly 'everything' from the neck down to the navel, leaving absolutely nothing to the imagination. Not wearing a bra, her boobs were as visible as though nothing covered them. As she entered the room, I introduced her to Prince Charles and spotted with glee the sparkling gleam in her eye. I then turned my attention to Prince Charles as he began talking to her. How he looked her straight in the eye, I shall never know… probably royal training. He kept his composure brilliantly – but I'm afraid I cannot say the same for all the other men at the dinner whose eyes and thoughts were elsewhere. I often wonder what HRH's thoughts were in the royal limo going back to the Palace!

Chapter 12

The City of London

"London pride has been handed down to us,
London pride is a flower that is free."

Noel Coward

People frequently ask me, "What is the most important function you've ever done?" to which my instant reply is, "All of them!" Every function at which any toastmaster officiates must be considered to be the most important he has ever attended because, to those involved in the celebrations, IT IS. From the most modest cocktail party or country wedding to any royal event, there is always someone to whom it is of the greatest concern at the time, and we must never forget it. However, if the question posed was, "Which is the most prestigious function you have ever attended?" it would be far more difficult to answer. Functions graced by Royalty are frequently very special, but not always, as they too are pleased to honour more modest events around the country which, although delightful, do not carry high prestige. So I suppose I would have to say that the City of London holds the more highly influential and colourful events in the calendar and at which I have officiated many times. But it was not always thus, and in recent years has become even less so... but more of that anon.

Between the two world wars and into the 1950s and '60s, the vast amount of the work of toastmasters was way outside the 'Square Mile' (which, in fact, it isn't – neither a mile, nor square!). Apart from London's West End, every county, city, town, village or hamlet throughout the United Kingdom had rooms and halls where functions could be held nightly, and they often were. There was a huge proliferation of all types of work and any toastmaster or MC worth his salt would always be busy during the season. This usually ran from the beginning of October right through to the end of June, with the summer months being rather barren and generally limiting the work to both Jewish and Christian weddings. For well over thirty years, this nine months was jam-packed full of engagements, most of which could be described as 'ordinary', but nevertheless lucrative and enjoyable.

My success in this area was growing steadily, resulting over a 25-year period from about 1960 in an average of around 320 functions every year. This included working every Christmas, Easter, Whitsun (when there was a Whitsun!) and all bank holidays as they were generally the periods for weddings. Consequently, my family and I missed out on all the traditional holiday breaks at which I would have been happy to entertain my kids. Alas! as we needed the money, this was not to be. Indeed, on one occasion, I actually officiated at three weddings at the same time!

In Finsbury Park, North London, there was a pub called *The Manor House* where the manager, a diminutive Welshman by the name of Trefor Evans, liked my work. It was only two tube stops from my home and he offered me all the weddings in his three small 'banqueting' rooms. The fee was around three guineas (£3.15p in today's money), and they were usually only about three hours long. On this occasion, he had three weddings to cater for, but had sensibly arranged that they arrived at different times to assist the single kitchen. The numbers were only about fifty or sixty at each one and, as I recall, it went like this.

At 12.00 noon the first bride and groom arrived and I lined them up for a receiving line, after which the guests were offered a sweet sherry and stood around drinking. At around 12.45, the second bride and groom arrived and I announced their guests in to another room, before again leaving them happily having a drink. I then went back to the first wedding, announced lunch, took the bride and groom in, said Grace and left them to eat.

By now, the third bride and groom had arrived in another room, and so I announced the guests and left them all with a glass of sherry. At this point, I returned to bride and groom Number Two and announced lunch, took them in, said Grace and left them eating. As bride and groom Number One were nearing the end of their meal, I announced the cake-cutting and speeches. Bride and groom Number Three, now being ready to go into lunch, were duly dealt with and, after Grace, I left them eating. It was now time to return to Wedding Two for the speeches and cake-cutting, which I announced.

The first bride and groom had by this time ended their party and were shortly to depart, which required my presence to take them out to the car and send them on their way. Being down to a mere two weddings, the rest was plain sailing. By 5.30 pm, all three brides, grooms, parents, bridesmaids and guests had cleared off, and Trefor and I collapsed into armchairs. We'd seen off three different couples into their married futures with no problems, complaints or difficulties, but when we looked back on what we had achieved, we simply couldn't believe it. For me it was something of a challenge that needed total concentration or it would have been a disaster. At the beginning of the day, Trefor said to me, "I don't care how you handle it, but for Gawd's sake make sure you get their names right!" I did. Of course, this was at a time when receptions did not go on well into the evening. These days, officiating at three weddings simultaneously would be inconceivable.

In my early years as a toastmaster, banquets in the City of London were a distant dream. They really were sewn up by the few toastmasters who had survived the war and who were mainly very formal and not specialist Masters of Ceremonies. Also, in the ninety or so Livery Companies which consisted of the make-up of the City of London at that time, the Beadles who ran the ritual side of each Company handled most of their events. Furthermore, The City Fathers were notoriously poor payers as the incumbents within the companies did not charge a large fee.

Norman Hall, a very successful solicitor in the City, was Clerk to a couple of companies and a Liveryman in the Worshipful Company of Butchers. Having seen me work, he phoned me one day and asked why I had not done any work there. I could only answer that I did not know why, except that I had been offered one function where the fee was ludicrously low. *Ring & Brymer* were the main caterers in those days, whose boss was Sir Lindsey Ring, a very prominent City man who eventually became Lord Mayor. One of his banqueting managers rang to give me a job, but when I told him my fee was five guineas, he nearly dropped the telephone and said, "But we only pay our toastmasters three-and-a-half guineas, less ten percent commission." I politely said, "Not me, you don't." I told him what to do with his job and heard no more. Norman promised to look into matters to see what he could do.

My Uncle Lenny ran a couple of butchers shops in Hendon and, during the war, while he was in the RAF, these were kept going by his wife (my Auntie Billie), my mother and their sisters – indeed, any member of the family who could pluck a chicken or drive a van. One day a shop agent for the meat industry, a Mr Ken Kenworthy spoke to Uncle Lenny and idly told him that he was running an event for the Butchers Charitable Institute (BCI) and needed a good MC. Uncle Lenny, true to family tradition, immediately sang my praises and persuaded Ken to engage me. I was about 18 and had been working a couple of years. I became a hit with the meat industry, which at that time boasted dozens of committees, associations, charities and societies of all kinds, all of which held functions. Over the years, the meat trade became one of my largest clients, and despite the severe shrinking of the industry, I am still involved with them. Norman Hall saw me working at these and made a suggestion which added yet another string to my bow.

The Beadle of the Butchers' Company was Mr Charlie Woods, an ex-military man of diminutive stature. He hated officiating at the monthly luncheons and needed outside help. Norman arranged with the Company that I become their regular toastmaster and a sensible fee structure was agreed. I fulfilled that capacity for very many years and, together with the multitude of meat trade functions, I established myself in the City of London. Being seen by senior officers of the Corporation who organised the major City events now meant that venues like the Guildhall, Mansion House and the Livery Halls came within my sphere.

It was around this time that Ann and I felt it would be a sensible idea for me to become a Freeman of the City of London. Ann's dad had owned several businesses there and she had been educated at the City of London School. For years they had lived and worked in the City and she knew and loved the whole ethos of the area. I had become well known in the appropriate offices of the Guildhall and had many friends who were Liverymen of Companies willing to propose me. In 1980 I took the oath of a Freeman in a simple and charming ceremony that had not altered by one single word for centuries and is conducted in the office of the Chamberlain of London.

As time progressed my work within the Butchers' Company grew to such an extent that I was virtually accepted as one of them; I knew many personally and they were very generous in the work they offered me. So the next logical step was to explore the possibility of becoming a Liveryman – a particular and singular honour. There were then around 90 Guilds or Worshipful Companies which make up the fabric of the City but I really was only known by one. I approached Past Master Norman Hall and Mr Ronald Lickorish, at that time the editor of the Meat Trades' Journal. Without hesitation they agreed to become my proposer and seconder and set my application in motion.

The Worshipful Company of Butchers' – number 24 – is one of the few of the older companies whose members are active practitioners in the 'Mystery and Art' of their profession; trades in many of the others have long since faded away, but the names and traditions continue. In my Company the rule is that 95% of all applicants must have direct connection with the meat industry only allowing a few non-meat-traders to join. Imagine my supreme pride and happiness when I was told that, as a direct result of my connection with so many, my application had been accepted. In 1984 I became the first ever Toastmaster to become a Liveryman of a City Company; a membership and honour I prize as highly as any I have achieved.

Every major Corporation of London event that is organised in The City is run by an officer known as The Remembrancer, a qualified barrister. The first of these for whom I worked was a fearsome man named Jeffrey Peacock, whose knowledge of procedure and protocol at the highest level was second to none. He recognised something in me which he thought suited the strictness and precision of the City of London and offered me many functions on behalf of the Corporation.

I recall vividly a correction Mr Peacock made to my dialogue which I have used and taught to all my students ever since. At a Mansion House Royal State Banquet in the presence of the Lord Mayor and sheriffs, a large number of civic dignitaries and a royal visitor, I led the main party to the top table. I announced, "Pray silence for Grace which will be said by the Chaplain to the Rt Hon The Lord Mayor" – totally correct phrasing, or so I thought. Immediately everyone had sat down, I was summoned by Mr Peacock who, firmly but politely, said, "Mr Williams, I must correct your last announcement. The words 'which will be said' are superfluous and should not be used. Simply say, 'Pray silence for Grace by...' That is all!" Great and very sensible advice which I have never forgotten.

Mr Peacock's successor was Mr Howlett who, thankfully, also looked favourably upon me and continued to offer me most of the major events of the Corporation. I enjoyed his patronage for many years until his retirement, during which time I met a long list of Lord Mayors and many world leaders.

When the head of any country or state pays a State Visit to these shores, there is something of a ritual during the three or four day stay. They are usually met by the Queen and entertained at a banquet at Buckingham Palace or Windsor Castle, where there are no toastmasters as it is all handled 'in house'. The following day, the City of London hosts a State Banquet to which the world and his wife and their children are invited. These are all prestigious, glamorous and highly spectacular affairs, consisting of the Lord Mayor, the Sheriffs, the Aldermen and Members of the Court of Common Council – which body actually runs the City of London – all in their robes and regalia of office, and very high-ranking dignitaries from both within and without the City. On the final day of the visit, a banquet is usually given by the country of the potentate on the State Visit at a venue of their own choice. They then go home.

Being now well in with The Remembrancer, I was hugely privileged to attend a vast number of these spectacular affairs, which were not particularly difficult but highly satisfying. But the acme of all City functions is the Lord Mayor's Banquet, held annually the Monday after his election, and at which the Prime Minister speaks.

For years the number one toastmaster – or announcer as we are known in the City – was a certain Arthur Richards. He had been a wonderful baritone and a close friend of my father; he also enjoyed a golf handicap of three! He sang regularly at City functions and, at the end of his singing career, became a toastmaster, principally within the City boundaries. It was logical that 'The Banquet' would be offered to him. In later years, another former employee within the City of London, Bernard Sullivan, assumed that role. He had worked for years in the Bank of England and, again, it was a logical progression that he would become a City toastmaster, which he did – a success he still enjoys today at over eighty years old. But way back in the 1970s, Mr Howlett wanted me for this occasion and the date was confirmed. It was a delight and honour to preside at the Lord Mayor's Banquet. If I am honest, I had hoped for more, but it was not to be. Quite rightly, Bernard Sullivan continued to do all the Corporation and Mayoral work and, when Mr Howlett retired shortly afterwards, a new Remembrancer took over with his own contacts.

As I stood behind the top table on that magical evening, surrounded by all the pomp, pageantry, glamour, traditions and trappings of that superb and very historical occasion, I vividly recall my thoughts at that time. From modest and humble beginnings at the Wood Green Chamber of Commerce, there was I, running THE event of the social calendar. As a professional toastmaster I had arrived. I was still only in my 30s and boy, were my parents proud of their 'little boy'.

The new Lord Mayor is sworn in during the very last part of the Lord Mayor's Show, always held on a Saturday morning in early November; I have been honoured to take part in two of them. The procession stops at St Paul's Cathedral where the incumbent is greeted by the Dean. The new Lord Mayor then proceeds to the Law Courts where he swears an oath of allegiance to the Queen and takes lunch with all the dignitaries.

The following Monday evening, the Lord Mayor's first official banquet is held in the Guildhall at which the Prime Minister speaks. It is always televised and the invitees are among the élite of the City of London, and Parliament. Around 800 attend, all dressed in full regalia, for this most glittering and formal of events. The Guildhall, dating back to 1411, is illuminated by candles and fully 'dressed' – all the antique golden artefacts are withdrawn from the vaults and placed along the tables, on small spotlit corbels and on shelves around the hall; the City constabulary, dressed in Victorian uniform, remain on duty inside the hall throughout to protect these priceless articles.

I have known John Owen-Ward and his wife Lois since my early days in Round Table. He followed me in as a member and, as I am about two years his senior, he has always been 'behind' me – we continue to be very close friends. When he sold his architect business in Palmers Green he went into the City in a big way as it really is his passion. He became a member of the Court of Common Council years ago and still enjoys that position, serving with great distinction on many committees and organisations. He also became the Clerk to two Worshipful Companies from which he was required to retire at the age of 65. His knowledge of everything connected with the City of London is encyclopaedic and that, coupled with an extensive knowledge of wine, are his two great loves outside his family.

I discussed my 'demise' within the City with him and he approached the Rememberancer about it, who rather lamely said that a very long time ago I had done one little thing he did not like and that was that, I was out for good. John tried to press him on the matter, but he was not prepared to divulge the reason. The fact that he had neither the courtesy, nor guts to confront me with it face to face both surprised me and made me angry. I cannot stand small-minded men who have not the courage of their convictions, but I was the loser in the long run. That man has now, thankfully retired, but my face no longer fits in the City and there are other and less expensive 'kids on the block' to handle the work, although, at 84 Bernard Sullivan is still doing much of it. Over the years he has built up a superb and much deserved reputation as a great toastmaster and is certainly one of the top two or three in the profession.

There are now 107 Guilds and Worshipful Companies within the City of London, each with their own number which they hold dear. The banners of the big twelve livery companies hang from the Guildhall ceiling in chronological order from the date they were awarded their royal charter. Each year at Common Hall a service is held in St Paul's Cathedral, the Masters and Prime Warden entering in that strict numerical order.

Being a lover of mnemonics, I remember the first of the big twelve companies thus: My Grand Daddy Found Gold; Sister Marie Theresa Had Stupidly Invited Violet Carson. Set against the companies, it looks like this.

1. My	Mercers
2. Grand	Grocers
3. Daddy	Drapers
4. Found	Fishmongers
5. Gold	Goldsmiths
6. Sister	Skinners
7. Marie Theresa	Merchant Tailors
8. Had	Haberdashers
9. Stupidly	Salters
10. Invited	Ironmongers
11. Violet	Vintners
12. Carson	Clothworkers

It is fairly well documented that The Skinners and Merchant Tailors regularly change their number. They were each granted their

Charter on the same day and could never agree which came first. It caused one helluva hullabaloo in the City and, when all the Burgesses around London found out, they declared that such was the muddle they were all 'at sixes and sevens' and the phrase stuck. They now alternate annually, their Masters entering the procession each year in a different position.

My mnemonic for champagne bottle sizes is a bit more daft, but it helps me:

Mnemonic	Name	Size
British	Bottle	1
Medical	Magnum	2
Journal	Jeroboam	4
Royal	Rehoboam	6
Masonic	Methuselah	8
School	Salmanazar	12
(for) Boys	Balthazar	16
North	Nebuchadnezzar	20
Mymms	Melchior	24

As I said, daft, but useful.

There is an ancient tradition at the end of all Lord Mayoral and Civic Banquets and most other City events which one must remember. Again I have taught this to my students and devised a mnemonic to remind me of the correct ending to a Lord Mayor's Banquet. It is GLC (Greater London Council, long since gone): G for Grace after meals, L for Loving Cup Ceremony, enacted at virtually every major City function, and C for Queen – yes, I know it's wrong, but it helps me and my students remember the correct order of events!

The Old Library in the Guildhall, only around 170 years old, is the room in which all the guests are received by the Lord Mayor and Lady Mayoress. The route from the cloakrooms is lined by men of the Honourable Artillery Company, the oldest army in the world and the Lord Mayor's personal bodyguard. Their magnificent uniforms include knee-length buff leather boots, scarlet tunics, breeches and gauntlets, while the width of the lace collars delineates seniority – the deeper the lace, the higher the office. Brown, wide-brimmed hats and twelve-foot spears complete the appearance.

The toastmaster stands by one door looking down the room, on either side of which are members of the Court of Common Council dressed in their blue robes carrying their staffs of office. They form a corridor down which the guests have to proceed towards the raised section at the far end. The members of the Court of Aldermen, brilliantly and spectacularly arraigned in their scarlet robes, are there to receive the newly-elected Lord Mayor and Lady Mayoress. The Lord Mayor is escorted by the Mace Bearer carrying the Mace of the City of London and the Common Sergeant carrying the City Sword. They lead the procession to the two thrones, in front of which the Lord Mayor and Lady Mayoress stand to receive the guests.

When all are in position, the toastmaster announces each guest, who then takes the long walk along that line of Common Councilmen and women to be formally received. The Lord Mayor, Lady Mayoress and Court of Aldermen then all process out of the Old Library to a private reception, the remainder making their way into the Guildhall for dinner.

On all other occasions, it is the norm for toastmasters to bang anything wooden with a gavel to gain attention. On State Banquets in the City, that is not necessary. There are three galleries in the Guildhall: the Minstrels', the Press and the Lady Mayoress's Own. Standing in the Press Gallery are four ceremonial trumpeters from the Household Brigade, with another four in the Minstrel's Gallery beside the eight-foot-high statues of Gog and Magog, representing Christianity. When the Lord Mayor and procession are lined up outside the door to make their formal entry to the top table, the toastmaster signals to the first trumpet quartet to blow a fanfare, which is immediately echoed by the other quartet, known in the City as 'Fanfare and Echo'. On the raised part at one end of the Guildhall and the extreme far end, long straight tables are laid. The centre of the Hall consists of what can only be described as a 'square horseshoe' or three sides of a square with the fourth open. Inside that section are many other sprigs setting out from the top table.

At the Lord Mayor's Banquet, there is a choice of two walks: the Long Walk or the Short Walk, the latter going straight from the entrance, along to the top table seats. The Long Walk means that the procession turns right down one side of the horseshoe, along the bottom ends of the long tables and turns left up the other side, coming into their seats from left of centre. It takes about five minutes to walk around Guildhall, and the Military Band play over and over, at a very slow tempo, the *March Scipio* by Handel, the Lord Mayor's March. When all are in place, the toastmaster announces Grace by the Chaplain. Everyone sits and eats. This tradition has been enacted, almost unchanged, for centuries and truly is very spectacular.

When dessert has been cleared, the banqueting manager informs the toastmaster, the trumpeters and military orchestra, and all take their positions. Silver Loving Cups containing wine, with a napkin tied to the handle, are placed in front of the Lord Mayor and at strategic positions at the ends of each sprig. The Chaplain to the Lord Mayor is then primed to say Grace after the meal, or it is a sung version from the *Laudi Spirituali* which is fairly commonplace in the City and at most Masonic functions. The toastmaster signals to the Trumpet Quartet to blow Fanfare and Echo and announces whichever of the two Graces are to be delivered.

After a further Fanfare and Echo, the toastmaster proclaims, "The Right Honourable the Lord Mayor and the Sheriffs drink to you in a Loving Cup and bid you all a hearty welcome," upon which he and the Prime Minister stand and take the first drink. That is the cue for all of the tables to begin drinking from their cups, which circumnavigate every table and every guest until returning to the original place, whilst the orchestra plays suitable 'drinking' music.

When each Loving Cup has been gathered in by the stewards, the toastmaster raps on the table or a block of resonant wood three times, very slowly, and the room becomes silent. The Lord Mayor stands, without any words from the toastmaster, and says, "The

Queen." They all stand, the National Anthem is played, they drink and sit down; this is repeated for each subsequent Loyal Toast. Coffee, port and brandy are then served. During this brief pause, the toastmaster checks the table with the lectern and microphones and prepares the new Lord Mayor for his maiden speech.

Traditionally, the first speaker is the Lord Mayor and, when the catering staff have left, the toastmaster again signals the trumpeters and announces the only full preamble – or 'allocution', as it is called in the City – to be used that night. It is simple and to the point, as are most things in the City. He says, "Prime Minister, Aldermen, Sheriffs, Your Excellencies, My Lords, Ladies and Gentlemen, Pray Silence for The Right Honourable the Lord Mayor." And that's it – no name, no decorations, no embellishments, nothing. As I say, complete simplicity, which is the perfect way to announce anyone!

The Lord Mayor then speaks. This ritual is followed for all the speakers and, when the last has sat down, the toastmaster makes his final announcement to lead the main party away from the tables.

As a Freeman of the City and a Liveryman of the Worshipful Company of Butchers, I still love the City and all it stands for, and I will defend its critically important position within Britain until my dying breath.

I am proud to number among my close friends, one of the greatest conjurors and illusionists in the world, Past King Rat, David Berglas. David is a very kind man and has been a guide and mentor to me throughout my years as a Water Rat. In the year that he was King Rat, Ann and I ran a garden party at our home and invited about 100 Rats, Ratlings and friends to a get-together. We frequently discussed magic and magicians, especially as he was, for several years, President of the Magic Circle. One who came under discussion was the remarkable Uri Geller. A former Israeli soldier, Uri is a proud man who commutes between England, Israel and the US, where he is considered a megastar. He is renowned for his amazing illusion of breaking an ordinary spoon or fork in two simply by massaging it with his fingers. David Berglas assures me that it is a conjuring trick and nothing else. I'm afraid I have to disagree, 'cos I've been there and seen it.

Uri Geller was appearing in cabaret at a barmitzvah celebration at a London hotel. I had met him several times, but never needed to be quite so close, as usually there was a freestanding microphone. On this occasion the mic had no stand, so when he invited the barmitzvah lad onto the ballroom floor to help him with the act, I had to hold the mic right under his nose. The three of us were side by side and he asked me to fetch an ordinary piece of cutlery from any table. I selected a fork. The barmitzvah and I watched, spellbound, as Uri simply rubbed his finger and thumb repeatedly up and down along the shank of the fork, holding it with the other hand, talking through the mic as he did so. After no longer than a couple of minutes, it suddenly began to bend and eventually broke in two with one bit clattering to the floor. The bit he was holding was blisteringly hot as he demonstrated by touching the backs of our hands with it. This is why I disagree with David Berglas; it *has* to be a special power! Doesn't it?

His next 'trick' was to place his hands firmly over the lad's wrist, upon which there was a very expensive watch. Uri checked the time first, clasped the wrist and asked the lad to concentrate as hard as he could on the watch. As Uri concentrated, he began to perspire furiously – after no more than two or three minutes he removed his hand… and the watch had advanced about fifteen minutes. I promise you, that was all he did. It was astounding. Call it a trick, call it magic, call it a power; I was as close as I could get and was very impressed.

Chapter 13

Associated Speakers

"It is better to keep one's mouth shut and be thought a fool
than to open it and resolve all doubt."

Abraham Lincoln

After the Second World War there were dozens of function rooms
all over the country, especially in the London suburbs: The
Yorkshire Grey in Eltham, Chiesemans' in Lewisham, owned by the
Chieseman family whose daughter married (Lord) Colin Cowdrey,
Pyne's Restaurant in Lewisham, where Ann had her 21st birthday
party, The Selborne Hall in Southgate, The Victoria Cross Galleries
in Wantage and dozens of others. Croydon alone boasted four
places of varying size and quality: there were two shops or stores,
Kennards and *Grants*, The Café Royal — not to be confused with the
one in Piccadilly about which much more anon — and The
Greyhound, a glorified pub with a huge ballroom. Ann and I still
joke, as we drive around the countryside and see an oddball hall and
say, "If ever you're doing a gig at the Welfare Hall, Little Puddle on
the Green, well — there it is," and, believe me, I have worked in
some weird ones, gaining a great deal of experience in the process.
Scout huts, boys' clubs, church halls, marquees, boats, ships,
aeroplanes, the lot — you name it, I've been there.

Working one night in Croydon, the guest speaker was Cyril Fletcher.
He was a famous radio and vaudeville comedian who spoke with a
very posh accent, but would change his voices for his Odd Odes.
He also dreamed up a catchphrase which was delivered in an oily,
cockney drawl, "Dreamin' of thee, Dreamin' of thee, Dreamin' oh

my darlin' luv, of thee." It then led into a silly poem. He and his wife Betty Astelle were great broadcasters who had their own radio programme. Towards the end of his career, he found further fame for several years with his large eyes and beaming smile in the Esther Rantzen programme, *That's Life*, before retiring to his own nursery in Guernsey. Cyril and Betty owned an agency called Associated Speakers which was run for them by a lovely couple, Dabber Davis and his wife Paddy. Dabber had been the manager for Bob Monkhouse and Dennis Goodwin and knew the agency and management market thoroughly.

As Cyril did not drive, I offered him a lift back from the Croydon job – this was the first time I met him. We discussed the after-dinner speaking business and he agreed to put me on his books; this launched me into another sphere which I loved and which taught me a great deal.

Associated Speakers had been in business for many years and the format was both clever and lucrative. They had hundreds of Ladies' Luncheon Clubs nationwide, from great cities to small hamlets and villages, all with varying budgets. My first speaking engagement was at a very smart Ladies' Luncheon Club in Torquay, and I set to the task of writing a 45-minute speech. Ann had the bright idea that, as I was a toastmaster, I should deliver my speeches in my full regalia. It was an instant hit; they loved me and it resulted in me speaking at nigh on 200 events for Dabber and Paddy all over the UK.

Every May, they would organise a Luncheon at The Dorchester Hotel in London's Park Lane. The ladies would buy tickets for their chairman and speaker secretary and 'make a day of it' in London. It began in the morning with coffee followed by an assembly at which the directors would talk about all their speakers, their names, their subjects, their prices, their popularity and everything the ladies needed to know. The speakers would then congregate in the lobby and be given name-badges. The meeting would end and the ladies would emerge with their notebooks. They descended on us like farmers in a cattle market, rarely looking us in the eye but at the name badge, saying, "Who are you? Oh yes. You must be the toastmaster." Obvious really, as I was dressed in full regalia. "How long do you speak for? Would you come to Brigg, or Scunthorpe, or Ashby-de-la-Zouch? How much do you charge?" (A question we were forbidden to answer.) "Do you take questions? Are you free on...?" and a whole lot more, whilst making copious notes in their little books. We really were just a commodity, but loved the whole business.

There were many well-known speakers on the list, such as Col John Blashford-Snell, the energetic and pioneering Army leader, Sheridan Morley, Michael Parkinson, together with actors, authors, musicians and anyone with an amusing story to tell. We speakers would chat amongst ourselves and the conversation usually ran, "Have you done Cambridge?" or "How did you get on in Boston? Funny lot there, weren't they?" "And what did you think of the food in Bracknell? Lousy, wasn't it? There was no mic in Rugby so I had to shout all the time. Then there was Runcorn! Speaking in a bloody restaurant, with other punters having lunch. What a bore." But really we loved it and were flattered when we were poked by a beautifully manicured, diamond-ringed finger and asked our names.

At the end of these little get-togethers, Dabber and Co would call us with a list of dates, way into the future, as they usually booked two years in advance, and so our diaries became full. The speaker secretary was instructed to send us a small contract on blue-and-white paper with every detail about time, venue, speech length, transport arrangements and fee clearly set out. We would sign the white one and return it, keeping the blue one which told us all we needed to know.

On the day, I would get myself to a London railway station, trundle to the town at which I was speaking, there to be met at the station by one of the ladies who took me to the hotel, or restaurant, or scout hut, or church hall, or village hall, or stately home, or marquee in a garden, or any venue which would take their numbers. Many clubs were strictly limited by how many could sit and have lunch in the only hall their town boasted; some as few as sixty. Every one was different, all were charming, and it was both enjoyable and rewarding.

I developed one basic speech but with variants liberally littered with little jokes, vignettes, stories and anecdotes. They loved to have 'names' dropped, particularly those whom they might know or could relate to and, in particular, Royalty. They all loved the Royal Family and enjoyed my relationships with them. My speech lasted about 35 minutes, after which I invited questions. It has always been my strongly-held belief that with question time you tell the audience what they want to know rather than what you just want to spout to them about, and invariably this session was more enjoyable than the speech.

There could be some rather odd introductions, often dependent upon the degree of nervousness of the chairman. After pudding and coffee, one lady said to me, "Are you ready to speak then?" to which I replied, "Yes!" She then said, in a rather stern voice, "Well, go on then!" and that was it. I introduced myself.

I also used to send them a flyer describing me and my speech. The introduction I dreaded was when they took that verbatim and simply read it to the audience. This was a damned nuisance, as contained within it were some anecdotes and bits of information I used as 'material' and from which I got laughs. So I developed the habit of saying to the chairman, "Tell them as little as possible. Something like, 'And now our speaker, England's famous Toastmaster, Mr Bryn Williams.'" That's all I ever wanted.

The food on these occasions was, at best, adequate. It certainly was not *haute cuisine* and frequently the chairman would apologise for it. One lunch in the Peak District began with thin, weak, not very hot carrot soup, after which we waited an eternity for two dollops of potato, a bit of chicken and about thirty peas. Having picked our way through that, there was an even longer delay which prompted me to suggest to the chairman that I go and see what was happening; invariably, I had to catch a train back to London which I dared not miss so really could not afford to be delayed. I went to the kitchen, saw the head girl and asked why it was taking so long to serve the pudding. She replied that they had had trouble with the cook but that the pudding was on its way. 'The pudding' consisted of a small dish of tinned fruit salad and a splash of cream. What took them so long to serve such a footling little dessert like that escapes me. It was horrible.

When I ended my speech and was just about to leave, a smartly dressed lady rose from the body of the room and in a strong, aristocratic, schoolmarm-type voice said haughtily, "Madame Chairman, I really must protest. But firstly, I must apologise to our wonderful speaker, Mr Bryn Williams, for causing him any embarrassment, but that meal we have just endured is quite the worst I have ever known. I have never eaten such dreadful rubbish and I propose that we do not pay the hotel. I must also insist that our luncheon secretary takes great steps to see that the quality of our luncheons improve in the future, or I for one will resign." It brought a roar of approval and the message was driven home in no uncertain manner. I wonder what happened, as one rarely, if ever, goes back.

The Ladies' Luncheon Club market died virtually overnight. I came to it rather late, but there were still many clubs with reasonable budgets. Some of the very large ones in big cities would meet every month and vary between a local speaker for expenses only, to professionals from all over the country. Others would hold six meetings each year with a special one at Christmas, at which I was very popular because of the colour of my uniform. Many of the members where middle-aged to elderly and dependent upon pensions and fixed incomes, so membership fees were restricted. Unavoidably, prices began to rise in the hotels, fares also increased, and the worst penalty of all was the VAT which many speakers had to charge. It was an iniquitous tax on these ladies and contributed to the ultimate demise of that market.

I don't know how many are left, possibly only the very big ones – I have only spoken at one in the last ten years. They were a great institution and it is sad that they no longer exist, but they provided me with wonderful experience in the art of addressing an audience, which led on to greater things.

* * * * *

JFK Airport, formerly Idlewild, the gateway to the USA, was nestled serenely under a blanket of white. As far as the eye could see, out of the small window beside my seat, everything was white; a few hours earlier, it had sustained a massive blizzard and was covered in snow many inches deep and our intrepid pilot was using all his great skill to bring us down to earth, literally, safely and without sliding all over the place. My first impression of the huge continent of America was white wherever you looked.

At last, one of my childhood dreams had been realised. I had arrived in what had always been 'the land of my dreams'. This was the first of what has become dozens of visits to that country and the buzz of excitement which engulfed me then never fails to do so each time I go there – I love the place. This landing began the first of several lecture tours I was to make over the next few years. It was the winter of 1974.

My life has been made up of coincidences, chance encounters, eavesdroppings and a whole chapter of unrelated events which have, over time, conspired to shape my existence. Two dear friends of mine – who have never, and will never, meet – shared the same lecture agent in America, Wally Dow, who ran the Dow Lecture Agency in Monkton, Maryland. The first of these friends is Past King Rat, Wyn Calvin, OBE – the 'Clown' Prince of Wales. Comedian, broadcaster, TV chat-show host and pantomime dame for over fifty years, he has been my friend and confidante within the Rats since I joined. I was privileged to be toastmaster at his wedding to his lovely wife Carole.

The other friend is the Reverend Canon Richard Tydeman, now retired and living in Suffolk, where he still writes poetry and regularly gives talks on his pet subject, Charles Dickens. Boasting a small beard, he dresses in the style of Dickens and speaks about him in the first person singular. He is also a leading Freemason and a wonderful lecturer on many Masonic degrees. He was for many years a minor Canon attached to St Paul's Cathedral at a church called St Sepulchre's Without, in Holborn. He took immense delight in telling the many American visitors that his church was restored one hundred years before 'Columbus sailed the Ocean

Blue' and discovered America. Wally Dow, when paying him a visit, asked, "What does 'without' mean?" Richard quietly replied, "It's the opposite of 'within'"! Think about it!

These two are both excellent lecturers and after-dinner speakers, and had made many tours of the USA under the guidance of Wally. Quite independently, they told Wally about me, which resulted in my being offered a two-week tour of the eastern seaboard of America, involving about ten speeches and lectures. Knowing that I would need many changes of my 'whites' (shirts, waistcoats, ties, etc), I bought myself a huge *Globetrotter* suitcase which I stuffed to capacity, and eventually found myself yellow-cabbing through the snow in search of my first talk.

A reverend (whose name, sadly, I have forgotten) was to be my host for the first night in New York. He was the Chaplain of The International Club, 42nd Street, New York. I have always boasted that when I went to America to speak and entertain, "I opened on Broadway!" Believe me, it wasn't that grand or spectacular, but it was a first. They ran these meetings monthly where they would give a few dollars to a special speaker. These usually attracted an audience of a couple of hundred members and guests. Sadly, on this night, the weather had been so dreadful that only about thirty turned up to hear this oddball toastmaster guy from the UK talking about himself. International it certainly was, as within that group there must have been ten different nationalities who had absolutely no idea whatsoever about me, my profession, my uniform, my job, who I was, where I came from, why I was there or what I did. Whatever else I had planned to say went out the window and I just chatted to them. I recall that we had a really great evening on a very informal basis. They loved my English accent and stories about 'The Old Country', while I did manage to explain a bit about what I did for a living.

It was there that I met a super lady with the stage name of Fredi Dundee. Her actual surname was Silver (I never did discover her full Christian name), but she hailed from Dundee and was a cabaret artiste in New York trying, like so many before her, to make her name in show business over there. We struck up a close friendship which continued for many years until, sadly, she died of cancer. On my first night there, she took me under her wing, and when I had finished my talk, we caught a cab to Greenwich Village and visited some jazz clubs. One especially will remain in my memory as the singer-pianist, the then legendary 'Chi-Chi-Girl' Rose Murphy, was playing and I sat right beside the piano as she sang, accompanied by her ever-tapping foot on a wooden block. Bliss!

Wally insisted that I would never make any money lecturing around America unless I was either famous or notorious; he said he had no trouble 'selling' to his clients if you were either a Member of Parliament or had been to prison. As I had neither qualification, I had to put up with anything that was on offer and be grateful. Long ago, I had decided that I wanted to tour the States, and I gave up two weeks' possible work in England to fulfil the dream, notwithstanding the finances. This meant that my travel arrangements had to be economic, so Wally bought me a round-robin ticket on the *Greyhound* buses which traverse the country. These are warm, efficient, reliable, run on time and are highly commended, but they are also very basic, and on the long hauls many people bring fast food on board that stinks out the damn bus.

My next two assignments were in Washington DC, and then on to a 'private' (what we would call 'public') school in Baltimore. This was a particularly tough assignment which nearly went sour. I was to address 600 boys immediately after assembly at 9.00 am. I arrived early, dressed in my toastmaster uniform ready for the introduction. Peeping out from the curtain, just before going onto the large stage at this school at 8.55, I saw, to my horror, that the place was empty; I feared the worst. I was assured by the headmaster that I need not worry as the boys *had* to come and hear me whether they wanted to or not! That's one way to get an audience. Five minutes later, when he went on stage for my introduction, every seat was full.

On this tour, I chose to make my appearance in a spectacular scarlet silk-lined black flowing cape with a gold buckle at the neck and a pair of black leather gloves. The impact on an American audience had what is now known as 'The wow factor'. Doffing both gloves and cape very slowly and dramatically, my full toastmaster uniform was revealed, generating a second 'wow' with a sharp intake of breath from the audience. It really had a startling effect.

I wouldn't wish a nine o'clock start to 600 totally bored and thoroughly sober, wholesome and well-scrubbed American sixteen-year-olds on my worst enemy. The implied criticism and lack of interest staring out from those 1200 eyes, defying me to entertain and amuse them, was tangible. As most of my talks related to British pomp, ceremony and ancient tradition, it was not really to their liking. My scheduled speaking time was 45 minutes, but after ten of those I felt I was sinking and trudging through treacle... it ain't a happy feeling!

Thankfully, I had two ploys to accommodate such potential disasters. I had taken with me a traditional Loving Cup with the intention of explaining its history and ceremony with 'audience participation'. Calling up three beefy lads from the front row, I told one that he was The Lord Mayor of London, another that he was the Lady Mayoress and the third that he was Princess Margaret. It worked! They loved it, and taking them through this quaint and ancient ceremony (having filled the cup with *Coca Cola*), the assembly erupted. When any of these 'actors' screwed it up, the others shouted encouragement. It was a riot.

My second ploy was to invite questions, which went like a dream, and when the headmaster interrupted one hour later to thank me, they were genuinely disappointed. One young man came up to me and said. "Sir, I just *loved* your talk. Please Sir, if I give you this programme, will you please get the Queen's autograph for me?" Nice thought. Nice guy. Nice school. No chance!

Whilst in Baltimore, I spoke at the world-famous Johns Hopkins University and at a beautiful house called Liriodendron. This had been the summer home of one of the four original doctors at Johns Hopkins Hospital. It was whilst in this great city that I made a visit which changed my life.

There have been many instances documented in this book about my belief that our lives are pre-ordained, that something or someone somewhere is watching over us and directing our actions. In 1970, I was called to work at a cocktail party in the Guildhall in the City of London for a group of women in the broadcasting world. They were American Women in Radio and Television (AWRT) and this was their farewell event after a European tour. I made myself known to several, and in particular the newly-elected president, Mrs Virginia Pate. All were perfectly charming and, in the usual friendly American style, some gave me their cards with an invitation to call them should I ever get to their part of the world. When Wally was arranging my trip, he asked if I had any contacts at all – I eagerly sent him these cards, but he was only really interested in one of them. Arriving in America, he gave me the whole itinerary for the trip, which included 'an oddball visit to a small town to go onto a radio chat show'. He had contacted Virginia Pate and arranged for me to appear on one of her radio stations.

As everyone knows, America is a huge country. Wally lived in a small town called Monkton, Maryland, while Virginia Pate's stations were in Havre de Grace, Chesapeake Bay, a fifteen-minute drive from Wally's place – a remarkable coincidence. He was disparaging about the lady and informed me that she had recently remarried and become Mrs Edward Pate Wetter, adding, "If you still want to appear for *your* Mrs Pate Wetter, for no money, just for the experience on her radio stations, then it's up to you." I agreed, he reluctantly arranged it and that was that.

I took a *Greyhound* to Havre de Grace, met Mrs Virginia Pate Wetter, did a thirty-minute broadcast to possibly a couple of hundred totally uninterested listeners, met her husband, Edward, and went on my way. I could not possibly have known then that that very brief meeting was to be the start of one of the closest of friendships Ann and I have ever had; since then we have become like brothers and sisters. We've toured the world together, paid regular visits to each others' homes, and carried on a lasting friendship spanning thirty years and 3,000 miles of Atlantic Ocean. Whatever power it was that shone on me at that Guildhall party in 1970, I shall never know, but it has given the four of us the happiest of times together. Sadly, Ed died in 2002 and we still mourn his passing.

Having ended my business in Havre de Grace, my charming hostess saw me onto another *Greyhound* to take me to my next destination, Colonial Williamsburg, Virginia, once described as '… an exquisite corner of America that is forever England'. This town has become, possibly, my favourite anywhere in the world, and if ever I chose to retire, I would love this to be my final resting-place. It is the home of William and Mary College, where Virginia and, coincidentally, Bibba (Wally's wife) had both been students. I talked to the alumni of the College as well as the local Rotary Club, and both speeches went fairly well.

From Williamsburg, the good old *Greyhound* took me the fairly short journey to Richmond, Virginia, where I was scheduled to make several speeches. If Richmond has any claim to fame, it must surely be through that epic film *Gone with the Wind*. There is one famous scene between the two stars filmed at the bottom of a wide and sweeping flight of crimson-carpeted stairs, indicating a rich and magnificent mansion. It is still there in the lobby of The Jefferson Hotel, and my first appearance in Richmond was on that staircase.

Wally Dow had alopecia and was totally bald. He stood about five feet tall, was just a little deaf, was as strong as an ox and had a voice like a foghorn. I have always likened him to Mr Magoo of cartoon fame, as he was equally vague. However, he didn't have a nerve in his body and when we were anywhere together, he would lead me up to someone, and whether or not he knew them, would say, "This is my good friend Bryn Williams. He's from England and is the Queen's personal toastmaster." (Not true. There isn't such a position!) I would try to interject, but to no avail, and to my acute embarrassment, he would prattle on in a very loud voice singing my praises to anyone who cared to listen. (Indeed on one occasion, going up to the tenth floor of a hotel in a very crowded lift, the poor passengers had no option but to listen… they were trapped.)

At the foot of that grand staircase in The Jefferson Hotel, Wally gathered around him anyone in the lobby and made me talk to them. It was a wonderful moment for me, standing on this magnificent and famous backdrop, where Clark Gable and Vivien Leigh had made cinema history, holding forth to a bunch of totally bemused Americans. I didn't let Wally Dow down! (No pun intended!)

Richmond is a proud, southern confederate town, with wide, tree-lined avenues and splendid, palatial, old-style American houses – indeed, it is the capital of the confederate states. It is a joy to visit and rich in history – many inhabitants can trace their ancestry back generations and are deeply protective of their heritage. There are many Women's Luncheon and Dining Clubs which have the luxury of their own meeting rooms with raked seating, stages with proscenium arches, full backstage amenities, microphones, lighting, stage curtains and every facility – the envy of any theatre. They hold regular meetings to which they invite speakers, all of whom are carefully vetted by a committee.

Wally Dow was extremely proud of his contacts with many of these clubs, especially The Tuckahoe, which was by far the most prestigious, and he was always pleased to be able to bring them speakers from England. At every high-profile speaking engagement, Wally would attend and give me the strictest instructions as to the style and content of my talk. They were all quite delightful and charming people, who adored any speaker talking about the UK and they were always so welcoming and hospitable. One lady once said to me, "Honey, I dunno what you're saying, but just keep on talking. I just luurrrve your accent." Such was my success that I returned on a later tour – this time with Ann!

At the end of this part of the journey, Wally called me to give me a choice. I have always loved the singing of Dinah Shore and have many of her records. At that time, she had a regular TV show and there was the vaguest possibility that I could make a guest appearance. However, it was only a slight possibility, and with my knowledge of the vagaries of TV companies and their broken promises, I was a bit sceptical. The second choice was far more attractive. I had gone down well with the William and Mary alumni and had been invited to return to Williamsburg to address another audience. What did I want to do? There was only one answer and, once again, I hoisted my now increasingly heavy *Globetrotter* suitcase into the hold of a *Greyhound*, giving me an unexpected return visit to the town which had captured my heart.

Williamsburg was the birthplace of the thirteen states of America wishing to secede from British rule. The Burgesses of that town met, argued, discussed and eventually chose to become totally independent and to cut all legal ties with the British Crown. It coincided in American history with the Boston Tea Party. These were momentous times and created great schisms amongst their leaders. It is a town steeped in history, of which it is very proud, and in the mid-20th century, John D Rockefeller donated millions of dollars to restore the central area to its original state. It was completed in 1950 with the result that colonial Williamsburg is now a wholly reconstructed and totally authentic area depicting the lifestyle of over two centuries ago. All the buildings are fully restored and functioning as they were then. The stewards (all volunteers) dress in the costume of the day, and the Corps of Fifes and Drums and the Militia give regular demonstrations of their music and marching. There are shops, museums, taverns, a court house, an armoury, the Governor's Palace, and halfway along the wide, mile-long Duke of Gloucester Street, is Bruton Parish Church, named by the British settlers after the town in Somerset. It was at that historic place that I was asked to give a talk to the local parishioners.

The Reverend Cotesworth Pinkney Lewis was the bright-eyed, smiling-faced, jovial and thoroughly charismatic Minister who made me feel that I was the most important person in his life. He had a beautiful shock of thick white hair and was a simply wonderful character, worshipped and adored by everyone. He reigned supreme and preached there for many years. When I visited recently, I learned that when he died, such was the reverence in which he was held, his ashes were put into a casket and placed permanently under the altar. All the pews have small brass plaques naming the famous early rulers of America who had worshipped there. Thomas Jefferson, George Washington, Patrick Henry, George Wythe and many others are named and, each time I visit, I marvel at its history.

My talk to these parishioners was pure joy and, as I was not being paid other than travel expenses, I was given several silver mementos, made in the silversmiths' shop in the town, as a souvenir of my visit. This had been set up by the Reverend Cotesworth Lewis. I was delighted to give these to Ann as a coming-home present.

My 14-day excursion along the eastern seaboard came to an end and I returned home with some wonderful memories and a deep yearning to return. I did make several more, much shorter tours, but they were becoming difficult to arrange as they had to be booked about eighteen months in advance, and Wally was getting older and frailer. However, I am eternally grateful to Cyril Fletcher for introducing me to the world of professional public speaking, and to Wyn Calvin and Dick Tydeman for recommending me to Wally, enriching my life in so many ways.

Prime Minister Margaret Thatcher was guest of honour at The Savoy Hotel Luncheon of The Saints and Sinners Club of London, a highly respected and influential club of 100 men in industry, sport, commerce and entertainment, founded many years ago by the brilliant crime writer, Percy Hoskins, and the famous bandleader Jack Hilton. They hold a lunch and a dinner each year and manage to attract some of the world's finest speakers. On this occasion, they were thrilled that the Prime Minister had agreed to attend, but we were all well aware that she had to leave by 3.00 pm sharp – and when her office said, sharp, they meant it... 3.01 just would not do!

The Club felt it another feather in their cap that Sir Robin Day, celebrated television and radio broadcaster, would address them. He, too, was aware of the time constraint and agreed to speak for ten minutes only. At 2.45 I introduced him, and the first half of his speech was warm, witty and very entertaining. But then he changed tack and began, obliquely, to talk about Margaret Thatcher in what was becoming quite unfavourable terms; he was banging on and on, taking a nasty side-swipe at the guest of honour, which was becoming embarrassing. I started getting very icy glances from the lady as well as similar glares from the chairman and secretary. By now it was about 2.59 and Sir Robin did not show any signs of stopping.

The PM signalled me over and whispered in my ear, "If you don't stop him now, I shall simply get up and walk out whilst he is on his feet. *It's up to you!*" And boy, she meant it. With a nod of approval from the secretary, I had the acute embarrassment, in front of 500 absorbed and very interested listeners, of tugging at the great man's sleeve and whispering in his ear, "Will you please stop NOW, Sir Robin, and sit down. The Prime Minister MUST leave a three o'clock and you've overrun your time." Knowing the volatility of that gentleman, I was terrified of a public reprisal. To my, and everyone's amazement, he simply said "Thank you" and sat down. At this precise second, gloves, speech and handbag already gathered up, the PM rose, glared at Sir Robin, said goodbye to the chairman and stormed out. I often wonder what she said at their next confrontation.

Chapter 14

The British Tourist Authority

"An odd thing tourism is. You fly off to a strange land, eagerly
abandoning all the comforts of home and then attempt to
recapture the comforts that wouldn't have been lost if you hadn't
left home in the first place."

Bill Bryson

The British Tourist Authority (BTA) supervised the tourist industry
in the UK for many years, and between the 1960s and the 1980s I
worked at numerous events organised by its many branches. There
were dozens of sub-committees, county sections, groups
promoting every area concerning tourism in their own category, for
which cocktail parties, luncheons, seminars, dinners and other
activities were organised to stimulate interest. As a result of
presiding over these various functions, I kept bumping into the
moguls at the head of the BTA and I knew them well. At that time,
Mr Frank Kelly and Mr Leonard Lickorish seemed to approve of
my work. Leonard was the brother of Ronald Lickorish who,
coincidentally, became my proposer into the Worshipful Company
of Butchers. They were both about 5' 2", and Ron, the then editor
of the *Meat Trades Journal,* was rather rotund with a twinkle in his
eye and a sharp sense of fun – he resembled the Tweedle-Dum of
that pairing and was a great champion of mine.

Frank, Leonard and some senior executives interviewed me about a
trip that was being planned to North America. It was to be called
'Great British Hotels' and involved representatives of eight of our
five-star hotels on a promotional tour. I got lucky and was invited

as both a toastmaster and kind of 'door-keeping' host to the American tour operators and travel writers who were to be invited. It proved to be one of the most fascinating and enjoyable two weeks of my career.

The Savoy, The Westbury, The Churchill, The Basil, The Grosvenor House and The Dorchester were among the eight who sent senior executives on the tour – the party also included a young chef. Our first port-of-call was Chicago, to be followed by Boston, San Francisco, Los Angeles, Houston, Atlanta, Washington DC and New York and, because of the nature of the tour, our venues were obviously the best five-star hotels in each city… it's a tough life at times! It really was a huge eye-opener to me of the way the rich and ungodly live when they travel; I had never known such supreme luxury, and I revelled in it.

Our fame had been well publicised and at each city we all went off in different directions to fulfil some kind of public relations exercise. My first was possibly the weirdest of all. I was erroneously billed as 'The Royal Toastmaster'. I wasn't. However, why waste a good opportunity for publicity, and the Americans certainly loved it!

On landing at 8.00 am at O'Hare Airport – at that time the largest in the world – I was whisked away in a plush limousine to The Drake Hotel. There wasn't much time to spare as I was due to appear on a radio phone-in programme at 9.30, the interview being conducted over the telephone from my hotel room. Nobody was in the room with me, but the producers insisted, unequivocally, that I be fully dressed in my red-tail toastmaster gear – God alone knows why! At 9.15 the telephone rang and a voice asked, "Is this Mister Berrryyn Williams, Toastmaster to the Queen?" "Yes," I replied. "Tell me, Mister Williams, are you wearing all your very colourful uniform that the Queen would see?" I saw no sense in correcting him and simply agreed.

"Well, Sirrrrr, it really is gerrreatt to have you in Chicago and I hope your trip was comfortable. We have a telephone presenter who will come on line in a minute, and at half-after-nine will go live on air and speak to you. You OKAY for this?" "Yes," I replied, "I have

HRH Prince Philip arriving at the NAT Royal Lunch 2002
That must have been a great gag

My dear pal the late Martin Nicholls
handing our cheque to Prince Philip

Companion Rats Prince Philip and Sir Donald Gosling, Rat Barry Cryer and Jim Davidson, Royal Lunch 2002

Wedding of Gloria Hunniford and Stephen Way, 1998

Three Great Singers

Kiri te Kanawa

Katharine Jenkins

A Brace of Bryns

Shirley Bassey,
before the 'dameship'

Jack Jones

The wonderfully
'bad' Eartha Kitt

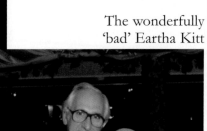

Phil Collins and cap at his
'surprise' 50th birthday party in
Zermatt

The fastest man in the world on two and four wheels, John Surtees

World class actor and world class bridge player, Omar Sharif

Linda and Pauline, 'Birds of a Feather', two smashin' gels

David 'Through the Keyhole' Frost at my 40th cocktail party

"I'm the greatest."
Take your pick!

"What idiot would
sit a Heavyweight
Boxing Champion
next to the Founder
of The British
Safety Council?"
James Tye and
Henry Cooper at
our Silver Wedding
in 1982

Water Rat Danny Kaye
Showbusiness Personality
of the Year circa 1974

Teddy, Joy and
Babs, 'The Bevs',
pals of Dad's and
mine for many
years, at my 40th
anniversary

Chaim 'Fiddler on
the Roof' Topol,
a legend and a
wonderful man

Kenny Ball and the boys

PKR Roger de Courcey, Jim Davidson, and Rat Bob 'The Cat' Bevan at the NAT Royal Lunch 2002

90-year-old Rat Sir Norman (Mr Grimsdale) Wisdom

Eric Morecambe, Ann and me

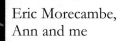

'Waddya think of it so far?' Eric, Ernie, and a couple of stooges

Band leader
Johnny Howard,
a life-long friend

King Rat Danny La Rue,
1987

Intronisation
into the Jurade
of St Emilion,
1989

Queen Ratling Carmen 'Allo 'Allo Silvera, and escort, Angela Rippon, and Sacha
Distel flanked by Past Queen Ratlings Valerie and Cheryl Garland (1997)

The NAT Royal Lunch
Ratling Ruth and PKR David Berglas, PKR Wyn Calvin, Comp Rat Bob
Potter (sitting), Past Queen Ratling Maggie and PKR Bert Weedon,
Barbara Leitch, Ratling Julie Rogers

President of the Cup of Kindness, Ratling Barbara Windsor
and Rat Bob 'The Cat' Bevan

Past Queen Ratling Ruth Madoc, a dear friend of Dad's and mine

Rats Tom O'Connor, Mike Craig and Jeremy Beadle,
Baby Rat Bob Hope in 1991, and PKR Roy Hudd with Ann

Four Generations

Three generations and two dogs

Our 30th Anniversary – we 'took over' Castle Howard

Me and 'er indoors

NAT Royal Luncheon 2002

had a wonderful flight and am ready for your presenter. What is his name?" To which the reply came, "Oh Geeez, I do lurrrrve your accent. It really is so quaint. Our listeners are gonna be thrilled. His name is Al." And off he went. Forty minutes later, having put the phone down, I had spoken to half of North America through 'Al'. In my best British accent, I answered a whole bunch of utterly inane questions, alone in my luxurious hotel room and fully dressed in uniform! It really was quite bizarre.

We were joined for the whole trip by the boss of the BTA in North America, a delightful man named Lewis Roberts, nephew of that great Scottish actress Rene Houston. Several functions had been laid on in each city, the first of which was usually a buffet luncheon to which a couple of hundred guests were invited. We had decided to be thoroughly British during these events, requiring me to greet the guests at the door and, after they had signed in, formally introducing them to Frank Kelly and Lewis. This was their first surprise, as it never happens at their formal functions. Stopping them at the door, asking their name and calling it out into the room knocked them sideways. "Oh Gee, ain't this great?" or "Hey no! You ain't gonna call it out, are you?" Generally they loved it and I confess to hamming it up more than usual.

When they had arrived, we presented the next item of pure British invention which fooled all of them; indeed, even the highly professional, hard-nosed British hotel managers began to believe it by the end of the tour. Having had a brief formal welcome from one of the BTA team, the chef paraded a sirloin of beef to be served. I was given a script which went as follows:

> "His Majesty King Henry VIII was hosting a banquet. When the succulent beef was to be served, it was paraded for all present to witness. One joint was of such supreme quality and taste that he commended the chef on its excellence. He enquired of the chef the name of the cut and was told, "Your Majesty, it is the loin of the animal!" upon which he called for his sword,

'dubbed' the piece of beef and proclaimed, 'Arise SIRloin and be served.' This is why, to this day, it is known as a sirloin of beef!"

Believe that, and you'll believe anything! Coincidentally, I was at The Tower of London recently and a Yeoman Warder recounted that story publicly as it is in their officially written dialogue. Such was our intent to impress, that we actually took on the tour with us a huge, very heavy, brass sword, and invited one of the guests to perform the ceremony. Try getting a four-foot heavy brass sword on a plane nowadays – you'd get chucked in the slammer!

During the afternoons the hoteliers and BTA representatives conducted formal seminars, addressing all facets of the hotel industry and tourism – I was not required to attend these, but was back on duty in the evenings when we usually held a small formal banquet or another buffet presentation for more guests. In most cities, many of us were invited onto either radio or television programmes, talking about ourselves, our hotels, Britain in general and any other appropriate topic to promote British tourism.

I had problems with my voice on this tour. Travelling around the US, you are so constantly in air-conditioned environments, the hotel room, the car, the aeroplane, that you never get to breathe fresh air and it began to affect me seriously. It has the effect of drying the throat so thoroughly that the voice simply disappears and there really is nothing you can do to cure it. As the tour headed towards Washington DC and New York, I was becoming quite dumb, literally, and knew that the last two venues were the largest and toughest so far as the hard-nosed journalists were concerned. Thank God, with the aid of incessant inhaling of *Crookes Karvol* and strong microphones, I managed to get by.

There was one interesting diversion towards the end of the trip. The hoteliers moaned that they were fed up with flying and asked if we could go by train from Washington DC to New York. It's not too far and we all boarded *Amtrak* for the last leg – first class, of course – which was relaxing and enjoyable. The whole tour was most memorable and is one I would not have missed.

Following the success of this US tour, Lewis Roberts invited me back for several shorter, but equally important, promotional visits. I was always booked in at The Pierre Hotel on Fifth Avenue, the finest hotel in New York, and I made many appearances, fully attired in toastmaster garb, on television. I actually counted my engagements on one of these trips. In four days, I visited Toronto, Boston and New York, and from the moment I landed in Canada until I flew out again from New York's Kennedy Airport, I attended no fewer than eleven events – luncheons, dinners, TV appearances, radio broadcasts and seminars. On the return flight I just crashed out and slept all the way home... I was exhausted.

I was privileged to do two important banquets at the Metropolitan Opera, in Lincoln Square, New York – alas! not on the stage, but in the huge vestibule where it is possible to dine many hundreds of people. My duties were minimal, but my appearance as a representative of the heritage of Britain was important. One of these events I remember with a shudder of embarrassment. The opera was the Zefferelli production of *La Bohème* which was absolutely sensational. Words cannot describe the mind-boggling second act of his production – it is not very long, lasting about twenty minutes, but during that time there must have been several hundred performers on stage. As well as the divas and principals, there were crowds in the bar where the main event takes place, and all around were costermongers, children playing, street-vendors and every type of street activity that a scene of that period would attract. Towards the end of the act, a full military marching band paraded across the stage and off into the distance. I have never ever seen anything quite so awe-inspiring, and at the risk of becoming boring, I can only repeat that it really was sensational. I am not generally a fan of opera, but this performance nearly made me change my mind.

It was a prestigious event to which about thirty ambassadors from around the world were invited, as well as four or five dukes from the UK. In my briefing, I had been told that the Duke of Norfolk, our senior duke, had cried off and would not be attending. The opera having ended, the 400 or so VIPs took their places and dinner was served. At the appropriate moment I began my welcome, listing all the ambassadors and their entourages, inviting them to stand to be acknowledged. I ended by introducing the four noble dukes from my own country, after which one of the American hosts spoke.

At this point, Frank Kelly came rushing around to me and said, "You've forgotten to introduce the Duke of Norfolk!" I said, "No, I haven't. He's not here. He isn't coming!" Frank said, "Yes, he is. Look, there he is, sitting over there!" Horror of horrors! I had publicly snubbed our senior duke. I immediately went over to him and said, "Your Grace, I really must apologise sincerely for neglecting to introduce you, but I had been expressly told that you would not be attending. Sir, I really am so sorry!" Such is the nature of the gentleman that he replied, "My dear chap, please do not fret yourself. I really do not mind. Yes," he went on, "I had said that I could not attend, but at the last moment, my plans changed and here I am. Please, please do not worry!" I then said, "Sir, I will be happy to go ahead and introduce you now, should you wish!" He threw up his hands in mock horror. "Oh no! Please don't bother. It really is not important. But thank you anyway!" One cliché I will allow myself is, "People who mind, don't matter – people who matter, don't mind." The Duke of Norfolk fell comfortably into the latter category.

There was a sequel. A month or so later in London, I met the Duke again – this time, he was with his wife. I repeated my deepest apologies for my indiscretion in New York, but he was such a genuine and charming gentleman that he reiterated his comments that it really had not bothered him at all and that I was to forget that it ever happened. He was the father-in-law of Sir David Frost who later became a champion of mine.

My son Tim was seriously courting Chloë when I was sent on another of these tours. Her parents, 'Dig' and Wendy Diggory, had branched out into New York and opened a shop on Fifth Avenue. I had not met them by this time, but plucked up the courage to pay them an unannounced visit. On my way from The Pierre to the BTA office just off Fifth Avenue, I found the shop called Cambrian Fly-Fishers. It had a huge picture window about twenty feet high and running across the entire frontage. (They were later to rue that window as some anti-Brits threw bricks at it and smashed it to smithereens.)

I asked one of the assistants if Mr Diggory was available and could I see him? She pointed to a man by the counter and said, "That's Mr Diggory." I approached him boldly, but with some trepidation and said. "Er... Mr... er... Diggory? My name is Bryn Williams and I believe that my son is hoping to marry your daughter!" His double-take at this astounding revelation from a complete stranger revealed his genuine astonishment at seeing me, 3,000 miles away from home. Our conversation was somewhat stilted, and having explained my reason for being in New York, I went on my way. Thus began a good friendship, which sadly ended on his too-early death at 69. He was a country gentleman in the true sense and a real character we all came to love.

Things tend to happen which occasionally add a little sparkle to my otherwise mundane existence. At around nine o'clock on a Monday morning, I walked down Fifth Avenue to the BTA office. Thinking of taking home a small gift for Ann, I looked in a shop window and spotted a charming necklace of ivory elephants on a gold chain but with no price tag. I opened the door and put my head inside to ask the cost. I was treated like the Prodigal Son by the people behind the counter. They invited me in, sat me down, offered me coffee, asked me what I was doing in New York, why I was there, did I come from England, what was my job, what is a toastmaster?... but nothing whatsoever to do with the necklace.

Eventually, after what seemed an eternity, it was brought from the window display and I was told that it was US$ 600 plus tax – way above my budget. They reduced it to $300 and then even lower, with them absorbing the tax. My protests that it was far too expensive were ignored. They pestered, they persuaded, they cajoled, they asked where I was staying – and I foolishly (or so I thought at the time) told them it was The Pierre. They put it into a small trinket box, wrapped it up and finally *gave* it to me and sent me on my way. Yes, they actually gave it to me with the words ringing in my ears, "You are an Englishman. We trust you to pay for it whenever you are ready!" By now, so far as I was concerned, the damned thing was hot and I hated it. I was too honest simply to steal it and really could not afford to buy it, but what to do? When I got to the BTA office, I met my guide and hostess, Marilyn Marx, and told her the story. Her reply was both casual and reassuring, "Okay!" she said, "No problem. Give it to me and I'll take it back for you. They won't mind."

Being Jewish, she explained an ancient superstition stipulating that the first person to enter their shop after a fast or a holy day must purchase or rent a product, or bad luck will follow. At nine o'clock on Monday morning I was the first person through their shop door and could not therefore be permitted to leave empty-handed, whether I purchased the necklace or not. Later that day, when I 'sneaked' past the shop I was pleased to see the necklace back in their display window, and hoped that they did not think too badly of that honest, upright, English Gentleman.

The American Society of Travel Agents (ASTA) is a vast society promoting tourism from coast to coast. Every year or so, they organise a convention somewhere in the world at which countries are invited to participate. They say that everything in the States is huge, and the ASTA Convention is one of the hugest. The year before I was invited to attend, it had been held in Rio, and was so highly regarded by that city that they built a special international airport to accommodate the participants flying in from over 150 countries.

In 1978, Lewis Roberts needed me for the four days of that convention and invited Ann to join me. It was held in New Orleans, and we were billeted at The Royal Orleans Hotel, on Bourbon Street, slap-bang in the middle of the French Quarter and all the jazz clubs and restaurants. It was four days of pure magic. BTA had created a British pub in the large ballroom of our hotel and sent out hundreds of invitations to tour operators. Three times each day we staged a formal presentation at which Gary Wilmot was the star. He was very funny and managed to adapt his act to encapsulate the 'touristic' and international feel of the event – the crowds adored him.

Ann was left to her own devices and had an open pass to tour all the 'countries' exhibiting. Fortunately, she met an Englishman she knew who chaperoned her and took her from place to place. She returned each day laden down with gifts, bags, badges, hats, souvenirs and paraphernalia from everywhere, and had a great time.

To provide some idea of the enormity of the event, I was told that the budget covering the convention was around 160 million dollars and that the British budget for the four days was approaching five million pounds. I also learned that in one of the vast convention halls, at the end of an afternoon seminar, Spain took it over completely. By mid-morning the following day, they had constructed a replica of an entire Spanish village with shops, bars, restaurants, street traders, gypsy and flamenco artistes and even a bullring, all built in about eighteen hours. This was just one example of the spectacular arrangements organised by all the countries attending.

Breakfast at *Brennans* is a must for everyone visiting New Orleans, and that world-renowned restaurant was immediately opposite our hotel; we paid it a visit and it really was exceptional – their Eggs Benedict are to die for! We also learned a piece of local history. They are all justifiably proud of their famous son Louis Armstrong whom they never cease praising. But call him 'Louie' at your peril. They all call him 'LEWISSSS'. Yes, Sirree, it's LouiSSSS Armstrong, not Louie! Geddit? We did!

We left that great city, with all its wonderful history of the Mississippi and jazz. We had sailed on *The Natchez*, a traditional paddle-steamer with the ubiquitous jazz band playing; we had witnessed, with much trepidation, a parade of a coven from the local Ku Klux Klan, clad anonymously in their white, peak-hooded robes – very sinister. We had travelled the length of Canal Street, fifteen miles dead straight; sampled some of the tremendous atmosphere of a typical southern American city, and brought home with us splendid memories and cases full of 'freebies'. We were both very sorry to see the devastation and havoc wreaked by hurricane Katrina in 2005; places we had visited and enjoyed were all totally destroyed – very sad.

The London Convention Bureau (LCB) was another small quango under the banner of the BTA. As its name proclaimed, it specifically promoted and advertised the convention potential in and around London. Conventions always have been a very lucrative source of tourism income, varying in size from a mere handful of participants to several thousand at a time, filling hotel and university bedrooms in an otherwise quiet period. Geoffrey Smith, the London-based organiser, devised a novel way of bringing together representatives of venues with potential European clients. Happily, this idea involved me in a most unusual capacity.

Paul van Weil was the LCB European representative who lived in Holland and whose knowledge was encyclopaedic. From as far north as Norway, down to Spain and Italy, he seemed to know every large organisation and potential client. The scheme involved Paul selecting several large cities in Europe, identifying the principal conference organisers and inviting them to attend an informal luncheon at one of the major hotels. Geoffrey Smith kept a low profile on the events, as did Paul, but my job was to act as a kind of chairman, or communicator at the table. I wore a lounge suit like the others, and apart from the Brits, none of the guests knew me or what I actually did for a living.

Luncheon began, usually around a large table, and seating was planned so that a British representative had a foreign invitee either side. Once the meal was under way, I introduced everyone, inviting them to say a few words about themselves and what they could offer or were looking for, after which I would start a round-the-table conversation about various facets of the convention and conference business. When lunch ended, the British representatives were able to make direct contact with potential clients.

These luncheons were held a couple of times a year for about four years, and involved us travelling to virtually every capital in Europe, usually doing two or three per trip. It was a delightful exercise for me as it was gentle, informal and very satisfying. It also gave us a few precious hours of leisure time in some of the most beautiful cities in the world and we all made the most of our freedom. Alas! it all had to stop. I was offered two more week-long trips to Europe – I was already busy with other bookings, so I suggested Lord Ponsonby of Shulbrede as a replacement. Tom Ponsonby was Chairman of the London Convention Bureau, a charming, feisty, very knowledgeable and charismatic gentleman. I knew that he would be ideal, and he was… so much so that I never got another look-in! That having been said, there were only a couple more tours before the BTA folded. We were all devastated when, shortly after these trips, Tom Ponsonby died, quite young, of cancer.

I have wonderful memories of trips all over the States and Europe 'selling Britain' in the best possible manner. I made many friends, plenty of contacts, and hope that I played a small part in persuading people to visit our shores. At one event, to fill in time at the end of a luncheon, and quite impromptu, I described, in detail, a journey from Heathrow to The Tower of London. I literally made it up as I went along, including all the historical places of interest. Geoffrey Smith was so taken with this that it became a regular slot in all future events. He called it 'A beautiful word-picture of our great city!'

A client of mine was friendly with Dali Tambo, the son of Oliver Tambo, the President of the African National Congress. Oliver Tambo's presidency covered the final years of incarceration of the Deputy President Nelson Mandela. My client called me one day and told me of a special cocktail party to be held in a modest house in North London, coincidentally about a mile from where we used to live in Muswell Hill. There were only to be about fifty people, but he needed someone to preside over it.

When I arrived at this house, it was full of activity – people tidying up, making the place spick and span and preparing a buffet, but it was in chaos. I asked if they would like some professional assistance so far as presenting the food was concerned; they agreed and I telephoned Ann to come and help. She took charge and presented the buffet admirably. We had been told that they were expecting a special guest of honour but were not certain whether or not he could be there.

Nelson Mandela had been released from prison only a week or so before and had travelled to England. Oliver Tambo lived in this house and Mr Mandela was hoping to visit. About thirty minutes before the official guests were due to arrive, the great man himself appeared amid a buzz of excitement and euphoria. He was happy, smiling and full of life, but years in prison had taken their toll and he was looking thin and gaunt.

After all the enthusiasm of his greetings, he retired to a drawing room where Ann and I were just sitting, waiting for things to begin. We were formally introduced to this wonderful man, who sat and spoke with us for about fifteen minutes – he was most charming and charismatic. He was gentle and kind and appeared to have absolutely no animosity towards his captors about whom he spoke with considerable respect. Eventually, guests began to appear and our audience ended. It left us both with an indelible impression of a very special and courageous man and we agreed that it was a privilege simply to be in his company.

Chapter 15

Some Special Friends

"To life, to life, l'chaim…
l'chaim – it means to life…"

Fiddler on the Roof

As Chairman of *Toastmaster Training Limited*, a job I held for twelve years, it was my responsibility to lecture on Jewish celebrations and traditions. I would begin by asking the candidates if they knew how many Jews there are in the UK, the answers I received being mostly in the millions. They were astounded to learn that there are actually no more than 350,000 Jews throughout the land, and that is an upper figure. Despite their apparent small numbers, their influence on the British economy is immeasurable and their ability as professionals in law, accountancy, medicine and the property market is legendary.

So far as my connection with the Jewish community goes, there is no other section of society that has been more influential, prolific or lucrative, and I am deeply grateful to them. Their flair for celebrating is second to none, their eagerness to hold a party, a banquet or ball is phenomenal, and they need little excuse to 'have an affair', their words for a *simcha* or celebration. And bless their generous hearts, they almost always use the services of a professional toastmaster.

In the fifty or so years that I have been privileged to officiate at these celebrations, I have come to know many families personally. I know what makes them tick, I know their likes and dislikes, I know their idiosyncrasies, and more than anything else, I have learned how to handle them; they really are unique. In celebrating with them, and even grieving with them, I feel honoured to have been accepted without question into their midst.

In my experience, I have found most Jews to be insular in their religion and in no way evangelistic; you are either a Jew or you are not, and they respect you either way. If anyone expresses a desire to become a Jew, they go to great lengths to dissuade them, but if determined, then they will do all in their power to educate, guide and advise. I have said repeatedly, if I was in need of spiritual guidance or personal counselling, I would seek advice from a Rabbi in preference to a Christian minister, and by saying this I mean no offence to my non-Jewish friends.

I am in no position to speak about other religions with such authority, simply because I have had so few dealings with them. However, the occasional functions I have done over the years confirms my view that they are equally generous and kind.

In addition to many weddings, barmitzvahs, anniversaries and funerals, I have been involved in various fund-raising events. The huge majority of British Jews are supremely generous, and the number of occasions when I see the same faces over and over again providing financial support is immeasurable. They often joke with me, saying that I am an Honorary Jew. I take this as a compliment, but reply, "I am not Jewish 'coz I simply can't afford it!"

I cannot abide anti-Semitism and will challenge it whenever I hear it. People who make defamatory statements about Jews and castigate them for their beliefs simply neither know nor understand them. I have heard hundreds of passionate speeches proclaiming that their one aim in life is peace. They are not by nature antagonistic, but they are stout defenders of what they fervently believe to be theirs, and will defend themselves and their families with every fibre in their bodies.

This is neither the time nor the place for me to be politically controversial, but I cannot allow any comment or book about my life to pass without expressing my deep thanks and gratitude to the many Jews who have taken me into their hearts during my long career.

I have worked in Israel several times, and met many of their great leaders. Prime Minister Golda Meir was a wonderful woman; I heard her speak several times and she was just magnificent. She was everyone's *Booba* (grandmother) – kind, intelligent, eloquent, a passionate defender of peace and a great leader of her nation. There was also Moshe Dayan and Menachem Begin, but the one I remember most clearly was Yitzhak Rabin. He was a gentle, kind and deeply sincere man whose one aim in life was to try to settle the disputes around Israel's borders. He paid for his deeply-held beliefs with his life, much to the sorrow of all who knew or who had met him. It was later my privilege to meet his widow who was particularly courteous and generous to me.

Two stories I wish to relate concern the same man, the late Sir Eric Miller who was a Companion Rat. His daughter, Linda, was getting married, and when he asked me to look after proceedings at The Dorchester, I asked, "Who's your band?" He replied, "Well, actually I have three bands: Kenny Ball and his Jazzmen during the reception, Judd Solo (another Water Rat), and The Count Basie Band from the USA." Seeing the surprised look on my face, he added, "The Musicians' Union won't let me bring in an American band unless I give work to British musicians, which is why I have three."

Count Basie had just about the hottest band in the world at that time and news spread that they were to play at The Dorchester. I have never seen so many musicians at one gig in all my life; there were dozens of them. When anyone asked who they were playing for that evening, they all said, "Judd Solo!" Judd, who normally had an eight-piece band, suddenly ended up with about 46 musicians if everyone was to be believed! The Basie Band was phenomenal.

Eric also invited Ann and me to a private dinner party in the River Room of The Savoy two days later just to hear The Basie Band. With only sixty guests and a twenty-piece orchestra, for two hours of great Big Band sound, it was simply fabulous. Some years later, Eric invited us to his son's barmitzvah in Jerusalem – it proved to be a memorable five days. A specially chartered *British Airways* jumbo jet flew 160 friends from London to Jerusalem to help celebrate Robert's coming of age. Aboard were Tommy Trinder and his wife Toni, Sir Douglas and Lady Bader, a couple of Labour politicians, and Lord and Lady Mais. Lord Mais had been the Lord Mayor of London and was Treasurer of The Venerable Order of the Hospital of St John of Jerusalem – more commonly known as St John Ambulance – this trip enabled him to pay the hospital a visit.

Eric was fundamentally a very shy man and more or less passed everything over to me to lead and guide his guests, particularly the non-Jews. On the day of the barmitzvah, I was to tell them exactly what was to happen, where they were to go, how they were to dress, how they were to behave, the format of the ceremony and everything connected with it. Throughout, they had to follow my lead, as most of them had no idea or concept of the celebration.

We duly left The King David Hotel on the Saturday, *Shabbat*, morning to begin the long walk to the Western Wall. Orthodox Jews do absolutely nothing on *Shabbat* but simply wash, dress, eat and pray – this meant that the only way to the barmitzvah was by 'Shank's pony'. We entered narrow gates into the hallowed area and walked down a slope where many Jews were praying, leaving little paper notes, prayers, in the cracks in the Western (Wailing) Wall. Down in the far corner was a small door, on the other side of which was an enormous cavern stretching about 100 yards. There were at least half a dozen other ceremonies and ours was at the furthest end of the cavern. Women are not permitted to enter that sacred ground, so Robert's mother and the other women had to stand behind a small railing. Their view of the ceremony was limited and it also looked most uncomfortable, but if you choose to have your *Simcha* in Jerusalem, such rules have to be observed.

At the end of the 90 minute ceremony – with no chairs! – we all left the Synagogue, for that is really what it is, and walked back to the hotel. Our route took along the *Via Dolorosa*, the route travelled by Jesus Christ to his crucifixion, which I was at great pains to point out to my 'followers'. It is now lined with merchants' stalls selling everything you could wish to buy in Jerusalem. The barmitzvah luncheon was formal with the usual speeches and prayers, but of course with no music, this being the Sabbath.

We were there for five days and Eric had arranged a variety of entertainments and outings from which we could choose. Ann and I selected Masada, a few miles from Jerusalem beside the Dead Sea, where a number of our party chose to swim. The sea is so strongly salty that it is impossible to sink although, interestingly, the river flowing into it is fresh water – no one has been able to explain this strange phenomenon.

About thirty of us went in a coach and on arrival climbed to the top of Masada which, perched as it is on a steep mound, is virtually impregnable – it is one of the most revered and hallowed places in the whole of Israel. The story is that the Romans discovered there were about one thousand Jews living a very successful and happy existence up there. Military leaders told their soldiers that Masada must be captured at all costs and so they camped around it. The encampments would have been clearly visible from the top, a terrifying ordeal for all the Jewish families outnumbered enormously and with no means of escape.

Gideon, our wonderful Israeli guide, related the story of Eleazar ben Yair, an elder, who summoned everyone together and gave an impassioned address.

As suicide is forbidden in Rabbinic law, the men killed the women and children, and then each other until Eleazar alone was remaining. He, being the last to be alive on Masada, then committed suicide. Two women and five children, who hid in the water ducts and tanks, eventually escaped to tell the tale.

Beneath a cloudless blue sky, under the canopy of Heaven in this most historic and religious nation, Gideon produced a small pamphlet containing Eleazar's Oration. Beckoning me over, he asked me to read it to the assembled company.

> Since we long ago resolved never to be servants
> to the Romans, nor to any other than to God
> Himself, Who alone is the true and just Lord of

mankind, the time is now come that obliges us to make that resolution true in practice... We were the very first that revolted, and we are the last to fight against them; and I cannot but esteem it as a favour that God has granted us, that it is still in our power to die bravely, and in a state of freedom...

... let our wives die before they are abused, and our children before they have tasted slavery, and after we have slain them, let us bestow that glorious benefit upon one another mutually for it will be a testimonial when we are dead that we were not subdued for want of necessities; but that, according to our original resolution, we have preferred death before slavery.

This was one of the most moving moments in my career, knowing the depths of tragedy it encapsulated, the horror and sorrow of over one thousand Jews from babies to grandparents agreeing to self-destruction, especially as this proclamation had been delivered, many thousands of years ago, on the spot where I was standing.

In the very early part of the 20th century, a refugee family named Moses settled in London's East End ghettos. Alfred Moses, the head of the family was, by trade, in the *schmutter* business; he was a tailor who struggled to make a living to feed his family. He built a good reputation of quality and reliability and enjoyed moderate success before passing the business on to his two sons.

One day a friend called upon one of the brothers and said, "Moshe, mein friend, I vant dat you lend me a' overcoat. I've gotta go to a funeral tomorrow; it's cold and I don't haf von! Please. Vot can you do for me 'coz I sure as hell can't afford to buy one?" After a brief thought the brother agreed, but suggested that his friend give him a shilling for the service so that he could get it cleaned. All was agreed. News of this new rental 'service' slowly spread amongst the very poor local Jewish community, which many used when they had to attend barmitzvahs, weddings and funerals.

The brothers decided to extend the rental business and go into it seriously. All was agreed – except the name. Moses Brothers did not seem right so they hit upon the idea of removing the 'E' from their name and calling themselves Moss. It was a very short step to the now famous name we all know – and *Moss Bros* was born.

Way back in the 1950s, I used to meet Harry Moss, his wife and their son Montague and wife Jane at The Grand Hotel, Folkestone, each Christmas and struck up a friendship with them. Monty is an extremely good after-dinner speaker and a great wordsmith whom I met many times at functions; indeed, his son Andrew and my son Tim went to the same pre-prep school together. He would recount many stories about the Moss family and their idiosyncrasies, one of which I loved to tell referring to all the articles of clothing they used to buy in to put into their rental and costume hire business.

Harry Moss stood about five feet tall in his stocking soles; small, feisty with a great sense of fun and a twinkle in his eye. The company would be inundated with dozens of articles of all types of clothing, which people wished to dispose of and would send to them to buy. It was a ritual enacted for many years and never varied. Every Wednesday, the Board would go into a special room, lock the doors and prepare to inspect the goods. Everything that was sent in would be piled high, and little Harry, five feet nothing, would put them on and model the lot! Yes, everything. It mattered not whether it was a jacket for a six foot six giant, a pair of jodhpurs, a shirt from a fat man, a pair of trousers with a 50-inch waist, a redundant nurse's uniform or anything someone wanted to sell – little Harry would stride up and down the room in front of his colleagues. From the way it 'looked on him', they could price accordingly – they never failed to hit the right price.

Chapter 16

Driving

"Every time 'he opens 'is marf, 'e puts 'is foot in it!"

Anon

I have been able to drive a car since I was about ten years old. Illegally, Dad used to allow me to drive occasionally, either on private land or quiet roads, and I never had any problems. At the age of seventeen and one month I had my first formal driving lesson from a bloke called Alf Coppen – you see, I even remember that 54 years later. He had a little old *Morris 12*, which was a delight to drive.

On my very first lesson, he asked me to sit behind the wheel and said, "Well, do you know what to do? Have you ever driven a car before?" Being brash and over-confident as I then was ('So, what's new?' I can hear many say), I replied, "Yes."
"OK. Start the engine and drive on."
I asked, "What, now?"
"Yes, now. You said you'd driven a car, so go on, drive this one."

To say I was astounded is an understatement, but I duly did as I was asked. I started the engine, found first gear, which I carefully engaged (of course, this was all double de-clutch in those days) and pulled away from the kerb. I confess to a sudden thought flitting through my mind that maybe I had made a mistake and that this was not a lesson, and that somehow I was already taking the test. Oh, the arrogance of the lad!

We drove along for about a mile when Alf told me to stop. He shattered me with his next remark. "OK. Just tell me, who have you ever seen drive like that?" It was back down to earth with a bump. Suitably chastened, I had to admit to 'nobody', to which his gentle reply was, "Fine. Now I'll teach you how to drive properly."

Alf Coppen was a super bloke whom I grew to like. At the end of the first hour, he asked how many lessons I had booked in advance, and when I told him three, he said, "OK. You can apply for your test right away. You'll be ready by then." I booked the test and arranged for a further three hours: one for a lesson, one for a refresher and the third for the test itself. So, I actually had only five hours of a professional teaching me how to drive.

The day of the test duly came. Alf had warned me that at the Wood Green Driving Testing Office there was one examiner who was a right bastard and who failed 'bloody everybody'. You've guessed it – when I signed in, I was told that he was to be my passenger for the next hour. Alf saw me walking out of the office and gave me a look as if to say, "Tough luck, old son. Better luck next time!"

Every inch of my test is indelibly imprinted in my memory; I remember every question; I remember in great detail the route, especially as it was all around Wood Green where I had played as a kid. When it came to the three-point turn I failed to notice a small barrow parked opposite, making a turn in three manoeuvres impossible. Notwithstanding this little problem, I did the first part, which put the barrow right in front of me. I stopped, reversed, and went forward again, in what was now a five-point turn.

My hill-starts were perfect, but I think the thing that swayed this miserable old geezer was what happened on the way back to the office. I had to stop on a hill before turning right as a bus was coming the other way. The driver stopped to let me go and, having completed an unscheduled hill-start, as I passed in front of the bus, I waved and gave him a courtesy 'thanks' – which I still do to this day. We got back to the office and pulled up. The examiner then asked me, "Why do you look down at the gear stick each time you need to change gear?" This nearly threw me, but I've since learned that it was something of a trick question. I thought for a second and replied, "I'm sorry, but I hadn't realised that I did. Thank you for letting me know, and I'll be more careful in future." This seemed to satisfy him, but if I'd have said something implying that I needed more time to get to know the car better, I could possibly have failed.

The examiner then said, "You'll be pleased to know that you have passed. Congratulations, it was a most pleasant drive." And with that he gave me a pink form – a yellow one was failure – and got out. I was over the moon with excitement and, as there was space in front of me, I actually drove the car twenty yards forward... legally, as I was now a qualified driver.

I saw Alf coming towards me from a café with some other instructors and I waved my pink form at him. He ran up and was as thrilled as I was. We parted company and I never saw him again, but I remember him with great affection. He was a man with whom I had spent only a few hours of my life but I shall never forget him.

My Uncle Lennie was a Master Butcher with shops in Hendon. However, he was also a dabbler in second-hand cars and would buy up any old heap of junk for a pittance, get it knocked into shape to sell and knock it out for a few quid profit. Dozens of cars must have passed through his hands and he loved the wheeler-dealer side of it. Words like selling ice cream to Eskimos come to mind. The trouble was that Uncle Lennie used to get these bangers, for that's all they were, from all over the place and he would say to me, "Brian (God! How I hate that name, but that's what it was in those days!), I've just paid a bloke a tenner for an *Austin Seven Ruby* over in Camberwell. Will you pop over and get it for me? There's the money to give him. All you've got to do is make sure it's got petrol, and bring it back here!" That's all? That was all!

Oh boy, what a car! The year was 1951 and there was little traffic around. Now *Austin Sevens* always were a problem, the main one being that there is absolutely no gap in the clutch between disengaged and engaged; you lift your foot up and Oooops, you're in gear, and if you're not prepared for it you lurch and stall. It was a peculiarity with all *Rubies*; I ought to know, I owned a couple. The trouble with the car I had to collect was that, notwithstanding this crummy clutch, there was no starter motor as it was broken! The only way it would start was with a starting handle already fixed to the front. That's why Uncle Lennie only paid a tenner for it!

So, on my way back from Camberwell to Wood Green, I kept stalling the damned thing, and every time I did I had to get out, swing the starting handle and rush back in before it stalled again. But that was not all. Oh no! What neither he nor I had been told was that the driver's door lock was broken and so the door just kept flying open. The only way to keep it shut was for me to put my elbow out of the window – which, incidentally, was also faulty – onto the outside of the door and simply hold it shut. So, what with a lousy clutch, no starter, a broken driver's door, a window that would not wind up or down and very dodgy steering, I learned yet another lesson in driving.

Uncle Lennie duly had it 'knocked into shape' and flogged it on for about £50. During my teens, I must have driven dozens of that type of car, which was great fun and terrific experience.

My vehicle ownership is hugely varied – *Austins, Vauxhalls* (about six), *Auburns, Willys Overland, Fords* by the handful, *Rovers* and many more. I had an *Armstrong Siddeley* 'Fluid Flywheel', and every time I went over a bump in the road, all the doors flew open. Then there was a small *Renault Dauphine*. When I called in to my local *Vauxhall* garage for some petrol, the owner, Roger Holmes, came over and said, "When are you gonna get one for the other foot?" People can be so rude at times!

One car I owned nearly got Ann and me a divorce… even before we were engaged. It was a huge, very old *Morris* 28-horsepower with a great long bonnet. It had belonged to the twenty-stone owner of *Hendon Hall Hotel* and his equally large wife. The bucket seats had sunk right down to the floor, making it virtually impossible for my 5' 2" girlfriend to see out of the front window. Ann and I went on a picnic; it rained and, oh boy, was it not a complete disaster! This great lumbering car was like a tank. I loved it, and driving along a lane, I saw a huge puddle so I put my foot

248

down and belted through it, thinking it would be great fun. WRONG! Ann got soaked, twice: once through the open sunroof (the sun was now shining), and once through the holes in the floorboards! She was not amused! She was even less amused when the car stopped and refused to move. Thankfully, as far as she was concerned, we were within 200 yards of her house, but this did nothing to dispel her embarrassment of being seen with such a disaster – the car, I mean, not me! The prop shaft had gone and I had to be towed all the way back from Dulwich to Wood Green, having had a lousy day and nearly losing the girl I loved. I eventually took it to the auctions in Alexandra Palace and saw the car I adored go under the hammer for £85 – I said goodbye to an old friend… not Ann, thank God.

I next bought an old *Austin Seven Ruby* – no, not the one from Uncle Lennie – and when I took Ann home in it, we would have a little 'snog' before she went indoors. Her mother said to Ann, "Will you please ask your young man not to park that dreadful little car outside our house? Tell him to go round the corner and leave it there." No, they weren't snobs, but Dulwich was a nice neighbourhood and thirty-year old bangers did not sit well with the image of the district!

One night I did park the car round the corner in a quiet, dark street, but this was not to save their embarrassment, it was so that Ann and I could indulge in a bit of nooky! Just as we were getting sweatily passionate and having a good old time, suddenly the church clock chimed the hour and came crashing in on the whole damned scene. It was a horrible chime, and more in anger than jest I said, "That bleedin' clock doesn't sound like a bell – it sounds more like a bloody sledgehammer bashing a steel girder!" Ann creased up with laughter and any thoughts of more passion went straight out the window. Whenever we think of that today – fifty years later – we never fail to laugh about it!

The car that Ann remembers with great affection was a 10-hp *Ford Popular* which got christened by our daughter Tracy as 'the bompety car'. It really was a gem. We had virtually no money, but Ann needed a run-around, so we asked Uncle Lennie to look out for something cheap and cheerful which might just do us a turn. He found this ghastly little black *Ford Popular* which we drove around Wood Green for a couple of days. It smelled horrible, rattled, wheezed, made funny noises – hence the nickname – but, fair play, we did persevere. That is, until one memorable day when Ann decided to take the kids for a drive up to Alexandra Palace. Big mistake. Just before turning into the Palace, the car began making very strange noises and started going slower and slower. She turned into a road, which happened to be a very steep hill, and it simply gave up. It wheezed to a halt and refused to move. There was Ann with two very miserable kids, in a strange road, with no money, a broken-down old banger and me gone to work. It was then that Tracy, aged two years old, said, "Mummy, I *hate* this car. It's a bompety car and *it smells!*"

Ann did what any sensible, angry, frustrated and worried young mother would do and knocked on the nearest door of a private house. The lady owner was wholly sympathetic, invited them all in, gave them a glass of water and allowed Ann to use the telephone. Uncle Lennie rescued them, got them home and that was the last we saw of the bompety car. Incidentally, he sold it on for £25!

I have always had 'wheels'. From the day I passed my test, I acquired one and have never been without. Our son Tim was always very interested in them, and from the age of three was able to recognise every make on the road. On getting his degree at Brunel University, he went to work for *Ford's*, remaining there for five years before starting his own business. He once counted the cars I had owned and I believe it is somewhere in the thirties, but at heart I have always been a *Jaguar* man.

For years I did all the functions organised for the Jaguar Drivers Club. I certainly could not afford to buy one, but was delighted to be amongst *Jaguar* owners, and was even happier when the Committee made me an Honorary Life Member of the Jaguar Drivers Club. This is a position I still cherish, especially as I now only drive *Jags*. I still receive their monthly magazine in which I have placed a couple of articles.

Apart from flirting with ideas of owning a *Rolls Royce*, I have only ever wanted a *Jag*. I eventually began buying new ones from Hadley Green Garage, with whom I have had a reciprocal working relationship for years. They were *Jaguar* and *Rolls Royce* agents, and when I went to see Paul Green, son of the founding Chairman, Douglas, he said, "Bryn, I wouldn't sell you a *Rolls*. You are essentially a *Jag* man and a *Roller* wouldn't suit you!" Ann heartily agreed with this, and she has gone on record loads of times saying that if I ever bought a *Rolls*, she would leave me… and I honestly believe she would.

Owning cars as a teenager meant that my mates and I were always mobile, unlike most of our contemporaries; owning vehicles at such a young age was unheard of in those days. I also had complete freedom of use of Dad's cars, usually great big, second-hand American beasts like *Buicks, Oldsmobiles* and others. If he wasn't working, he would let us take the car, so long as we filled it with petrol. At five bob a gallon (25p in today's money), times were great, and divided between four of us it meant that we had reasonably cheap transport.

Paul MacDonald, John Dickens and Jimmy Denyer were my closest friends at that time. We went everywhere and did everything together for years. Our favourite sport was ice-skating. We loved it and went at least twice a week, mainly to Harringay Arena – alas! no longer there. We became quite good skaters and had some great times. We also supported the Harringay Racers ice hockey team. There were about ten in a league in England, and we were ardent supporters, although it was all a bit weird really. Ice hockey certainly ain't a natural English sport, so virtually all of the players were from Canada, with a few from the USA.

Being the fastest team sport in the world, it was wildly exciting and we never missed a match, even hinting at trying to play the game ourselves. As skaters we were certainly good enough, but, like all dreams, they were shattered and it never happened. However, ice-skating did introduce me to the only other girl I thought was nice and with whom I felt I could build a relationship.

As I have said elsewhere, my mother was fiercely protective of 'her little boy', and even the mention of a possible girlfriend was seriously frowned upon. I can only recall one occasion in my early years before I met Ann, that I actually told her of a girl who was a friend rather than a 'girlfriend'. Her name was Shirley Whiter and we were at Pitman's College together. I brought her home to our flat on one occasion with my parents there. They liked her, but it never developed and that was the end of it.

This overt protection meant that we four pals never even discussed 'girls' in the presence of my parents. As a change from Harringay, we began to go over to Wembley Ice Rink to skate, and it was here that John and I met a couple of lovely girls – the one I liked was called Pat Taylor. She was quiet, shy, diffident and pretty, and I became quite fond of her. We would meet every Sunday evening and she told me that she worked for a perfume company in the 'blending' department. However, as her job was secret, I never knew the name of it. I visited her home a couple of times and met her parents. Regrettably they were not on the telephone, so I could not contact her between skating 'trysts'. It could possibly have developed until...

Whereas I was a good driver – or so I thought – I had never been schooled in the art of handling a skid. Returning home from Wembley one night with Paul and Jimmy in my Dad's massive *Oldsmobile* 30-hp, the traffic lights at Hoover Corner decided to change from green to red. It had been raining and the road was still a bit wet, so when I put my foot down hard on the brake, the wheels locked and this huge monster of a car slewed round sideways and smashed into a traffic light, knocking it over. There we were, stuck, with a dented wing, wheels buckled and completely locked into the traffic light, so that was that.

However, the big snag as far as I was concerned was that we were not supposed to be in Ealing where it happened. We had told my parents that we were playing table tennis in a club in Edmonton. Jimmy worked for the Gas Board and was a member of the Tottenham Games, Athletic and Sports Club, or 'GAS Club' as it was called. We spent hours there playing table tennis and snooker.

"So what the b******g hell were you all doing in Ealing?" The truth had to be told that we had been ice-skating… I did not dare mention Pat Taylor or the balloon would have gone even higher.

We got home, the car was repaired, and I had to find £150 to pay for the traffic light. So far as cars were concerned, we were grounded. Yes, "No more cars for you, my boy, until further notice!" 'Further notice' was several months hence, making it impossible for us to go far, especially as far as Wembley. As I had absolutely no means of contacting Pat, I could not tell her what had happened. When we eventually got our 'wheels' back, we went over to there to skate again. Oh yes, Pat and her friend were still there, but alas and alack! the old spark which she may have had for me had long since fizzled out and it was not the same. We drove home very carefully and never returned.

I often wonder what happened to Pat. She was lovely and I still feel it might have developed. It certainly was not serious, just very pleasant. As I have told Ann many times, whereas she had many boyfriends with real possibilities of a future together, I only had one, gentle fling with a girl I met no more than a couple of dozen times and with whom I never went out. Ann really has been the only love in my life.

* * * * *

The second half of this chapter also concerns my love of driving – driving in the guise of golf. A tenuous link, I admit, but it's my book, so you're lumbered. And for those not interested in golf, if you've got this far in the chapter, you might as well read on!

Around 1946, my parents met someone who gave them an interest in golf and they were persuaded to take a look at Muswell Hill Golf Club, which vies with The North Middlesex as being the nearest golf club to either the City of London or the West End. My parents were instantly hooked, found the money to join and began a love affair with the game which took them all over the UK and lasted for well over thirty years, by which time Dad boasted that he had played on over 200 courses and, as he had a photographic memory, he could remember individual holes on most of them. For years they went with my Auntie Lillie and Uncle Bernard, and played golf and bridge all over the place from the north of Scotland to the depths of Cornwall. The four of them had been married at a double wedding and remained close all their lives.

I was introduced to golf when I was 14, and I appeared to have an aptitude for the game. It was about then that another of my mother's 'lame ducks' came into our lives in the person of Matt Forster, a Geordie ex-Tottenham Hotspur footballer who was exactly the same age as Dad, bar one month. He was a glorious golfer, playing off a handicap of one, and was a brilliant ball player at any game he touched. But in life he was one long failure, and the term 'no fixed abode' virtually applied to him. So what did my mother do? She invited him home to supper one evening – twelve years later he left... to get married to a lady thirty years his junior! There were two beds in my small room, and Matt had one of them. Anything like that happening today would be unheard of, but he was a friend in need and we provided the accommodation. There was one consolation... boy oh boy, did I learn about golf!

Matt was a regular first team player at Muswell Hill, which could field eight players with a handicap of two and better. They were glorious days as the club kept winning prizes. Matt bought every book published on the game and would read them avidly in bed every night. In return for our hospitality, he instructed all of us and we became accomplished golfers. Dad's best handicap was around 15, and Mum almost got into the Ladies Silver Division with a handicap of 18. She was well built and hit the ball a long way; she represented Muswell Hill in inter-club matches dozens of times with much success.

As I grew older with loads of time on my hands, I joined them playing courses throughout the country. We toured Scotland, and I remember some wonderful games at St Andrews, Troon, Carnoustie and all the great courses in the home of golf. Our golf was good and we had some memorable times. I eventually got into single figures and could regularly knock around the course in the high 70s. I teamed up with four or five other chaps about my age and we played every Saturday or Sunday morning for years – our handicaps were all between 6 and 8 and the competitiveness was fierce.

As Matt was a student of golf, he experimented with different grips, styles of swing and other variants as advocated by the great and the good of the game. He would frequently ask me to try the overlapping, the double-palm, the interlocking and Vardon grips, and we used to practise our golf swings in the long passageway in our flat, resulting in the ceiling being covered in smudges as we over-enthusiastically 'followed through'. We didn't care; after all, it was only a lick of paint.

Reg Horne was a good club professional at Hendon for many years. He saw me playing one day and asked my parents if they would allow me to become his assistant and be taught as a professional – apparently, he thought that I had potential! This was a huge compliment as he was in the top flight of British golf, having played in the Ryder Cup. Coincidentally, I had already been approached by the pro at Dunstable Downs with a similar offer, but my potential as a toastmaster was apparent and it was wisely pointed out that if I became a golf pro, my hobby would be my profession, as opposed to making a living elsewhere and still playing the game I loved for fun. I therefore declined, but felt flattered to have been asked. It was a wise decision.

While I played a lot of golf in my twenties and thirties, I did not sustain the standard that I had achieved. Oh yes, I still have a natural swing, and when, infrequently, I go on a course, I still strike the ball quite well, but as in every sport, practise is essential if standards are not to deteriorate. Work commitments meant that golf had to take a back seat, but I still find it highly enjoyable to play the occasional round with one or other of the societies of which I am a member... although, sadly, this is becoming less often with age!

Another of my mother's lame ducks was Jack Cullen, a single-figure golfer and a rep for *Dunlop*. Despite living in Bristol, Jack was a country member of Muswell Hill, and we often played together. As his employer supplied most of the golf balls used in the major tournaments, Jack had the less than onerous task of having to attend. Jack was the clothing rep. for *Dunlop*, and so he took packages of trousers, jackets and other clothes. As he had to go to the Open Championship in St Andrews with a carload of golfing paraphernalia, he asked if I would help share the driving. It would be an all-expenses trip for about four days, paid for by *Dunlop*. Needless to say, for a 17-year-old like me this was an opportunity not to be missed.

We arrived on the first practice day and checked into our hotel. Things were vastly different in those days and, as there were no fund-raising pro-ams, the competitors would simply have the odd round to test lengths and conditions, or would spend time on the driving range. It was so casual and so totally different from today's high-tech, highly efficient, highly financed competitions.

I had my clubs with me and was standing idly on the first tee when three English pros came out for a practice round – Peter Alliss, Harry Weetman and Bernard Hunt. They teed off, saw me standing there and asked, "Would you like to join us for a few holes?" Oh boy, oh boy, oh boy, what a question! Would I? Wow! "Yes, please, yes I would." And so I played the first six holes at St Andrews with them. It was bliss, especially as I didn't let myself down. Their method of 'practising' for a major tournament was simply to play two or three more shots if their original shot did not please them. It's all yard count, distances, pin placements and a whole load of other statistics which now dominate the top class game – it has become far too technical for my liking! I had had the most wonderful experience of my young golfing life, thanks to Jack Cullen, a 'lame duck' friend of Mum's.

I owe a lot to golf, for which I am grateful, but it also became my downfall and taught me an important lesson. John Paramor, son of the late Norry Paramor, was and is a lovely golfer, having the distinction of winning both the Middlesex Amateur and Professional Championships. He married the daughter of one of our members at Muswell Hill and is a super bloke. Apart from being Secretary of the Volvo Golf European Tour and its senior referee, he is the organiser of the dinner immediately prior to the English Masters at Wentworth at which I was the toastmaster for a number of years.

I also used to work at an annual Golf Ball at The Grosvenor House chaired by The Earl of Derby. As it was run on behalf of the Professional Golfers' Association, quite a few pros would attend. In the fateful year to which I refer, Europe had won the Ryder Cup when it was played in Spain. The non-playing Captain, Bernard Gallagher, was at the ball, at which The Cup was proudly displayed. When he came to the floor to make his speech, the crowd gave him a well-deserved reception. It was then that the devil must have got into me.

Commercialisation had reared its ugly head, and stringent contracts with *Sky TV* meant that absolutely no coverage of the Ryder Cup appeared on any other channel. There was a lot of money involved, but it meant that the vast majority of the British population without *Sky* did not see a single shot of our great achievement. Being somewhat peeved at this state of affairs, I took the unprecedented step of using the microphone to vent my feelings, saying something like: "Isn't it a pity that the powers-that-be who govern what we watch on television did not allow one single shot of the Ryder Cup to be shown on terrestrial TV? I heard that Nick Faldo's approach shot to the 17th on the final day was one of the finest of his life, and most of us were prevented from seeing it!" Not a great career move!

I received a huge round of applause from the vast majority who agreed with my spontaneous outburst, and who, like me, did not own cable television. But boy, did I say the wrong thing as far as the PGA and European Tours were concerned! Months had been spent negotiating the contract for exclusive coverage and all the *Sky* bosses were there. Not only were they furious with me, but there had been no provision for them to reply.

I was and to this day remain totally unrepentant, and as people left the building, dozens told me how much they agreed with what I had said. A former Tory Minister for Sport echoed these sentiments, as for months he had been striving in Parliament to protect the 'Sports

Crown Jewels' for the nation, ensuring events like The Ryder Cup, Wimbledon, the Boat Race and the FA Cup, among other national sporting treasures, remained on terrestrial television. It is a testimony to his efforts and possibly my indiscretion, that very shortly afterwards a law was passed to that effect, and that those competitions we value are available on our usual channels. All test matches are now on satellite television, with none on terrestrial – a huge financial reward for cricket, but lousy for the supporters!

I received a very strongly-worded letter from the Secretary of the PGA; I had burnt my boats as far as the professional golfing world was concerned. It is also significant that the ball at which all this occurred ceased to be held, and I believe the organisers got into some kind of hot water. I remain unrepentant!

When I was speaking regularly on the Ladies Luncheon Club circuit, I sorted out stories which I knew they would enjoy hearing – whether I was personally involved in them or not did not matter. I regularly recounted one which I heard and which they loved, as it always made them laugh. It was actually told at a banquet by Prince Philip about himself and referred to a trip he and the Queen made early in her reign. They were both very young, but even in those early days he had the propensity of 'putting my foot in it'! I tell it as I heard it, but would add that several times since, I have mentioned it to him and he concurs that it is true.

> The Queen and I were to make an official visit to Canada. After long discussion, it was decided that rather than fly to various cities, we would begin at the east coast and travel west by train, stopping at towns and villages along the way, thereby enabling us to meet more people of that great country. The format was simple and more or less the same at each stop.

258

The train would pull into the station and, after our security chaps had checked things, the Queen, dutifully followed by me, would step onto the platform to be greeted by all the civic dignitaries. We would meet The Mayor, The President of Rotary, Chief of Police, the leading Church Minister, heads of all the local committees and anyone else they thought important. We would spend a happy hour or so strolling around their town, possibly have a cup of tea and a biscuit, and return to the train. Having said our farewells, we would board the train and the signal was given to move on to the next port-of-call. At that moment and at each town, as the train moved away, the local town band would strike up a tune to play us out.

After about the seventh, or it could have been the tenth, time this occurred, it struck me as being rather sad for the local band, who had probably rehearsed one particular tune for weeks for our benefit, that we never actually got to hear it; rather recklessly, I chanced to mention this to the organisers!

At the next stop, the ritual was repeated; the train stopped, security guards leapt out, followed by the Queen and me and our entourage. We met the Mayor, the President of Rotary, The Chief of Police, the senior vicar, committee chairmen, and anyone else they thought important, ambled up and down their main street, had a cup of tea and biscuit and eventually returned to the station. On this occasion, the message had got ahead that we would like to hear the band play. So, instead of boarding the train, we all remained standing on the platform chatting away merrily. At this precise moment someone cued the bandmaster to begin playing their pretty little tune – which they did …whereupon, the train pulled out!

So, you see, I was capable of opening my mouth and putting my foot in it even in those early days.

Chapter 17

Stars and Stripes

"Come fly with me, let's fly, let's fly away."

Sammy Cahn

There are four Inns of Court: Lincolns, Grays, Inner Temple and Middle Temple, and for one year their Chairman or most senior person is known as The Treasurer; a tradition based in the mists of time. Sir Martin Nourse, a former Deputy Master of the Rolls, was Treasurer of Lincoln's Inn. I have known him and his wife Lavinia for years, not least through her organisation of many functions – she used my services for everything she ran and one particular event stands out in my mind as being 'different'.

Lavinia had been asked to run a huge charity bash in New York to coincide with *Phantom of the Opera's* opening night on Broadway. Andrew Lloyd Webber had already had great success with the show in London and it was to start a long, record-breaking run in the States. Adding glamour and glitz to the occasion, the newly-married Duchess of York was to be the guest of honour. It was one of the rare occasions when Ann came with me, and we also took our daughter Tracy for a few days' break.

There were three levels of guest depending upon how much they had donated. Curtain up on *Phantom* was timed for 7.30 pm, and the first level of guests was invited to a cocktail reception at six o'clock to meet HRH. Eventually, we all made it to the theatre, and Ann, Tracy and I were given seats in the front row of the dress circle. We had all seen the production in London, and Ann and

Tracy were thrilled to attend this great opening night. However, I didn't like it the first time and had no desire to watch it again, so I returned to the hotel to oversee things for the dinner.

Guests in the second category were entitled to meet HRH privately in the interval; the third group, who had paid very large sums, joined the royal party and stars of the show for a dinner at the Waldorf Astoria afterwards – a grand affair which went on until 1.00 am.

Over the coming years, I was privileged to be involved with many functions with which the Duchess of York was connected and she frequently wrote to me, signing her personal notes, "Bestest Love, Sarah." She is passionately devoted to her own charity, *Children in Crisis*, which she founded. She has raised millions of pounds for it and makes regular visits to those places all over the third world where the money has been directed and she does wonderful and essential work.

Many years ago, I did a function at The Dorchester for the *Boeing Company*. A banquet was held every year to coincide with the Farnborough Air Show – every other year, it is held in Paris. A lovely lady called Jan Graham ran the *Boeing* office at Heathrow and was virtually their sole agent over here. She was given the task of running this dinner and I was duly engaged. The chairman and top management of *Boeing* had no idea what I did, or why I was there, but agreed that, as they were dining in London, it would be a typically English banquet. This entailed a formal receiving line where I announced all the guests to the chairman – they were tickled pink by this, as they had never seen it done before. They also loved it when I announced dinner – in the US, people simply drift to their tables when they feel like it. It can be hell!

They had the full works: accompanied by a military band, the VIPs were led to the top table for Grace, and after dinner I persuaded them to have the Loyal Toast as well as a Toast to the President of the United States of America. I also introduced the speaker and, with the band on stage, I invited the chairman and his wife to begin the dancing. All this tradition and tarradiddle was totally alien to these Americans and they adored it. I did this function alternate years for a long time, and all of them loved to see me there to 'Do all that English traditional, formality stuff!'

The chairman was a Mr T Willson – in all the years I worked for them, I never discovered what the 'T' stood for. I tried guessing, asking around, probing, poking my nose in, but to this day I do not know what it is, although I believe – but only believe – it is something like Theophilus. Anyway, who cares? He and his wife were simply delightful and made a huge fuss of me every year.

Jan Graham called me one day and said that T was due to retire and the company were putting on a farewell dinner for him in Seattle, the home of *Boeing*. As a surprise for T, they wanted me to be there as toastmaster, together with the Band of HM Welsh Guards who regularly had played at The Dorchester dinners. All was arranged and dates were fixed.

It transpired that my trip to Seattle was the day after the New York *Phantom of the Opera* engagement. Ann and Tracy stayed on a couple of days in New York before flying back home, but I flew up to Seattle for a three-day stopover. I met Jan and The Welsh Guards at The Westin Hotel where the banquet was being held, and we planned what we were going to do at the dinner.

In over 55 years in the business, I have never seen anything like the arrival and reception part of this banquet for 650 guests. The enormous reception area had been totally transformed into the reception hall of 'The Grand Hotel' – a fictitious hotel, but with a long reception desk with concierges and receptionists. Guests went to the desk and gave their name, but instead of reading a table plan, or being given a place card, they were presented with a large brass key and disc, upon which was stamped their table number, while on the reverse was the logo of *Boeing*. I still have mine as it is unique. They were so well organised that they had had time to engrave over 650 keys with table numbers, thus making it impossible for any alterations if things went wrong.

Dressed in full red regalia, I went to the reception area to await the arrival of T and Mrs Willson. The look of absolute amazement on their faces when they saw me will live with me forever. To say they were surprised is an understatement; they were bowled over and greeted me more like a son than a toastmaster. The whole trip was worth it just for that momentary reaction.

It is the duty of any toastmaster to liaise closely with the banqueting management of the hotel; it is standard practice and any toastmaster who doesn't do it is courting disaster. I spoke to the Maitre d', who had never worked with a toastmaster before and was rather sceptical about my abilities. In the US, dinner is never announced. If the invitation states 7.30, then they arrive at any old time and wander into dinner whenever they feel like it; how they manage to run anything on time escapes me!

I asked the Maitre d', "What time is dinner to be served?" to which he replied, "Who knows? Whenever they get up here, I suppose. I guess around eightish." My reply was, "I thought it was scheduled for 7.30, but even that is tight as we have a special cabaret. Would you like me to have them seated promptly for 7.30?" He simply said, "Bryn, this is America. You'll never do it. Americans ain't like that. But sure, go right ahead and try!" In the area where 650 guests were chatting and supping champagne, I found a strong box, laboriously climbed up onto it, and hollered at the crowd for silence. There was a deathly hush – they'd never seen or heard anything like it before, and from that moment they hung on my every word. In stentorian British tones, I began with, "Your Royal Highness, My Lords (although neither of these were present, I gave them the full works!) Ladieeeeeees and Gentlemen, may I have your attention. Gentlemen, will you please put your drinks down and take your partner's arm. Dinner is now ready to be served upstairs in the banqueting hall and I would like you to escort your ladies to the dining tables right away. Thank you!" The roar of laughter and applause was huge, but to the great amazement and delight of the Maitre d', they obeyed my every command. Grace, or Benediction as they call it, was said at 7.30 pm precisely, possibly the first time in the history of banqueting in Seattle.

The next surprise for T was the performance of the Band of the Welsh Guards who, as usual, did a magnificent thirty-minute display of marching and counter-marching. There were to be two speeches, followed immediately by a surprise cabaret. I knew that it was Mel Torme with his full orchestra, an artiste, musician and singer I had revered for years. To think that I was to meet him and introduce him into cabaret was another dream come true. Whilst the last speaker was on, I went backstage and met Mel Torme. He was rather nervous, but perfectly charming and we had a chat. However, we both had half an ear on the speaker, who droned on and on for over thirty minutes, boring the pants off everyone. He was the worst speaker I had heard for years. Eventually, to a highly soporific and bored-stiff audience of international guests, his final words were, "So congratulations to T and Mrs Willson."

As if he had not done enough damage, he then went on to destroy the surprise of the night by saying, "We are now going to be entertained by a Mr Mel Torm!" (He left out the 'AY' bit!) Mel Torme turned to me in utter amazement and said, "Was that it? Was that my introduction? Did he actually say 'Torm'? Geez! I'm not even ready yet. I've got to get a 15-piece band on stage and tuned up!" He was furious, so I told him to leave it to me and I went to the front of the curtains. At the sight of this red-coated Englishman, whom they had come to like and who would certainly brighten things up after the previous speaker, I received a warm welcome. I started with, "This may come as something of a surprise to you, but contrary to popular belief, I am *not* Mel Torme!" It immediately raised the flat, lifeless atmosphere of the room. I continued, "We need a couple of minutes to prepare backstage, so chat among yourselves and I'll be back soon." Five minutes later, Mel Torme and band ready, I went out front again and gave him the build-up an artiste of his standing merited and, to a rousing ovation, he started.

Afterwards, I had some important domestic announcements to make and I took pleasure in teasing the crowd, making them giggle a bit, and I spoke in the purest English I could achieve – Ruth Conti would have been proud of me. It is my firmly-held belief that English people could read the telephone directory to Americans in perfect English and they would hang on every word. Frequently, on my trips to the States, people have said to me, "I don't care what you're sayin', Honey, but just keep talkin'!" I brought the evening to a resounding close with the promise of a highly unusual day on the morrow.

It has long been the custom with the *Boeing Company* (not Corporation as I used to think) that when they produce a newly designed aircraft, or a major modification to an existing one, they organise a special event known as a 'Rollout'! To celebrate T's retirement, they planned a rollout for two aircraft, the 747 and the 727, and we were all invited. To say that they are spectacular is an understatement; they are *sensational* and anyone privileged to attend will experience an event they will never forget. All 650 or so who attended the banquet, including the Welsh Guards Band and me, were classed as VIPs. You may not think that is very special, but when I tell you that all the workers at the *Boeing* factory were invited – some 12,000 – it puts things into perspective.

After breakfast, we boarded coaches from our hotel and were taken to one of the enormous airfields and led into a vast aircraft hangar. We were told that it was the largest unsupported roof in the world, and when you consider that in that huge factory they assemble several jumbo jets simultaneously, you can begin to imagine the size. After coffee and pastries, we were invited to sit facing an enormous display of single-colour drapes, alternately a red one, a white one and a blue one. Each had a drop of 100 or so feet, were at least thirty feet wide, and there were about a dozen of them across the end of the hangar. Above them, just below ceiling level, were several vast screens.

The *Boeing Company* is extremely staff-conscious and quick to praise the work done by members at every level. During the hour before the actual ceremony began, the screens projected pictures of every employee who had played any part in the construction of the aircraft, no matter how small. Accompanying the picture was a dialogue explaining that person's job. For example, the lady who stitched the covers of the seats, the electrician who wired up the cabins, the technician who had installed some small but vital part of the engine, the painters, the carpenters, the draughtsmen and women, the cleaners – the list was endless – but every employee who played any part in its construction was mentioned and thanked.

As the time for the ceremony approached, a procession of managers paraded on a stage just in front of us. Each was carrying a large banner with the logo and name of airlines around the world, with a commentary telling us how many aircraft they owned. For example, *Piedmont* 15, *Virgin Atlantic* 12, *British Airways*, etc. I forget the precise numbers, but there were dozens of them.

On the dot of eleven o'clock, all the lights were dimmed, fanfare music began and ever so slowly those red, white and blue drapes were drawn aside, gradually revealing one of the most majestic and awe-inspiring sights you can imagine. Behind them was a brand new, silver *Boeing 747*, brilliantly lit from all sides, shining and glittering like some gigantic mechanical bird. We were only a few feet away and so needed to look up at this great leviathan, gleaming in all its natural metallic glory. All new aircraft are silver; it is only when they are purchased by airlines that their particular livery is painted on. All around this hangar were the 12,000 employees and guests, roaring with delight at the splendour of this scene. It really was breathtaking. We could all see the underside of the wings and fuselage, and the great wheels and undercarriage were there right in front of us. It was impossible to absorb it all in the time available and, after a brief speech of thanks to everyone concerned, congratulations to the designers and builders and a farewell note, the ceremony ended, but not the entertainment of the day.

For the guests, there was to be a second rollout that afternoon at another airfield about thirty miles away. How do you move 650 people quickly? By bus of course! I have an everlasting impression of one particular but very small incident that occurred on that momentous day in Seattle. It demonstrated to me, with the utmost clarity, the total lack of hierarchical snobbery seen in many companies, especially in the UK. It amplified the genuine and sincere desire of the *Boeing* Board to subordinate themselves as simple employees of a great company and not a bunch of 'suits' who live in an ivory tower. My experience of British companies is for the management to be ferried by limousines or posh cars in descending order of seniority, each with a liveried chauffeur and containing two people. Not *Boeing*.

As I boarded one of the dozens of coaches – they call them buses – I was surprised to see T Willson and his wife waiting in line. I said, "Good morning, T. Where's your limo?" He said, "Oh, hi Bryn. Good morning. Limo? What Limo? I haven't got a Limo?" So, rather tamely, I said, "So you're riding with all of us!" To which he replied, "I work for *Boeing* just like everyone else, so I and all the board travel with them and our guests. Is there any other way?" He seemed genuinely surprised that I should think otherwise.

At the second airfield, we were directed to a roped-off area in a corner of another massive hangar; there were dozens of tables and chairs and a very long buffet. We duly collected our lunch from a display of superb food and drinks, and again found ourselves rubbing shoulders with board members, Vice-Presidents and *Boeing* staff all jostling for the tastiest bits. Not for them the private lunch, silver service by butlers and waitresses with vintage wines and all the trimmings. No! They were just employees of a company of which they were justly proud and they were delighted to mingle in with everyone else.

After lunch we were treated to another impressive rollout, only this time when the silver 'bird' was revealed, albeit a smaller one, it was well back behind the screens and literally rolled towards us. It was being towed by wires, and rolled at an oblique angle along a corridor until it was right in front of us with the nose and port wing immediately above. And there it stopped. It was a different presentation, but equally breathtaking and spectacular. To see this great silver beast rolling towards us in all its magnificence was just awe-inspiring and we all gazed up in wonderment and stupefaction. To quote an appropriate metaphor, we were flying high, thanks to an unforgettable day as guests of a wonderful company.

A further misapprehension was corrected for me that day – I assumed that *Boeing* staff received 'freebies' in the form of free or subsidised flights. I was wrong. Their very sensible philosophy is, "We sell them aircraft and make them pay for them. We do not think it is fair, therefore, to scrounge free flights as well. The airlines have to make a profit to be able to buy our product, so why should we make life difficult for them? No. Whenever we fly, whether in a *Boeing* or another make of aircraft, we pay!" Great and very intelligent thinking!

By eleven o'clock that night I had boarded my *PanAm* flight to London – first class, of course, thanks to *Boeing* – and slept the entire journey home. A wonderful way to conclude a memorable trip.

* * * * *

Bryan Langton (CBE came later) was a young trainee manager at the Café Royal. I met him when he was just out of catering college and learning the business, guided him along and watched him develop. Many years later he became the Chief Executive Officer of Holiday Inns International and was one of the many young lads I have known 'wot done well in the business!' He was a feisty Northerner, a real John Blunt, who deserved all his success as his knowledge of the hotel industry was exemplary. In 1981 he called me from Atlanta, Georgia, and told me he was the Chairman of the British Olympic Committee in the city which was to house the forthcoming Olympics and therefore in charge of fund-raising for our athletes. At that time, HRH Princess Anne was the Chairman of the Olympic Committee.

Bryan asked if I would be willing to come over to his hotel and look after a couple of fund-raising events that he was putting on in various cities, mentioning *en passant* that Princess Anne would be attending. The whole event was to be sponsored by *Coca Cola* whose directors were there in large numbers to keep a watching brief. "Would I?" I replied, "Just try and stop me," and we indulged in our usual friendly banter over money.

Somehow or other I screwed it up at Atlanta airport as I did not find the car they had sent to meet me, so I took a very expensive taxi ride to the Crown Plaza Hotel; more gentle flak from Bryan about spending 'his' money, but I could live with that. My room was on the executive floor and I learned later that Princess Anne was to be sleeping in the adjacent bedroom with inter-communicating doors – very heavily bolted with a detective sleeping outside! So, no chance there I thought. She arrived around mid-afternoon, was fêted, fed, watered and prepared for a large banquet and ball in the evening. About 500 attended the event which Bryan had organised specifically in an English style.

Many years ago, I invented my own system of organising raffles at banquets and other formal occasions. It consists of small, square cards upon which is printed:

RAFFLE TICKET
NAME ....
TABLE NUMBER ......

Utter simplicity, and I get them printed by the quarter million. I have used them hundreds of times and raised millions of pounds with that system, one which has now been copied by many of the larger national charities. Bryan asked me to bring a supply over for his functions and I set them up in the normal way, which is to place sufficient tickets into an envelope for about three per person at the table. During the dinner, I appoint a table 'Captain', usually with a gag or stupid method, who then sells the tickets around the table at the selected price. When they have done that, they write on the envelope the amount received, put the money into it, bring that and their tickets to me by the stage and hand it all over. As I said, it is utter simplicity, a system I have used in the presence of Princess Anne many times. Indeed, she now knows it so well that, whenever we are together at a charity bash, she gets on with the sale of the tickets without waiting for my directions. All she needs to know is what is being charged.

There was one instance somewhere, sometime, when she was drawing the tickets for a raffle. She had a look at one and put it back in the drum. I said, "You can't do that," to which she replied with a mischievous grin, "Oh yes I can. I cheat!" and laughed. You don't argue with a Princess!

At the Olympic Banquet, the raffle went very well and Bryan, always the extrovert, auctioned a dozen items and raised much-needed funds for our athletes. Princess Anne was in great form, as always, and made a wonderful speech. I never fail to be amazed at the sincerity and intelligence of that fine lady. Many times when we have met she has probably had three or four events during the day at which she possibly had to speak; her knowledge of the subject at each and the people she has to meet, is totally dedicated to that event. She has a sharp wit and is aware of everything that is going on around her. She is undoubtedly one of the more popular royals, certainly one of the busiest, and I thoroughly enjoy being at functions in her presence. It is not too conceited to say that we know each other very well and, as such, she 'trusts' me as a toastmaster and has confidence that all will go well.

I recall one very large banquet at The Grosvenor House for merchant banks where they spend money like snowflakes and raise around three quarters of a million pounds for the Save the Children Fund and Riding for the Disabled. On this occasion, they had told me that Princess Anne would be drawing the five raffle prizes and that they would be drawn, '... in reverse order of value, ending with prize number one.' I said, "You can't! It's illegal," but they were adamant; that was what they had decided and that was what they would do! During the dinner, I spoke with the Princess and said, "Ma'am, I understand that you will be drawing the raffle. I also know that they are planning to draw the tickets in 'reverse order of value' from number five up to the major prize." To which she immediately replied, "You can't! It's illegal." End of discussion. We compromised, drew them in the correct order, but announced them in reverse order which satisfied both parties. Toastmasters have to be diplomatic in every situation!

Back in Atlanta we were scheduled to visit two more towns in the US before returning to England. At 6.00 am we had breakfast and at eight o'clock were taken, in royal convoy with motorcycle outriders, to a private airport owned by *Coca Cola*. We honked, blazed and sirened our way through hugely congested commuter 'drive-time' with the police motorcyclists opening great gaps between the almost stationary vehicles. We loved it.

It was to my huge delight that the representative invited to attend this trip was that great Olympian oarsman Sir Steve Redgrave, and we were bracketed together throughout the trip. As you would expect, he is one of the nicest guys around – a genuinely great man who is a delight to know. He only had three Olympic medals at that time, which had been shown around the tables at the banquet, and they got lost. Someone had put them down, we could not find them and Steve was anxious that they might have been stolen. They were found in a strange place giving a strong impression that they had been 'misappropriated' with the intention of being picked up later.

The cavalcade of long, black, shiny police-guarded limos swept into this airfield where we disembarked and boarded a small aircraft, the official plane of the *Coca Cola Company* in Atlanta. There were about a dozen of us on board and the hospitality was quite superb. It was one of the most luxurious aircraft I had ever seen, with gold decorations, soft, expensive, expansive, comfortable armchairs, and the hospitality was just perfect. Apart from Steve and me, there was Bryan Langton, Princess Anne and her Lady-in-waiting, the usual attendant security guards, the CEO of *Coca Cola* and various hangers-on. We took off and sat back to enjoy a comfortable couple of hours' flight.

Our destination was Philadelphia, Pennsylvania, where luncheon for about 250 people had been planned. Yet another cavalcade blazed its way through heavy traffic to the hotel where we had about half an hour before luncheon. Again, Bryan had asked me to arrange the raffle, which I had done. However, to complicate matters, there were to be two raffles running together, both using my system. What was also critical was that it all had to be over by 2.30 at the very latest as the Royal Party had to attend another function planned for that evening in Boston, Mass.

To explain to an American audience my raffle, which was totally alien to them, was tough enough. To explain two at the same time, but using different-coloured tickets and different prices was even worse. The usual raffle was modestly priced at around $10 for three tickets, for which there were about a dozen simple prizes. The second raffle was $100 per ticket but the prizes were worth thousands of dollars and were really worth winning. They included complete holidays for whole families for weeks at a time at the expense of Crown Plaza Hotels, which Bryan had sponsored. In the US, Americans can claim tax allowances for spending large sums of money for either raffles or auctions at charity events. What a great idea. Chancellor of the Exchequer, please take note!

The smaller raffle was to be drawn by Steve Redgrave, but to help 'sell' the larger raffle, I asked Princess Anne if she would agree to draw it and have her photograph taken with the winners of those three prizes. She agreed wholeheartedly; she has an eye for making a quick 'buck' when the situation arises. It worked, and the sale of the tickets went like a dream with the local committee doing a great job in helping me.

There was a delightful moment when Princess Anne was with Steve Redgrave in the middle of the room whilst I stood on the stage with the microphone. She selected a ticket and Steve called out the name, to which there was no reply. I repeated it, but nobody came to claim the prize. Somebody then called out, "He's left. Had to go back to the office." After a moment's pause, I said, "So! He ain't here to collect his prize, eh?" Princess Anne, Steve Redgrave and 250 American businessmen and women all looked at me questioningly to see what I would do. "In that case," I said, "TOUGH! 'E's 'AD IT, AND WE SHALL DRAW IT AGAIN." They roared, and Princess Anne gave me one of her huge grins, as if to say, 'Great, well done,' and plunged her hand back into the raffle drum.

I learned later that we raised well over $30,000 for British athletes at that luncheon graced wholly by Americans, and they were all thrilled. Unquestionably, the main thrust of their enjoyment was lunching with a real live Princess as well as a great Olympian. Again, Steve had been proud to show – not send this time! – his three medals around the tables and take the much-deserved plaudits of the American guests. They really do love a great champion, no matter what nationality.

At 2.30 we rose from the table, the Royal Party leading out. When we got outside the room, Princess Anne said to me, "Are you coming to Boston with us?"
"No Ma'am," I replied, "I'm due back in England tomorrow and cannot afford the time."
"Well," she said, "What a pity – we shall miss you. You've done a wonderful job over here and thank you very much. Have a good trip home. See you in England!"

As a lad from a very modest background, I prize those moments dearly. To have such praise from someone like her is wonderful. To spend a couple of days in the company of one of the greatest English sportsmen ever born was a huge bonus. As Steve is diabetic, he carries around medication which he needs to apply at any function. It seems so unjust that one so fit and healthy as he, as well as being married to a doctor, should be so afflicted. He treats it very casually and does not make a fuss about it, but I think it is a wee bit sad.

Being too busy, I had had no time for any food at the lunch, so I asked the chef to make me a sandwich, which I could munch at the airport. He did. It was one of those huge, squidgy, spongy, gooey egg-mayonnaise concoctions which I took to the airport and gorged down. I mused over the rather pleasant irony of the situation. Here was I – an English toastmaster who had travelled across America, lunched and dined with Royalty and an Olympic sportsman, raised tens of thousands of dollars for British athletes from admiring Americans – here was I, scoffing a huge sandwich, drinking *Coca Cola* given to me by a grateful sponsor, all on my own in a quiet, lonely corner of an international airport, and nobody either knew or cared. I still have that small box which housed a six-pack of *Coke*, which I now use for my raffle tickets! Ain't life funny!

As a postscript to this trip, whilst in Atlanta itself, I had a whole day free with unlimited access to my own chauffeuse-driven limo. It was recommended that I visit the *Coca Cola* factory and museum somewhere downtown, which I did. It is an amazing place and incredibly well organised. When they discovered who I was (fame at last!) and why I was there, I was given the full VIP treatment – a personal, private tour of the place, unlimited information, some lovely little gifts which I treasure to this day, and an unforgettable morning's entertainment.

However, my abiding memory of that place was in the entrance hall. Above the main door to the building is a huge, red, neon-lighted display. Above, it proclaims: "THIS IS THE TOTAL NUMBER OF *COCA COLAS* SOLD SINCE THE FOUNDING OF THE COMPANY..." I have never seen so many digits in one number, at the end of which there was one which was spinning unreadably, like the hundreds digit on a stopwatch. That figure was recording the current and immediate sale of *Coca Cola* worldwide. It is mind-numbingly awe-inspiring to see the billions of *Cokes* that have quenched the thirst of millions of people worldwide over the years, and it is growing at an ever-greater pace.

I was also privy to a small piece of Atlanta political correctness to which I refused to bow. My limo chauffeuse was a very attractive black lady. She was charming, witty, knowledgeable, kind and, in every way, very good company. On our arrival at the *Coca Cola* building, I invited her to come in with me on the tour. She immediately declined, stating that because of her colour it would be frowned upon. My private response is unprintable, but I asked her if she had ever been inside and, if not, would she like to accompany me? She said that she had not been to the *Coca Cola* museum and would enjoy seeing it. So, when I went to the desk and told them who I was and that I wished to invite this lady to accompany me, without demur, they agreed. Such was the prejudice in that town, it was only due to the influence of a white Englishman that they consented – whether reluctantly or not, I never did find out, but she had a great tour.

Pauline Quirke and Linda Robson, the stars of the wonderful TV series, *Birds of a Feather*, have been mates since they were kids; indeed, it is this friendship which made the series quite magical. The girls then embarked on a programme called *Jobs for the Girls*, where they tackled activities in which they had precisely no experience but were taught by professionals how to do them successfully. One of these was to organise and run a Royal Charity Dinner and Dance. They wrote to HRH The Duchess of York who had recently created her own charity, *Children in Crisis*. Sarah Ferguson immediately agreed to be a part of this programme and help in any way she could, especially as her pet cause would be the beneficiary.

I received a call from the producer of the show asking if I would consider being part of it. He surprised (and flattered) me when he said that The Duchess of York was only willing to accept the agreement on condition that I was the toastmaster in charge of the evening and fund-raising. I had been involved with many of her events and she knew my style of working. Of course, I leapt at the idea and agreed to attend meetings and discussions with 'The Girls'.

Understandably, Pauline and Linda had no idea of what to do or how to get it off the ground. All they knew was, they had a royal supporter, a venue (the *In and Out Club* in Piccadilly), a producer and a willingness to learn. They did not know how to obtain prizes, sell tickets, discuss menus, obtain other sponsors, book cabaret, or – and this is where I came in – organise fund-raising on the night. Their knowledge was nil, but their determination was total; the difficulty was that, because of tight TV schedules, they only had a few weeks to set it all up.

After several meetings with just the three of us, we put an evening's programme together in conjunction with all those involved, including The Duchess of York's office, caterers, photographers, musicians, cabaret artistes, TV producers, management of the venue, sponsors, and anyone who was to play their part in this education of Pauline and Linda. And, of course, TV cameras took shots of everything.

The girls were thrilled when Curtis Stigers agreed to be their cabaret act, and it was the way they threw themselves wholeheartedly into the scheme. They wrote personally to many companies asking for prizes, sponsorship or to buy tickets for the dinner, and they spoke to bands and artistes about entertainment – they really worked hard to ensure the success of the event.

We all arrived at the venue early on the day of the dinner to go through all the 'nitty-gritty' of setting up a charity banquet. Believe me, they don't just happen; they have to be planned meticulously and there are a thousand and one details to monitor – the seating arrangements, the display of prizes, discussions with the auctioneer, checking that the champagne has arrived, overseeing the caterers, advertising displays, flowers, decorations, lighting, PA equipment, photography, speeches, etc – the list is endless. And, of course, there is also the royal protocol: who is to meet The Duchess at the door, and then there are the precise timings of the whole evening from arrival to departure so that everyone is aware of what is to happen. Linda and Pauline had to be closely involved in all of that if their learning about running a charity event was to be complete.

At last all was ready and we eagerly awaited the arrival of HRH The Duchess of York. She is a delightful lady and a very loving and devoted mother to her children. She is also passionate about the charity she founded and which has now raised millions of pounds for projects for children abroad. I once asked her if she would be willing to accept patronage of another large and very deserving charity. Her immediate but very sincere reply was that she really was not interested in adding her name as patron to a large list of deserving causes as she did not feel she could genuinely devote the time to it that it needed and that her one major charity was *Children in Crisis*.

As The Duchess stepped out of the car, she was met by the Chairman of the Club – as protocol dictates – who introduced her, formally, to Linda and Pauline, by now quaking in their beautiful new frocks and fancy shoes. This was all very open and a bit stiff and starchy, as they already knew each other very well, but it has to be seen to be done as respect for any member of the Royal Family. The entourage made its way to the reception and the party began in earnest. Dinner was called and the programme, so diligently prepared by the girls, went through with total precision and great entertainment for the 160 or so guests who attended.

Well over £60,000 was raised for the charity. Peter Stringfellow was a most generous supporter, paying a vast sum of money for a dress that had been presented for auction… and into which he tried – unsuccessfully – to persuade The Duchess of York to change and model. He offered to pay an almost obscene sum for that great privilege, which alas! was not taken up. However, he grabbed my microphone during the auction and invited everyone to Stringfellows after the show as his personal guests – "Just turn up and mention my name: the drinks are on me!"

Formalities over, fund-raising completed, entertainment enjoyed, The Duchess of York took her leave, after which dancing continued into the early hours. Again, tradition dictates that The Duchess is escorted to her car by the hosts of the evening, and there were some very girly hugs and kisses as these three super young ladies said goodbye. By now, any nerves they may have felt were totally dispelled as it had gone so well. Everyone was thrilled with the whole event. It was 'put to bed', as the saying goes, by the BBC and was shown to the viewers months later – huge amounts of the footage taken over the weeks ending up on the cutting room floor! It was certainly one of my more memorable evenings and gave me two more super 'gals' in Linda Robson and Pauline Quirke to number amongst my show business chums.

Chapter 18

Valued Clients

"Dentopediology is the science of opening your mouth and
putting your foot in it; I've been practising it for years."

HRH Prince Philip... and me!

It makes sense in this long narrative to explain the phraseology of
'Toastmaster-speak'. The words 'did' and 'do' refer to the action of
officiating at any event. For example, I 'did' the wedding of Gloria
Hunniford and Stephen Way, and I shall be 'doing' various
functions in the future. It is a common phrase and less clumsy than
the alternative of 'officiated at'. There are four clients for whom I
have 'done' work, spanning virtually my entire career.

The British Safety Council was founded nearly fifty years ago by
James Tye, a left-wing, highly controversial and charismatic
journalist. He developed a passion for safety in the workplace and
was appointed by the government to form a quango to identify the
subject under the chairmanship of Dr Douglas Latto, MBBS,
FRCOG, FRPS. All those letters meant that he was a
Gynaecologist and Obstetrician by profession, but a Fellow of the
Royal Philatelic Society by choice, as it was his hobby. He was an
eccentric 'braw' Scot who, even well into his last years in the 1990s,
was still charging his consultation fees in guineas. He was a leading
authority on philately and had one of the world's largest collections
of extremely rare and valuable stamps, and was proud of the fact
that such were his dealings in them that he was registered for VAT.
He once showed me a stamp he was about to sell, from the

proceeds of which he would take his children and grandchildren for a fortnight's holiday to Hong Kong; it was worth over £15,000.

James Tye and his wife Rosalie became good and loyal friends for whom I worked regularly from the early days of the Council, which then consisted of safety officers and managers. He appointed people in industry whose main interests were in safety, and began lectures and training courses for any company who felt the need to learn more. The results were that successful candidates qualified for a Diploma in Safety Management and functions were organised to present them. For the first few years, luncheons were held in the Churchill Room at the House of Commons and I was invited to run them. It is my proud boast that nearly forty-eight years later, they are still being held several times each year and I am still involved, particularly at a very large Safety Awards Banquet held annually at The Grosvenor House.

James was one of the most remarkable men I have known. He was wholly unpredictable, especially in his office, and his staff tell me that on a daily basis they had no idea what was planned for that day. He did not have a nerve in his body and would hold forth on safety wherever and whenever he chose. He had no qualms about criticising anyone – from the Queen and Princess Anne downwards if he felt they were not leading by example in the realms of safety. He roundly criticised the Queen for horse-riding without wearing a riding hat, and Princess Anne for driving a car without wearing a seat belt – that was before it became law! He was banned from the Royal Albert Hall, proclaiming it was the unsafest building he had ever entered. On various visits there, he noticed that safety regulations were being violated with emergency doors being chained up and safety access points blocked. He published this in the national press and was forbidden ever to go there again. He loved boxing and one evening when a bout was being held there, James totally changed his appearance; he slicked his hair down with *Brylcreem*, grew a beard, wore a false moustache, dressed like an eccentric vagrant – and got in. He made a note of every unsafe point in the building and published it. The result was that those in charge of the Royal Albert Hall addressed his concerns. It is now as safe as any building in the UK. His methods worked and he didn't care how he achieved them.

He was renowned throughout the world and spent many months lecturing to safety officers and companies in dozens of countries, especially the USA and the Far East. The Council grew enormously as safety in the workplace became fashionable and was carefully studied by hundreds of companies. Even today it is growing at a remarkable pace with the result that they are still organising many events to reward individuals and companies who have qualified for diplomas. The teams and format have changed somewhat, but they are still continuing the great work for safety that James began.

James's daughter had purchased a pair of jeans from a high-class shop in Kensington, but they had soon fallen to bits. As she was too frightened to return them, one Saturday morning James went to the store, which was packed with shoppers, climbed on a chair in the middle of the display, held up the offending garment and in a very loud voice, proclaimed, "I would like to speak to the person who sold this load of rubbish to my daughter!" It had the desired effect!

It is, of course, unquantifiable, but there is no doubt that, as a direct result of his tenacity and perseverance, millions of lives have been saved. My 48-year connection with the British Safety Council was something I prized. They were my oldest client and I will never forget the many years I enjoyed the courtesy and company of their founder, a truly charismatic man.

Ann and I invited James and Rosalie to celebrate our Silver Wedding in the Café Royal in 1982. It thrilled him to bits that I seated him next to our great British heavyweight boxer, Henry Cooper. A press photographer spotted them together and next day their photograph appeared in one of the papers with the caption, "What weirdo sat the head of the British Safety Council next to a Champion Boxer?" Me!

In 1997, in the Armourers and Brasiers Hall in the City of London, James and I were talking before a presentation luncheon. Our conversation was desultory and about nothing in particular.

Suddenly, he seemed to walk in front of me and then quietly rolled down onto the floor, not even spilling the orange juice he was holding. He was dead before he hit the floor. Oh yes, he was taken to hospital and given all the revival treatment and was proclaimed dead a few days later, but in my humble opinion he simply died in my arms! At the age of 72 he was doing what he loved best, preparing to give awards to people whose lives revolved around safety.

* * * * *

In 1946, the *Barclays Bank* London Branch Managers Club started two functions which became annual events – a dinner-dance to which wives and friends were invited, and a banquet for over 1,000 guests, strictly for members and their more influential clients. Dad was involved from the outset and was invited to provide the band and other entertainment. A great clarinettist and broadcasting band of those days was Nat Temple who played at every one they ran. He is now over 90 and we still remain close friends to this day.

In addition, small departments of *Barclays Bank* ran functions in their own ballroom in their Bishopsgate head office in the City of London, which I did together with my own five-piece band. The organiser, Mr Laurie Topp, was a tall, bald, stooping, angular man with a beak-like nose. He paid the fees on the night and always in brand new ten-shilling notes.

Sadly, economics caught up with matters and the Bank found it impossible to sponsor the Ladies' Night, which ended, as did the small, local functions. However, *Barclays* continued to underwrite the banquet. My father did that dinner every year from 1946 until his death in 1983, when it was handed to me and I am still doing it to this day. Consequently, the event spanning over sixty years has had only two toastmasters, father and son, a fact they are happy to acknowledge each year.

* * * * *

The Association of Hydraulic Equipment Manufacturers (AHEM) was founded in 1956. Captain Payne organised their first dinner and dance in the Orchid Room of The Dorchester, at which I was not present. The following year, he took over the ballroom as numbers had grown and he needed a toastmaster. He also needed a band for the event so I was asked to do the job and provide the music. Thus began a friendship which exists to the present day. After Captain Payne's retirement, Mr John Nosworthy ran their annual banquet and we became firm friends. When he left, Mr Neil Percival took over for the next fifteen years before retirement; again, I value his friendship and that of his wife Rae. A few years ago, they changed the name from AHEM to the British Fluid Power Association, BFPA.

Nat Temple provided the music for the first few years but I later changed the band to Johnny Howard, who is still doing it. John Nosworthy was asked to provide a thirty-minute entertainment slot during the evening to cover the band's refreshment break, and he and I had great fun in choosing the cabaret. It became the tradition that the Chief Executive and I were the only two who knew what the entertainment was to be, as the crowd all seemed to love the surprise on the night. For years he chose a military marching display band alternating between bands from the Brigade of Guards, the Royal Marines, the Royal Artillery and the Royal Air Force, all of which were quite supreme. It was decided that variety was needed and thereafter we varied our selection. Amongst the changes were steel band with limbo, acrobats, conjurors and several dance troupes, the most popular of which were The Tara Dancers. These were so well received that, by popular demand from the membership, they were invited to return. They actually come from Glasgow, consisting of about thirty girls (the youngest being eight years old and the oldest, her mother!) dressed in traditional very colourful Irish dresses – velvet, embroidered tabards – who dance traditional Irish dances ending with the sensational Riverdance routine. They are the only cabaret I have seen who receive an instant standing ovation when they end their programme.

Next year (2007) will be my fiftieth involvement with that association. The event is without doubt one of the nicest in my calendar, which both Johnny Howard and I love doing. The members and guests are quite charming and demonstrative in their appreciation, so different from the type of person who now frequents London banquets. Sadly, behaviour has deteriorated dramatically over the past few years, and it is refreshing to find a crowd who represent old and valued standards. They love me, I love them and hope that the relationship will continue for many more years.

* * * * *

I have known Derek and Beryl Roston for over fifty years. They were enthusiastic caravanners, as were my parents, and they occasionally met in that connection. In 2002, I did their grandson's barmitzvah at The Savoy Hotel, and whilst discussing this, Derek said with a broad grin, "I was sitting on the lavatory this morning thinking about you!" Talk about word association! Somewhat taken aback, I replied, "Oh yes? What was that all about?" "Well," he said, "I suddenly recalled that you were toastmaster at my wedding to Beryl in 1954 – it must have been one of your first engagements! You then did the barmitzvahs of our two sons. You were also toastmaster at both their weddings and you have now done the barmitzvahs of *their* three sons. It has to be some record that one toastmaster has been connected with one family for fifty years!" I sent this information to Ned Temco, the editor of the *Jewish Chronicle,* which he published.

I only mention these last four events as they are unique. As I am, by a very long way, the longest-serving active toastmaster in the profession, they will never be beaten. I am proud of these associations and the fact that I must have got something right over the years for them to retain their trust in me.

George Howard, the time I first met him, was the Chairman of the BBC. A quiet, diffident, modest and unassuming man, he was the owner of that magnificent Vanburgh-built pile, Castle Howard, just outside York, an establishment I was destined to visit oh so many times. He was always complimentary about my work and on one occasion enquired about my Toastmaster Association. He told me that his catering director Ian Martin was a good toastmaster and would we consider him for membership. I contacted Ian and eventually he joined our ranks; but, far more importantly, he became a dear and close friend. Ann and I soon got to know him and his smashing blonde wife Susan and their two young kids Charlotte and James – yes, you've guessed it, James Martin, the gorgeous handsome TV celebrity chef of great acclaim. We paid many visits to their lovely little cottage in Coneysthorpe in the valley below Castle Howard on its estate, as I did a whole heap of work there for Ian. He was a workaholic, ran some quite stupendous events and always enlisted my help.

Before Castle Howard, Ian had a few jobs – a policeman, a licensee – running, with Sue, their own pub – and professional toastmaster. Following a passionate interest in wine, he became one of the two legally required Englishmen on the Jurade of St Emilion. He became the Chancellor of the Jurade, a position he held for over 25 years.

> "Formed in 1199 when King John granted a charter giving the Jurade power to govern the Province; in return for that power they had to supply a certain amount of wine each year for the English Crown. Two English members were put there to ensure that the French did not add all sorts of unmentionable fluids into the hogshead. They had a lot of power and could elect Magistrates. The Jurade was

abolished by the French Revolution. It was reformed in 1944 by Daniel Querre of Chateau Monbousquet and Jean Capdemoulin, of Ch. Cap de Moulin."

Each Jurade member has the power to invite anyone with an interest in wine to be 'intronised' or inducted as a member. If accepted, the nominee is required to visit that beautifully picturesque part of Bordeaux to attend the *Bans des Vendages* or proclamation for the Vintage.

In 1989, Ian told us to keep the second week in September free and broke the exciting news that I had been accepted and was to be 'intronised as a *Vigneron d'Honneur*' into the Jurade of St Emilion wines: a rare and singular honour. We fixed to take Tim and Chloë, their business partner Phil Forrest and wife Berna, and our American friends Ed and Virginia Wetter.

At 10.00 am, the sixty or so inductees, their families and friends assembled in the grounds of an old chateau all a'buzz with anticipation. As a jangly old clock in the tower chimed the seconds away, the centuries-old tradition of the formal parade of the forty or so Jurade members, elegantly clad in their long scarlet robes, white silk shawls, and their neat crown-like matching headgear, filed past. We searched eagerly and spotted Ian sombrely walking with his *confrères* to lead us all into a large open, grassy square surrounded by crumbling cloisters. We sat and the ceremony began. It was conducted in unintelligible classic French, and one by one we new inductees were called.

Each had individual citations proclaiming our worthiness read out to the assembly, and we approached *M. le Premier Jurat* at his table. We were 'gowned' in the same uniform plus a white, ermine epaulette called an epitoge, which was ceremonially affixed to our shoulder and which we were required to wear throughout the day – it is about fifteen inches long, wider at the bottom than at the top where it is about three inches wide. We were then presented with a framed scroll proclaiming our membership; it now hangs in pride of place in my home. The whole atmosphere was serious and sombre and, within the spectacular and historic surrounds of the chateau open to the heavens with the autumn sun beating down, it was deeply moving. The ceremony over, the scarlet-gowned Jurade, whose sensitive and delicate palates determine each year's vintage of some of the world's finest wines, paraded out, leaving the new clutch of *intronisées* and guests to their congratulatory hugs, kisses and snaps.

A church service followed which Ann and I chose to attend, but which didn't mean a great deal as it was all in Latin and weird classic French. But for me it was a time of quiet reflection during which I recall with disconcerting clarity one poignant moment. The walls of the ancient, small, slightly decaying Catholic church were devoid of the usual epitaphs, tributes and icons, except in one spot. High up on the wall beside where we sat, was a Crucifix about three feet tall, set back in a recess which had been there centuries. A shaft of bright sunlight from a small opening high in the ceiling shone, like a celestial spotlight, illuminating this symbol of Christianity. I found it quite unnerving as it further added to my awe of the whole event. But more was to come, stirring even greater emotions.

We rejoined our crew to attend a pre-prandial reception when champagne – yes, champagne in St Emilion – flowed like the Rivers of Babylon. Lunch was called and we took our seats at tables set in a vast cathedral-like dining room; and boy oh boy, what a lunch! It was unbelievable.

French cuisine is legendary; they take their food extremely seriously, especially banquets. Anyone who has experienced dining or lunching at a wine chateau will concur that these feasts are exceptional. I will restrict myself by saying that we sat down at 1.00 pm and rose from the table at 5.00, eating throughout. 'Butler Service' means that butlers offer you a large platter from which you help yourself. What you are not told is that the butlers return two or three times for each course encouraging the unwary to take another helping. At our gargantuan feast there were eight courses all offering 'seconds'.

I have never seen so many wine glasses on one table in my life. Each course – I repeat, each course – was accompanied by at least two different St Emilion red wines. It is the custom that every year, selected *viniculteurs* provide their finest wines for this spread and the glasses are filled full. Eventually, glorious, rich, succulent, aromatic French coffee arrived and we were all stuffed: we could hardly move. But, this remarkable day was not yet over. There was one final disarmingly emotional ceremony to experience.

The small town of St Emilion is built on two hilltops with a kind of steep valley or rift dividing them. A single bell tolled sonorously, summoning all to attend. We took up casual places at the top of one side to see across to the other hill – or *cotes* as they are known in wine-speak. From seemingly nowhere, like silent, scarlet spectres, the Jurade began their final act of thanksgiving. Attired like bishops and surmounting several hundred well-trodden, steep, narrow steps, they processed to the other side at the summit on which was situated the ancient, ruined Chateau de Roi – Castle of the King. As the bell chimed its dreary monotone, we watched in wonderment these gentlemen, some quite elderly, slowly approaching their eyrie for the dénouement of this very important day.

In most, if not all, vineyards across France, the annual *Bans des Vendages* takes place when all the grapes have been harvested, the wines selected and secured and the vintages established. When the vital hard work of gathering it all in has ended, it is time to relax, reflect, rejoice and, above all, to thank God.

At precisely 6.00 pm, the far *cotes*, colourfully emblazoned by each crimson Jurade member standing in reverent silence, the bell ceased its tolling. Its echoes fading down the valley in the weak evening sunlight, the Jurade Chancellor read a tract in French, thanking the Almighty for his goodness, grace and love, rewarding their loving, painstaking labours with a good and healthy harvest. He then read a long list of names of oenologists, vintners, vineyard owners, members of the Jurade of St Emilion and wine producers who had died in recent years.

It was devastatingly moving and I freely admit to blubbing like a baby at the pure magnificence and sensitivity of the entire event. My son Tim is not, in any way, a romantic or emotional guy, being thoroughly pragmatic and down-to-earth, but he too was so deeply moved that he made a point of acquiring not one, but two, copies of that tract in English and French which he later had framed and which hang in his home.

At the close of the day, although full to busting with great wine and wonderful food, we were emotionally drained. There is a light-hearted twist in the tail. Throughout the four days, Ian had arranged for us to visit many of the classic chateaux for *degustations* and French hospitality – all wonderful experiences. In the evening of this great Sunday, we were invited to yet another of these. So! Yes! You've guessed it... 7.30 pm – having downed an eight-course banquet and consumed a lake of wine – saw us visiting our umpteenth chateau for yet more tasting, with their brand of grape produce and a vast Bar-B-Q of various meats all cooked slowly over vine branches and vine leaves, giving it that special, delicate 'winey' flavour. We soldiered on manfully and womanfully, and accepted the proffered largesse of these kind, generous and hardworking wine-farmers.

Our gratitude to Ian was unequivocal and sincere. We had all enjoyed a quite sensational weekend, which none of us will ever forget and I have the scroll and *Epitoge* (which means shawl or cape) to prove it!

Chapter 19

Speakers' Corner

"Did you hear about the member of the House of Lords
who dreamt he was making an after-dinner speech,
and woke up to find that he was!"

Anon

'Who's the best speaker you have ever heard?' is arguably the question I am asked most often, but answering it is not simple. I estimate that I have listened to – in the vast majority of cases, painfully endured – thousands of speeches, of which well over 90% were dreadful and highly forgettable. Of the remainder, only a few fall into the category of memorable. A further difficulty I have is in which area of professionalism do I place each speaker – are they amateurs who have a natural flair? Are they professional entertainers who get paid to do the job anyway? Are they politicians who speak for a living? Or is it a person who may make only one speech in their whole life, prepare properly and deliver great words of amusement and entertainment, never to return to the podium again? It is wholly invidious to brand them all together and select just a few, as the competition is unfair.

Professional comics are, of course, high on the list, but that is their job. Even here there are differences as the majority use the same speech over and over again – it is their act, whether from the top table or the cabaret floor. Many names that leap to mind are Tom O'Connor, Bob 'The Cat' Bevan, Rod Woodward, Roger de Courcey – especially when he brings out Nookie Bear – Jim Davidson, Ian Irving, Adrian Walsh, Johnny Casson, Jimmy Bright,

Frank Carson and dozens of others who always make me rock with laughter. But, supreme in this region has to be my good friend and brother Water Rat, Barry Cryer who, for one specific reason, reigns supreme. Not only are all his speeches hilarious, but each one has been tailored for that particular event. I have been fortunate in that Barry has been kind enough to speak at several functions on my behalf – not just professional engagements – and each has been personalised, usually ending with a specially-written poem. I can never really express my deep gratitude to him for the many times he has responded to my call to speak. Occasionally I send him gags and one-liners and if he repeats them on, say, *Countdown*, he is always thoughtful enough to mention my name as his source of supply.

There are any number of comics now on the after-dinner circuit who are charging big fees and working hard. To list them all would fill another chapter. Many are fabulous, but to place them in the category of 'the best speaker I have ever heard' would be impossible and quite unproductive. But I have one inviolable rule by which I judge them all, and that is the content of their material, especially in its use or otherwise of foul language or the vernacular. Every speaker I consider to be worthy of mention would never indulge in filthy humour. Their talents are far too finely tuned to need to sink into the morass of the liberal use of four-letter words, gags about personal bodily functions, racist jokes or any type of scurrilous humour which becomes offensive.

These so-called entertainers are simply not worthy of the adjective 'great' and none of them can live in the same company as the hundreds of semi-professional and professional entertainers who, nightly, all over the UK are entertaining audiences without being blue. As far as I am concerned, the moment a comic begins using filthy language, particularly if there are ladies in the audience, I simply cease to listen. Sadly, it is becoming all too prevalent today with the range of 'alternative comedians', and the sooner they realise that they are not funny but simply dirty, the better it will be for entertainment.

Another very popular section amongst audiences nowadays is professional sportsmen and women talking light-heartedly about their sport. One of the few ladies in this genre, and one who has been a very successful raconteuse for many years, is Rachel Heyho-Flint, whose experience and knowledge of women's cricket is second-to-none. Incidentally, there is an interesting trivia question I have occasionally posed with a surprise answer: "Which English cricketer has played the most times for England?" Most people deliberate about all the well-known men in the game. The answer is Rachel H-F!

Among those whose talents I rate highly is that superb England and British Lions rugger player, the gigantic Martin Bayfield. At 6'10" he is now making a great name for himself as Robbie Coltrane's body in the *Harry Potter* films. Geoff Miller and Duncan McKenzie, former professional and international footballers, are very funny, and all of them tell true stories about famous names with whom they have played. PKR Sir Henry Cooper gives a very good account of himself and is loved by everyone. There may be others I haven't heard, but it is yet another area of public speaking.

Members of the Royal Family are trained and polished speakers, but none are really earth-shattering or remarkable. Of course their background and upbringing makes them wholly reliable, and they all have the great merit of never speaking too long. If I had to choose my favourite, it would have to be HRH The Princess Royal, whom I have heard on so many occasions. Her approach to the specific subject is total and sincere, but she also has a great sense of humour and fun and is not afraid to 'ad lib' if the situation requires – and these are as funny as any professional comic.

Politicians, despite having to make any number of speeches to enable them to get to the House of Commons in the first place, do not, in my view, necessarily make memorable after-dinner speakers. Certainly they can *ad lib* forever and talk themselves out of a paper bag, but that does not automatically make them great orators. At most events where I meet them, their speeches are usually written by civil servants or private secretaries, from which they have to read for fear of imparting the wrong political viewpoint. The content of these is invariably 99% waffle and 1% substance from which their audience can take any lasting information. I recall very few memorable speeches delivered by MPs – with a couple of exceptions.

In his prime, Edward Heath was excellent. One speech I heard, which went on for the best part of an hour, was funny, informative and entertaining, as well as being full of pathos, occasionally actually making you *want* to weep, it was so moving – quite brilliant. And all he had was a piece of paper upon which he had scribbled two words around which he wove this tremendous piece of oratory. He really was an oratorical genius. The other who falls into my list of a truly 'great' speaker is William Hague. He too has to be acknowledged as one of the finest speakers anywhere to be found today. Usually speaking extemporaneously, he is spell-binding, simply grabs his audience by the throat, makes them listen, imparts a great message and always with enormous humour. There are few orators that I have heard who come anywhere near William Hague for quality, genius and audience appeal.

Gyles Brandreth has been known to end his speeches talking about Australia and standing upside-down with his head on his chair. But I mention him for another reason. Many years ago he asked me if I would do him the favour of acting as 'referee' in his attempt to beat the record of the world's longest after-dinner speech. My co-referee was to be Robert Birchfield, the Editor of the Oxford English Dictionary. This was held at a venue in Ashridge Park near Berkhamsted, and lasted for four-and-a-half hours. He later did another lasting eight hours. However he asked me the same favour years later when he and another longstanding friend, Nicholas Parsons (now a brother Water Rat), were to go head-to-head to see who could speak the longest. It was a verbal 'challenge to the death', the first to sit down, or run out of material, being the loser.

The *Guinness Book of Records* had set out the rules – it was arranged that they were to speak in adjacent rooms in The Hyde Park Hotel. Sixty or so guests were invited to dinner at 6.30, and at eight o'clock precisely, the two protagonists went to the lecterns in their rooms and began. My colleague, Martin Nicholls, assisted me and we took it in turns to visit each room and listen to the speakers. One rule which had to be observed was that not only was there to be a dinner beforehand, but that the audience in each room had to be more than nine people. It had been well advertised and throughout the night, other invited guests popped in to listen for an hour or two before leaving again. Another rule was that each speaker was only allowed five minutes' break every two hours for obvious refreshment, otherwise it had to be continuous. And so began this marathon.

Throughout the night, they just talked and talked and talked. The morning dawned and still they prattled on and on, until at around 7.30 the hotel manager called me away and told me that the rooms they were occupying were needed for another function that morning and that it was essential that it ended. I became extremely unpopular with both when I sent them a note saying that, as referee, I would have to stop them both at eight o'clock and proclaim a draw. And thus it was that after exactly twelve hours of non-stop verbiage, they sat down to weary acclaim of the few remaining listeners.

There were two mildly contentious issues at that event. The first was that Gyles' father, who had spent some time listening to Nick Parsons, complained to me that, rather than delivering a basic after-dinner speech, he was quoting huge tracts of Shakespeare and that it should therefore not be allowed – Nick had been a Shakespearian actor. However, I took the view that within the structure of the whole event, it was but a very tiny part.

The second problem was the size of the audience. By around 6.00 am, there were exactly nine people in each room, three of whom were my ageing parents and daughter who wished to leave. Had they done so, it would have nullified the competition. So when it became necessary for me to call a halt, it saved what might have been a tricky situation.

Both Gyles and Nicholas have to be numbered among the best speakers I have heard. Gyles began his talk by saying that he had divided it into letters of the alphabet and that he would begin with the letter 'A'. When I stopped him twelve hours later, I learned that he had only reached the letter 'O'! So, heaven knows when he would have sat down.

Now we come to what I call 'non-professionals', those who have other occupations but, because of their supreme talents, are frequently invited to speak. There are several who come to mind over the years, a few of whom are sadly no longer with us. The first has to be that wonderful surgeon Arthur Dickson-Wright – whose daughter Clarissa is now a member of my Livery Company. His fame and renown as the best speaker in the country was legendary and I was privileged to hear him many times. He never used a note, was caustic, critical, charismatic, insulting to all and sundry, but side-achingly funny. Anyone old enough to remember those halcyon days might still recall his verbal dexterity and brilliance.

At the annual Remembrance Day Service at the Royal Albert Hall, the commentator for years was a gentleman by the name of T Humphrey Tilling. A businessman with a deep voice, a gentle, lugubrious, self-deprecating sense of humour, he held his audiences spellbound. He spoke on many occasions at functions given by the Lords Taverners and comes well within the top one percent of oratorical greats. Around at the same time was Lord Mancroft, who was equally brilliant; he gave the appearance of being able to speak off the cuff, without a note anywhere to be seen, giving a speech full of wit and knowledge. I congratulated him on the apparent ease with which he spoke so casually and without any preparation. His reply was surprising; in measured tones, he said, "My dear Sir, how kind of you to say so, but actually you are quite wrong. I will let you into a secret which I trust you will not divulge. Every word I utter has been written, prepared, read, re-read, rewritten, many times and eventually learned by heart. I have never delivered what you call an *ad lib* in my life!" I was surprised, but honoured to share that closely-guarded secret.

Many years ago two well-known speakers were invited to the Water Rats Ball – Terry Wogan, who can be extremely funny, and Pam Ayres. At the time she was far less famous than today, but she was renowned for her poetry and her own special accent and style of delivery. She spoke first and simply delivered her poem, *The Black and White Minstrel,* which to an audience of show business professionals, went down a storm. They roared with delight.

It is always hell for any speaker to follow such a storm and standards have to be tremendously high to live with it. Sadly, dear Terry, a loveable and genial gentleman, although well received by the sympathetic crowd, simply could not match Pam's magic. On the Wogan programme the next day he was brutally honest about his apparent lack of success and full of praise and congratulations for Pam Ayres.

I must also mention Philip Sellers, formerly Deputy Chairman of the Post Office, who was a naturally gifted speaker. But, of the hundreds of speakers I have met and heard, I have two absolute favourites whose friendships I value. The first is Peter Molony who, despite several different careers, was on the professional circuit for many years, although he has now retired to continue with his academic writing. I have listened spellbound many times and know of no one who can handle an audience with such skill. He graduated with degrees from four universities all beginning with the letter L – Leeds, Leicester, Lancaster and London. He then pursued Holy Orders, with a view to becoming a monk, but this was not to be his calling, so he joined the army in the Dental Corps. To his and everyone's surprise, he won the army boxing championship at his weight (he is a small, slight man), but as this was not appropriate for the Dental Corps, he became an officer in the SAS. On his return to Civvy Street, he became a teacher in the Toxteth area of Liverpool, "… where they teach English as a second language!"

A devout Catholic, Peter is frequently invited to preach. His way with words is remarkable – wise, witty, considered and thought-provoking. Being such a gifted man, I was surprised when he told me that his sermons were 'insanely difficult' to prepare and that he agonised over them for days. As Peter now spends more time with his business interests and academic writing, he is sorely missed by the many who would dearly love to hear him again.

Two others who do not really fall into any specific category are former US President Bill Clinton and the late Archbishop of Canterbury, Robert Runcie. In November 2005 I was at a fund-raising event in St Petersburg, Russia. Bill Clinton made a brief appeal on behalf of the charity. He was quite sensational, without a note, and with warmth, wisdom, persuasion and great personal charm, he squeezed over £2 million out of that audience.

Robert Runcie was an absolute natural. After his retirement he became a regular visitor to the Saints and Sinners Club in London where he was invariably asked to say a few words. He is about the only man I know who, 'in a few words', can bring tears of laughter to a tough, hard-nosed audience of businessmen and leave them wanting. Recently passed away, he is sorely missed.

Whilst on the subject of the clergy, two other notables are the late Dean of St Paul's, Martin Sullivan, who was quite superb, and my good friend Canon Roger Royle, who certainly fits into my list of the finest after-dinner speakers.

Into this category I also must add my very dear, but late lamented friend, Isabel Grainger. Surprisingly, this feisty, amusing and beautifully spoken lady had a sister named Bryn! Isabel and sister lived in a tiny cottage in Hampstead, and I really didn't get to know her until she was well into her 70s. She was passionate about girls who got themselves into trouble with crime, drugs, pregnancy and any other misdemeanour, and was an ardent prison visitor; she became such a regular at Holloway that the staff all knew her well. Some of her anecdotes about conversations with these girls were hilarious, and as an after-dinner speaker she was right up there with the best I've heard – tremendous humour mixed liberally with pathos to bring tears to the eyes. Isabel had been deeply involved with the NCUMC, from where we acquired our *au pairs*, but had fallen out big-time with the then Secretary, Pauline Crabbe.

Isabel asked if I would be willing to talk to one of her regulars – for a fee of course! – the 'army' of the St John Ambulance Brigade. Every year they held a training convention in Loughborough University and on the Sunday morning invited a guest speaker to address them before lunch. On one of these occasions Isabel had done so well that she received a standing ovation. She persuaded them to book me the next year, and I absolutely stormed them – they raved and banged on the table... but did NOT give me a standing ovation. She went back the following year and got yet another standing ovation and challenged me to see if I could do better. I went back – and you've guessed it... I did NOT get the hoped-for acknowledgement. We laughed and teased each other about that every time we spoke.

I conclude this chapter with my all-time favourite after-dinner speaker, Joe Dindol, in his heyday unquestionably the funniest man on two feet. A small, East End Jew whose business was *schmutter* – "I sell ...no, sorry, I *stock* men's and ladies' jackets and dresses" – Joe had a stall in Wood Green market. In a slow, lugubrious monologue he says, "I'll tell yer where my shop is! You go to Oxford Street and walk dahn Bond Street to *Aspreys the Jewellers*. Jus' opposite *Aspreys* there's a bus stop. You jump on a 46 bus to Kings Cross Station where you take a train to Kettering where you take anuvver bus to Rushden. An' that's were where my shop is, Rushden, in Northamptonshire!"

We became great friends and I was able to use him professionally on many occasions to the riotous delight of his audiences. For my fiftieth birthday, Ann and I took forty people to a hotel in Cheltenham, owned by two friends, Paul and Mary Sparks, with whom I had worked when they managed the *Derry and Toms* restaurant in Kensington High Street. Joe Dindol was the last speaker, paying a tribute to us both.

I simply switched on a tape recorder and let it run. It produced one of the funniest tapes imaginable – so much so, that if I play it in the car whilst I am driving, I have to stop for fear of having an accident as I am laughing uncontrollably.

Joe is soft-spoken with a typical East End humour. He began quietly by greeting everyone with, "L'chaim!" to which we all replied, "L'chaim!"

Equally quietly and lugubriously he repeated, "L'chaim! ...L'chaim is a Hebrew word which means 'to life' ...And I ought ter know, 'coz I got a bruvver doin' chaim!"

He continued, "The date 1066, the place, Hastings. King Harold is inspecting his troops and calls out, 'OK men, I see you're all in great

299

shape. Don't forget: tomorrow morning, Battle of Hastings, nine o'clock; be there!' Suddenly he spots this little Jewish man holding a great six-foot bow and arrow. 'Ah! my man. Tell me, who are you and what you do?'

'Vell, Sir, I'm Cohen – I'm only a jobbing tailor from Stepney. Shouldn't be 'ere reely. I make buttonholes and cuffs. So I don't know what I'm s'pposed to be doin.'

'Well,' said Harold, 'Let me see how you use that bow and arrow. Can you use it?'

'Not velly well, Sir.'

'Well, show me what you can do. See that barn door over there? Well, hit it.'

'I'll do me best, yer Majesty, but like I said, I'm really a buttonhole-and-cuff man.'

So he fires off three arrows at the barn door – one goes off to the left, the second goes way over the top and the third hits the ground. Useless. So King Harold says to him, 'Not very good, are you? You'd better be careful with that thing tomorrow, or you'll 'ave some bugger's eye out!'"

I make no apology for including some of Joe's great material which all my friends and family just love.

I am not sorry to be away from speaking engagements despite Ann's view that I could so easily emulate and, in most cases, be better than, many I have heard; but I am terrified of failure, the bitter taste of which is impossible to digest. There is one aphorism I quote which states, "Those who can – do. Those who can't – teach," and with that thought in mind, several years ago, I tried my hand at teaching and ran a few seminars on 'The Alphabet of Addressing an Audience'. I also produced a book to go with it, each letter containing several facets relating to the subject.

There is absolutely no doubt that well over 90% of the male business population are lousy speakers. Most of them will not admit it as they think that when they talk to people, they are some kind of 'Jack the Lad' who can hold forth on any topic they choose to the enjoyment and amusement of all listeners. Most are wrong and become colossal bores. It is not easy, as anyone who has had to do it will agree. Winston Churchill once said the three most difficult things a man can attempt are climbing a fence leaning towards you, kissing a lady leaning away from you, and making an after-dinner speech.

And so I decided to put matters right and eventually ran about twenty seminars. The success rate of producing fairly competent and confident speakers was total. The day-long format consisted of lectures from me based on the pamphlet with each student speaking several times before a video camera, and afterwards seeing their performances and having them criticised. I also ran corporate seminars, training members of staff and I remain convinced that, despite being successful in their own sphere, many business people could benefit from coaching in the art of making a speech.

So, to answer the question, "Who is the best after-dinner speaker you have ever heard?" I can only repeat, "That depends…" But I cannot resist the opportunity to end this chapter with another contribution from Joe Dindol, in the form of a poem he read at one of our parties.

As I awoke this sunny day, to greet this special morn,
My heart was filled with love and joy to behold this wondrous dawn.
I opened wide my window – with air my lungs to fill,
When a tiny little Robin came and landed on my sill.

He looked so bright and perky, and brought me so much cheer –
And sung his song so joyfully, for all the world to hear.
He was so sweet and gentle, with his chest a fiery red.
So I slowly closed the window… and crushed 'is bleedin 'ead!

They don't write 'em like that any more.

What do you give a man who has everything for his seventieth birthday – a man who owns large slices of London and who is one of the country's most generous philanthropists? The answer is 'No Presents Please', which was clearly emblazoned on the otherwise spectacular invitation the 400 guests received to Sir Charles Clore's birthday bash at The Dorchester. He stood and shook hands with them all as I introduced them, and we all sat down for dinner. The Dorchester ballroom had been divided into two 'gazebos', side by side, with a small dance floor in each.

As a surprise, his family had invited the legendary Andy Williams, one of the most famous recording and cabaret stars in the world at that time, to come and sing *Happy Birthday*. They took him secretly to his table with his back to Sir Charles, and when the birthday toast was proposed, he made his majestic appearance and sang his tribute. It stunned and delighted the entire company – a magical moment.

Before that surprise, a mini-drama occurred which caused quite a stir. The second course had been served and gentle music was playing in the background when suddenly, a slim, pretty, blonde and petite young lady got up from her seat, walked casually round to where Sir Charles was sitting, stood in front of him and casually stripped off – shoes, dress, bra, panties, the lot – and for a brief moment stood there starkers. She then hurried out of the room amid a buzz of amusement and amazement. I was immediately summoned to Sir Charles' presence, who demanded, "Who the hell was that? Who arranged it? Go and find out, at once. I must know!" And so I was sent off to find the streaker.

She had gone into the ladies' cloakroom, and a man who had followed her out to give her back her clothes was waiting for her. Sir Charles then came out and called for both his own and The Dorchester's security guards, intending to have her 'dealt with'. To say he was furious was an understatement – he was boiling with anger and demanded an explanation from the man.

"Who are you, who is that woman, and what are you doing here?" he roared. Names were given, as well as their contact with the company.

"So what made her do such a disgusting thing at my party?" continued Sir Charles.

"We did it for a bet," was the tame reply.

"A bet... *a bet?*" roared the birthday boy.

"Yes, I bet a friend that she wouldn't dare to do it."

"And how much was the bet for?" enquired Sir Charles.

"£1,500."

Sir Charles thought for only a few seconds and then said, "Right. I want £1,500 from both of you, which I shall give to charity. You'll sign a promissory note and then be escorted from the hotel. If you do not settle, I'll take further action. Do you understand?"

In front of a lobby full of security men (burley ex-coppers), the man, and the woman, now clothed, agreed and apologised for the embarrassment. A nod and a grunt was all they received from Sir Charles, who turned to me and said, "Right, let's get on with the party!" As we walked through the reception, he uncharacteristically put his hand around my shoulder and, with a huge grin on his rather craggy face, said, "I got three grand out of the bastards and I couldn't be happier. It's made my evening!"

Chapter 20

Music – Music – Music!

"I'm playing all the right notes...
...not necessarily in the right order!"

Eric Morecambe/Eddie Braben

In the 1950-60s, Theresa Brewer sang a great song:

Put another nickel in
In the nickelodeon,
All I want is loving you and
Music, music, music!

The last two lines apply unequivocally to me. I love my wife and music – in that order, although, because of my devotion and my constant listening to it, Ann sometimes questions the order! "...You love Rachmaninov more than you love me!" is the oft heard *crie de coeur* in our house!

(Here I'm reminded of a story about a lifelong Arsenal supporter who drove his wife mad. She said to him one day, "Arsenal, Arsenal, Arsenal, that's all I ever hear. It's nothing but Arsenal all day long. I bet you love Arsenal more than you love me!" To which the nurd replied, "When you go on like that, I love the Spurs more than I love you!")

Music of all kinds surrounded my upbringing because of Dad's deep love of it and his wonderful voice. As soon as I could walk, I was put to the piano and, whereas I occasionally play a bit, I was never brilliant, only reaching Grade VII in my studies, but I can still knock out all three movements of Beethoven's Moonlight Sonata when I think about it; but not very well.

My tastes are eclectic and I frequently listen to a wide variety of different types, enthusing vociferously about performances to anyone who is prepared to be bored by my rantings. I do not have one particular favourite kind of music, but as I was brought up on Victorian and Edwardian ballads, those are possibly at the top of my likes. I have piles of Dad's music, some of which he sang, but many more of the tenor range which did not suit him, and I still play those accompaniments. These are full of beautiful music, virtually unknown and unsung today, but as I can hear the melody line in my brain, I do not need to have them sung.

Dad was passionate about brass band music, and whilst he was at the Royal Academy, made annual visits to the Royal Albert Hall for the finals of the National Contests. He would sit and listen to twenty or more bands, all playing the same test piece, and love every moment. I, too, worked at a couple and found it a blissful experience. In my view, there really is no purer sound than that produced by a brass band. No, I do not mean a military band, but a band consisting simply of brass instruments.

Dad's tutor, Prof Thomas Mukes, used to ram Gilbert and Sullivan down his throat, filling him with a lifelong dislike of it. I actually like a lot of their stuff and have seen several of their operettas. One of my favourite Sullivan works is *The Long Day Closes* which is sung at many show business funerals; it is beautiful and so moving, and I hope will be sung at mine!

Dad loathed opera in all its forms and refused to sing any – I agree wholeheartedly. In the entire repertoire of that genre, I suppose there are about three pieces to which I can listen. The rest either make me laugh – especially when sung in English – or bore me to tears.

I adore the more romantic classics: Tchaikovsky, Rachmaninov, Saint-Saëns, Grieg, Delius, Vaughan Williams, and many others of that period, and can weep openly at great performances. My main loves are the large orchestral pieces and concerti for the piano and violin; there is a whole world of great music which, if I had it all on disc, would last me the rest of my life. I also love to hear different recordings of the same piece and compare techniques and performances.

I do not like baroque music and really cannot get to grips with Corelli, Vivaldi or Bach. In my view, Bach has far too many notes: a whole heap of demi-semi-quavers which don't seem to get you anywhere and go on for ever. I feel the same about oratorio.

As a kid, I used to go, as often as I could afford, on Sunday nights to the London Palladium for the Ted Heath Swing Sessions. The drummer, Jack Parnell, was related to the boss of that theatre, Val Parnell, and I am sure had something to do with these shows. This was undoubtedly one of the finest bands of its kind in the world, as was acknowledged when he did his first concert at the Carnegie Hall, New York. It was a riot and the Americans simply went wild for his music, which at the time, rivalled the other greats like Stan Kenton, Count Basie and Glen Miller. Only a few years ago, a bandleader friend, Johnny Howard, and I went to the final concert of the Ted Heath Band at the Royal Festival Hall. It was a night full of nostalgia and we had the cheapest seats in the chorus, right behind the stage. As the twenty or so musicians walked on to take their seats, Johnny pointed to many of them and said, "He used to work for me... and him... and him... and him," as virtually all of them had played in his bands over the years. I, too, used to run a small 'gig' band and booked the musicians through a sax player called Vic Reynolds. He was 'star-struck' about jazz musicians and would frequently book many of the greatest names to 'sit-in' on one of my jobs. So I can boast that Tommy Whittle, Bob Efford, Don Lusher, Pete Hughes, Cliff Townshend (father of Pete of The Who!) and many other great musicians used to play in *my* band! Ha... but quite true!

On piano at that farewell concert, was a fabulous pianist, Brian Dee, with whom I had often worked. I have a beautiful *John Broadwood* grand piano at home in perfect condition and it needed playing – properly. So after the show I asked Brian if he would come to my place one evening and play for me. I told him I would invite a few mates with like minds to hear him, to which he readily agreed. A few weeks later, about forty pros from the business all descended on my home and Brian held the fort. It was a purely magical night – one which I would love to repeat. Also at that party were Kenny Ball and his bass player John Bennett. They play a type of jazz which is also among my favourites.

That brings me to my next passion: great pianists, both jazz and classical. I adore the talents of such legends as Art Tatum, George Shearing, Oscar Peterson, Teddy Wilson and so many more, especially André Previn, whose brilliant talents comfortably span both types of music. Art Tatum's recordings of Gershwin's *Liza* and another of *Tea for Two* send me into ecstasies.

Mervyn Conn was the finest entrepreneur of Country Music this side of the Atlantic. It should not be called Country and Western, although many people do call it that. For over twenty years, Mervyn put on an enormous Country Music show at Wembley Arena. He took the place over for the whole of Easter, and each night invited the top names from Nashville, Tennessee, and other towns with that kind of music, to perform there. The concerts were a sell-out each year and were sensational.

Every Maundy Thursday, Mervyn ran a large banquet to which all the stars, as well as sponsors, musicians and other Country enthusiasts were invited; he asked me to run them for him, which I did for about ten years. They were memorable, purely because of the artistes who attended and who performed privately for us. They really are delightful folk; highly talented, kind, clean-living, charming and extremely friendly, and were a joy to meet. I list with much pride such names as Don Williams (who never removed his hat!), Johnny Cash, Tammy Wynette, the Everley Brothers, Dolly Parton, Kris Kristopherson and Glen Campbell. On one occasion I had to introduce Glen Campbell, who had brought along his three-year-old son. As he went onto the floor, lad in arms, he handed the boy to me and said, "Don't drop him!" I was literally left 'holding the baby', a memory I treasure!

These concerts bred in me a liking for that kind of music. No, not a great enthusiast, but I love its simplicity and purity, and the fact that I met so many from yesteryear gives me nostalgic memories. Mervyn Conn ran these concerts all over Europe. He was famous in *The Grand Ole Opry* in Nashville as he did more to publicise their music in Europe than anyone before or since, and was honoured by being given recognition in their Country Music Hall of Fame.

Alas! nothing is eternal and its popularity faded until these concerts ceased. I still see Mervyn occasionally and we spend hours reminiscing about the golden days of Country Music.

In a long career of great events, one of the most memorable was spent with my family at the Royal Albert Hall. It was an evening concert given by the Red Army Choir and Dance Ensemble, an occasion of the most brilliant musical entertainment I have ever encountered. The choir of over 200 soldiers, the 60-piece band of Russian musicians, and the team of the greatest Gopak and Trepak dancers were all truly sensational. I could almost write a whole chapter on their brilliance – alas, space and your interest don't permit. However, they produced a CD of their songs which I play regularly, and their performance of a solo singer and the choir singing 'Annie Laurie' makes me weep buckets every time I listen to it.

Also high on my list of adored music is what are generally known as 'Standards'. Melodies written by such brilliant composers and lyricists as Cole Porter, Irving Berlin, Richard Rogers, Hoagie Carmichael, Johnny Mercer, the Gershwin Brothers, Sammy Kahn, Oscar Hammerstein and many British exponents like Don Black and Tim Rice – it is a very long list. I have a large collection of tapes and CDs and can listen to their wonderful compositions for hours. In their own field, all were geniuses and have given years of pleasure to millions of people. The world would be a much poorer place without their talents. It is regrettable, because of the present demand of younger folk, that the music regularly played on most commercial stations nowadays is noisy, tuneless, banal, ghastly and, in my opinion, quite frightful. Popular demand for that kind of crap has pushed the really talented, lyrical sounds virtually off the airwaves and it is only thanks to the likes of David Jacobs, Desmond Carrington and a few others, that we can still hear them on the BBC. We should offer our thanks to some recording companies who are still prepared to produce them on disc so that we can enjoy them privately.

One of the real 'downsides' of my work currently, is the horrendous noise that the bands are now required to play. I will not dignify it by calling it music, as it isn't. It is a cacophony of coarse, garish, over-amplified sound which is deafeningly hideous. When I began my career, I took a couple of medals in ballroom dancing – the kind of dance where a gentleman holds a lady in his arms and, with varying degrees of ability and talent, manoeuvres her around a dance floor. OK, so some ladies ended up with very sore toes or an aching back, dancing with a guy pushing her arm backwards, but at least it was sociable and pleasant. It is noticeable that over the past twenty years or so that kind of dance has almost completely disappeared. When the band strikes up its mindless, tuneless roar, people skulk onto the floor, stop on one spot, frequently with a fag or lager bottle in their hands, and simply wiggle or gyrate their bodies in grotesque movements or jump up and down. There is no charm, finesse, gentility or meeting of minds or bodies, just gymnastics-to-a-tuneless-beat. It really is quite horrible. Fortunately, at many functions I now do, I leave when the formalities have ended so do not have to endure this horror.

I am grateful for all the musical memories I have loved over many years. I can switch off the last lot when I get into my car to drive home and can choose from my very wide range of musical loves to calm me down and 'soothe the fevered brow!' Music is a very important part of my life and I still enjoy playing my piano.

This brings me to another small area of music which I enjoy: hymns – mainly Welsh ones with glorious harmonies. I often play them just for my own pleasure. I have fond memories of family musical evenings in my aunt's tiny North Wales cottage – it was filled to the gunnels with relatives who each sang in their own range. Uncle Will was a deep basso profundo, Dad was a baritone, Cousin Griff was a light, lyrical tenor, Ann and Aunt Ceridwen (Dwd to everyone) were deep altos, and cousins Sarah and Catherine were sweet sopranos; any English people there just shut up and listened – they couldn't compete! Dwd owned a small American pedal harmonium, which we took in turns to play, choosing a hymn for all to sing. These were wonderful evenings and proved beyond any doubt, if ever there was any, that in the words of Dylan Thomas in *Under Milk Wood*, 'Thank God we're a musical nation.'

I frequently indulge in a daydream of picking my eight favourite pieces of music to take onto *Desert Island Discs*. The task is impossible! I can pick eight one day and then next a completely different bunch. I really do not know where my favourites lie, but it is a pleasant little exercise.

So as long as I can play and listen to discs and radio, all will be well. Music will always be with me and I am grateful for that. Life would be drab and empty without it.

As stage doorkeeper at the London Palladium, George Cooper was a legend. He zealously guarded that very special office for many years – the litany of the greatest names in the world of entertainment that he looked after would fill several volumes. Ask any performer who has had the great thrill of appearing there, and they will tell you their particular story. I only met George infrequently but was always treated with respect and kindness.

I recently delivered a pair of shoes, which had been left at my home by a friend who was appearing in a variety show at the London Palladium. They were in a plastic bag and I asked the doorkeeper to inform him. My friend told me later that this young man had said to him, "Some grey-haired old fart named Williams has just left a plastic bag with a pair of shoes in it for you. What do you want me to do with 'em?" Such respect!

Way back in the 1960s, Tom Jones was at the height of his career (he seems to go on for ever), and to have secured him for a cabaret appearance would have been both difficult and expensive... however, fairground proprietors had persuasive powers. The Showman's Guild was a lively organisation consisting of families who owned and ran fairgrounds, showgrounds and fun palaces of all kinds. They were a close, family-orientated group with much inter-marrying. They worked extremely hard in their everyday business, but loved to play equally hard at their social gatherings; and boy, did they know how to spend! Johnny North was their organiser, and he booked me for their banquet and ball at the Café Royal. I clearly recall one member ordering the wine and drinks for his table. Having requested several bottles of both red and white wine, he said to the waiter, "To begin with, I'll have a couple of dozen bottles of lager and you'd better also bring a couple of dozen bottles of light ale. We'll also have a bottle of scotch, brandy, vodka, rum and gin, two or three dozen tonics and bitter lemons, and a few jugs of fruit cup and *Pimms*... I'll let you know when we've run out and need some more." "Very good," said the waiter, "By the way, Sir, how many are there in your party?" "Ten," was the monosyllabic reply.

The function began at 5.00 pm and was scheduled to end at 4.00 am, and there was not a moment's respite during the whole evening. The nine-course dinner was followed by the usual speeches, and on this occasion there were ten speakers either proposing or replying to toasts. I expected them to last for hours, and was astounded by the fact that the combined length of them all was no longer than twenty minutes – yes, less than two minutes per speech. Marvellous!

Their evening dress was impeccable! The ladies wore expensive and glamorous *haute couture* dresses from the most exclusive houses, while the dinner suits were all Savile Row-tailored and must have cost a fortune; they were all absolutely immaculate.

The cabaret was a secret, but Johnny North told me that at midnight Tom Jones would be appearing for half an hour. This was astounding news, as I knew how impossible it was to get him. But, as I said, they have their ways and Johnny told me how. The day before, three of the committee went to the Palladium and chatted to George Cooper where an 'inducement' changed hands, gaining them entry into Mr Jones's dressing room. They spoke to him and offered him substantial financial persuasion to '…pop into the Café Royal on your way home tomorrow night and give us a few songs!' The deal was done; musical backing was discussed and the great man agreed to 'pop in'!

To give everyone a better view of the show, I needed to get those whose tables were at the back to come and sit down on the ballroom floor, thus creating a cosy semi-circle facing the band. At midnight I uttered the magical words, "And here he is… MRRRR TOOOOM JONES!" They went wild with delight. He sang his heart out and twisted, squirmed and gyrated to great effect. He was wearing a pair of trousers that were so tight, they not only showed his sex but also his religion; and the women loved it … to such an extent that some of them sitting on their bums in their *Christian Dior* ball gowns on the floor felt a burning desire to touch him as he sang. They began to slide slowly but surreptitiously forward, getting nearer to Tom, and I had to try to keep them back. I was wasting my time as they kept coming! I hastily found Johnny who had spotted it anyway. I said, "You must stop them or there could be a disaster." His immediate reaction was to summon four blokes – that really is the best description – saying to them, "Right, 'Arry, Fred, Charlie, Joe. You see them women? Well stop 'em!" And four fairground bouncers, scar-faced, broken-nosed, cauliflower-eared, dressed in 500-guinea suits stood like four pillars of Hercules between Tom and the sex-motivated women.

His show nearly over, Tom Jones came to his last number and ended with rapturous and adoring applause from the audience – they were going mad. Expecting him to return to take the customary bow with possibly an encore, they all stayed in their seats. But, as he came past me, he handed me his microphone and said, "I'm not coming back on! It's too dangerous out there. But how can I get out?" I pointed to a small door into the kitchens and said, "Go through there and lock the door behind you when you get out!" He did. Suddenly there was pandemonium. The women realised that he was not coming back and at least a dozen of them hurled themselves at that little door, scrapping with each other to get out of the way. Dresses were torn, one lady fell down and sprained her wrist, and they were screaming, "TOM, TOM, TOM!" It was pure madness. I had never seen such mass hysteria... but he had got away.

Things quietened down and dancing resumed. Later, I took some of the principal wives to see him and he was most courteous and friendly. I shall never forget my one and only meeting with the legendary Tom Jones.

Chapter 21

Forty Years in the Red!

"An autobiography is much the same as a biography…
but without the last chapter."

Anon

As mentioned earlier in this narrative, the painful memories of the Perforated Paper Company and the other two 'starters' have never left me. Of the thousands of subsequent and extremely successful dinners, dances, weddings, barmitzvahs, 21st birthday parties, cocktail parties, Royal functions, fund-raising extravaganzas and a myriad more, most totally forgotten, those three are still alive and well in my nostalgic archives. In the ensuing years a number of milestones had been reached, but these passed without special recognition, so when 1990 approached the celebration of forty years in the business seemed a good idea and Ann and I set about planning it. By now I was well established and had built what modern terminology would describe as 'a good database' of names and addresses of clients. We therefore decided to hold a cocktail party in March, inviting as many people as we could afford. This was to be the launch of a much larger banquet to be held in September – but more of that anon.

I worked at the Café Royal, Regent Street, dozens of times each season and was their preferred toastmaster. My Seminars on 'The Art of Addressing an Audience' had been held there and my friendship with the management was very strong. Furthermore, the Forte family who owned it were very good friends and I did a lot of work for them and the Trusthouse Forte Group. I had recommended The Grosvenor House for many large and lucrative banquets over the years, and now felt it was time to call in a favour or two. Steve McManus, the banqueting manager at the Café Royal, took my request to the board and brought me the great news that Rocco Forte had agreed to pay for the drinks and that the food was to be charged out at cost, a great saving to me and very generous of them. And so 15th March 1990 was the chosen date, forty years after my first job.

But who were we to invite? Ann and I went through all our records and we sent over 850 personal invitations to attend a cocktail party at the Café Royal, all with pre-paid return acceptance postcards. It was an eclectic list involving members of our large families, industrialists, MPs, Freemasons from dozens of Lodges, entertainers from stage, screen and radio, Lords, Ladies and Gentlemen and many others. As the replies came in, we were delighted to see the acceptances piling up and eventually the day arrived.

To spice up the venue, we took with us photographs, brochures, menu cards, letters of congratulation and boxes full of souvenirs I had collected during my career to display around the room. My cousin Jean, always a champion of mine, took a visitors' book around to all the guests for them to sign. It was to her horror that she spotted many people taking away armfuls of the precious memorabilia which had coloured my career. She was furious and stopped them, but many had already disappeared.

We felt it courteous to receive the guests and stood by the door shaking hands – which proved to be a huge problem as the queue to meet us stretched down two floors. The toastmaster was a very dear and close friend, Malcolm Clayton, who was trying to push us along when suddenly there was a bit of a furore. Sir Edward Heath had arrived to greet us and steadfastly refused to queue; so in he came along with about a dozen Lords, a whole list of show business personalities, Sir David Frost, and my guest of honour, Lord Tonypandy. Malcolm kept a count of the numbers who attended, which was in excess of 480. You can imagine just how proud we felt.

Adrian Goodall, the husband of one of my clients, was a young artist whom I felt had great talent and wonderful skills with the brush. He painted a portrait of me to be 'unveiled' at this party. My family – and in particular my mother – hate it as they say it makes me look severe, morose and unsmiling. I like it for those very reasons as I feel it is a thoroughly honest portrayal of how I look when I am at work. Sadly, it now rests in my attic as I do not have a wall large enough to show it.

I had asked Lord Tonypandy to say a few words on the night, and he delivered a really wonderful speech. My son Timothy was the second speaker, and he was also quite superb and very kind in his sentiments. I spoke last and, apart from thanking everyone for attending, I explained about the banquet I was planning in September. The cocktail party was a great success in every way and gave us some wonderful memories.

The Great Room at The Grosvenor House has been my 'spiritual home' since my early career. This was the venue I chose for the major celebration of my forty years, and having worked there hundreds of times, I knew all the staff. All the proceeds would go to various charities, but as I was involved with so many, it was difficult to choose which ones. The final choices were The Prince's Trust, SPARKS, NCH, Birthright and The Ravenswood Home.

It was now time for Ann and me to start sending out invitations to try to sell tickets for the banquet. At the time, no royal guest had agreed to attend. I learned very early in my career that if you invite a senior royal personage to a party who refuses, you can only send any further invitations to a less senior royal – you cannot go upwards! Prince Charles and Princess Anne were unable to attend, but as HRH Princess Michael of Kent was the royal patron of SPARKS, I sent her an invitation. Ann and I went on holiday and on our return the first letter I opened was from Kensington Palace saying that Princess Michael of Kent would be delighted to attend, which was just thrilling. Having agreed certain details with her office, a few weeks later I received a telephone call asking, 'Would it be alright' if her husband HRH Prince Michael of Kent came too? *Would it be alright?* I was delighted. Suddenly my fortieth anniversary bash was now a Royal fortieth anniversary bash.

You have no idea just how much a royal guest at an event helps to sell tickets. On 21st September 1990, just under 1,000 guests attended The Grosvenor House to celebrate my forty years 'In The Red'.

As mentioned elsewhere, Fred Finn was famous as the world's most travelled flier, having clocked up several million miles, with dozens of trips on Concorde. He introduced me to a 23-stone giant named Micky Finch who, amongst his many other occupations, was a publisher and promoter who proved to be invaluable. At most of these large events, it is customary to produce elaborate and expensive brochures which hardly get looked at and are of little value to the advertisers who spend large sums of money. My choice was to produce a diary which had information about the event and in which advertisers would contribute. Micky Finch handled all of this and produced 1,000 diaries for the guests and advertisers. Many of my friends still have them as souvenirs and did not actually use them as diaries. In addition, he was happy to present a substantial cheque to the banquet from the advertising revenue to go to the charity fund.

Fred Finn offered me a prize of a Kenya Safari trip for two people – worth about £6,000 – which gave me an idea for pricing my tickets. The total costs for running the event were around £50 per head, based on 500 attending. This included food, entertainment of special guests, bands, cabarets and production costs, but I had determined to make a profit on the sale of tickets so these were priced at £95 each, quite high at that time. This released £45 per ticket as charity donations. The Kenya Safari was the 'door prize' so that everyone who paid top price to attend had a chance to win it. It also helped in another way as I had a few friends who really could not afford £95 but who were prepared to pay £50, which was the cut-off price. It just meant that they did not qualify for the Safari prize draw. It was a simple expedient; the tickets had a perforated tear-off section which was collected on arrival and placed in a drum to be drawn later. It is a great idea and I am surprised that other organisers have not pinched it for their own events.

Prince and Princess Michael of Kent arrived at 7.30 and were taken into the VIP reception area where they were introduced to other guests, including the cabaret artistes and senior representatives of the five charities. When dinner was announced, we four made a formal entry to the top table. I had written to various toastmaster organisations around the UK offering them special terms if they would be willing to attend to form a guard of honour into dinner. Forty attended, making a spectacular and colourful line in their red tailcoats with arms raised, holding gavels in their white-gloved hands. We processed down this column, and The Princess loved it, speaking to many of them on the way to the table. I had also sent open invitations to 'stars' of several of the TV soaps who responded generously and were pleased to accept. Several came from *EastEnders* and *The Bill*, as well as many entertainers from all branches of the business. This made it possible for me to seat a few 'faces' at tables around the room so that the guests could meet them in person.

Long speeches are not popular at these charity events, so I restricted them to two – me and one other. Barry Cryer was my first choice and agreed at once, and, as I suspected, was screamingly funny. For other entertainment, I had selected all my favourites – after all, it was my party and I could do what I liked! Johnny Howard's Big Band played Glen Miller music during the dinner, and immediately after the speeches, the raffle was drawn, the auction held and the main entertainment began. Incidentally, the auctioneer was the masterly Nicholas Bonham.

The late and much loved entertainer, Roy Castle, a brother Water Rat, was one of the greatest of artistes. His talents were almost unlimited – he could sing, dance, play about ten instruments, tell stories and amuse audiences for hours. We had been friends for years and he agreed to come along. He was wonderful. Just before he died, he involved me in a charity called ASH – Against Smoking for Health – and we did several TV shows together, talking about cancer being caused by 'passive smoking'. He had never smoked in his life, but eventually died of lung cancer, having inhaled smoke from other people's cigarettes in the many venues he had worked. He crusaded passionately to bring it to the notice of tobacco companies, doctors and the government, right up to his last breath, and there is now a special research unit in his name.

Being Welsh, there had to be a strong flavour from the Principality, so I engaged the Band of the Welsh Guards to perform their usual marching display. When they eventually stood to attention, not one but two Welsh choirs appeared on the stage, The Gwalia Male Voice Choir and the London Welsh Male Voice Choir – some ninety voices in all. They were asked to sing a couple of my favourite hymns in Welsh. With the accompaniment of the band, the sound was heavenly. As a finale, they combined with the band to sing the usual flag-raisers – in English – *Rule Britannia* and *Land of Hope and Glory*.

To add further lustre to this display, I engaged about ninety small children to appear in the show. Babette Langford – the mother of Bonnie – ran a dance school with dozens of kids from the age of three upwards. For my party, she dressed them all in Yeoman Warders (Beefeater) uniforms, gave them all wands and banners, and choreographed a marching display around the Guards Band. The crowd adored them. They made their entry from either side of the top table, and as the little 3-4 year-olds went by, Ann and the Princess were almost in tears as they were so gorgeous.

Whenever people ask me, "What's the cabaret tonight?" my usual reply is, "The Red Arrows!" Guess what I had at my fortieth anniversary bash? Yes, you're right... The Red Arrows! But 'How?' you may ask. Fred Finn had organised the whole thing. At the end of the musical part of the cabaret, as the last chorister left the stage, the Great Room was suddenly thrust into total darkness. In the ceiling were erected two very large TV screens and, on cue, a three-minute film of the Red Arrows Flying Display team was shown performing all their spectacular flying tricks and manoeuvres filmed over the clear skies of Cyprus. It was breathtaking and, when it ended and the lights went up, there, on the stage, were the ten Red Arrows pilots standing to attention. The crowd was euphoric. As the pilots appeared, Ann and Princess Michael were peering forward, with eyes sticking out like chapel hat-pegs, staring open-mouthed at these handsome, charming young men. Princess Michael leaned across me and said to Ann in a whisper, "You pick any five you like and I'll have the others! Aren't they gorgeous!"

For an auction prize, Fred Finn had also arranged a day with the Red Arrows at Scampton, including flying on one of their practice trips. Doug Lockyer bid £10,000, and he and a friend actually flew with the Red Arrows. He had a wonderful day… and had never been so sick in his life! Apparently, the G forces have that effect on anyone who goes up for the first time! All the pilots and their wives were guests at the banquet. Knowing Prince Michael's keen interest in flying and veteran cars, I placed the captain and team leader of the pilots next to him on the top table as they had so much in common.

Dancing began to the Johnny Howard Band, and Ann and I had the great honour of opening the ball and actually dancing with Royalty. The final band had to be Kenny Ball and his Jazzmen. Thanks to raffles, auctions, profit from the tickets, advertising in the diary/brochure and other donations, a total of just under £70,000 was raised for the five charities.

It had not been possible to sort out the finances on the night, so when the accounts had been settled, I needed a venue to present the cheques to the charities. I chanced to mention this to Peter Worthy, the General Manager of *Madame Tussaud's* where I had worked occasionally. He immediately said, "Bring them here – I will give you a champagne buffet for the presentation." So, a week or so after my party, I invited about fifty people to The Garden Room at *Tussaud's* and handed over five cheques to very grateful recipients. It had been lot of hard work, but the memory of that night will always remain with me.

Here I must add a personal tribute to my good friend and accountant for many years, Charles Niren of *Niren Blake*. He masterminded all the finances of these events and saved me a great deal of work and heartache. Charles has been my financial guru for many years and Ann and I value his advice and friendship.

There are many who loathe flying and the thought of spending 22 out of 24 hours in an aeroplane can be horrific, but this happened to me and with no less successful and charismatic a gentleman than Sir Richard Branson (although the Sir-dom came much later). It all happened a long while ago.

Unsurprisingly, in view of his penchant for flying, Fred Finn was very friendly with Richard Branson and they both benefited by the publicity Fred received for his travels. I've lost count of the number of millions of miles Fred has flown, but he was to achieve another milestone in a flight to Los Angeles, which was to coincide with the opening of a new gateway into that city for *Virgin Atlantic*, and I was engaged to officiate.

A dinner party was organised at an exclusive Sussex hotel the night before for the VIP guests who were to travel on the new route. The following day, we all assembled in the *Virgin Atlantic* first-class lounge at Gatwick Airport and prepared for a memorable flight. Richard Branson masterminded the whole trip and led us to the plane. We settled into our seats in the first-class compartment where the champagne flowed freely. Once airborne, we ate, drank, met friends and went onto the flight deck to talk to the crew; there were hairdressers, manicurists, masseuses to look after our comforts, together with a fabulous buffet. The eleven-hour flight passed in a flash.

Richard was in his element as he really is a 'people person' and he had a great trip. The plane was full in economy class, but when we had achieved a certain 'mileage', I was allowed to make an announcement through the cabin PA system – something I had always wanted to do – to tell the passengers about Fred's latest landmark and what was going on 'up front'. It was another small dream come true.

It is a tradition when flying on *Virgin Atlantic* to give passengers an ice cream. On this flight, the passengers had the privilege of receiving theirs from the hand of the boss himself; they were astounded to see Mr Branson walking up and down the aisle, handing out goodies and chatting to everybody. He is very hands-on and knows the importance of getting the opinions of his customers firsthand. Indeed, he even asked me to sample two starters he was considering for future first-class meals. I pondered on them both, chose one as being better than the other, and gave my opinion, to which he replied, "Thanks for that. I agree. You've just saved me a couple of million quid as I shan't use the other one!"

A cocktail party had been arranged for when we landed at Los Angeles... and I was needed to run it. I had the intriguing and extremely cramped experience of changing from casual clothes into full evening dress in the loo of a Boeing 747 – not easy – and in my haste I lost my collar stud down the lavatory and had to use a safety pin!

An enthusiastic crowd of fans, airline dignitaries, airport officials and press were assembled to greet Fred Finn, Richard Branson and our flying guests, and I had to introduce them to the VIPs. It was a highly successful public relations operation – the downside was that, with the exception of Richard and me, the others were staying over for a few days, but we had to fly back home. Reluctantly, we left the party, jumped into our limo and within about ninety minutes of landing we were back in the first-class compartment of the 747, now fully restored to its pristine comfort. Twenty-two hours after we had left Gatwick, we were back there again.

I slept all the way home and, as we touched down, Richard and I discussed the trip and the general comfort. This pre-dates the current luxury of beds and lounging seats where you can stretch out, but I had to agree that we had slept well and were quite refreshed. So ended a round trip of about 9,000 miles.

Shortly after, *Virgin Atlantic* opened a gateway into Boston, Mass. There was not the same razzamatazz this time, but Richard Branson invited about fifty American travel journalists to his home in

Oxfordshire and felt the need of a toastmaster to control matters. I arrived early and enjoyed the casual delight of a cup of tea and piece of toast with him in the large kitchen of his beautiful home. He told me that he was planning on teaching them the rules of cricket – absolutely crackers, but that's Mr Branson... zany, impulsive and unpredictable.

On their arrival, they were fêted and fed with champagne and a magnificent buffet; as usual, his hospitality knew no bounds. After a couple of hours of socialising, I began the virtually impossible task of explaining to a gang of semi-inebriated, tough-cookie, hard-nosed American travel journalists the gentle, complicated and oh so English rules of cricket. It was quite preposterous and impossible. A cricket pitch had been marked out on the lawns and about fifty of us went out to attempt to play the game. It was as hilarious as it was disastrous, and Richard entered into it with huge gusto and enthusiasm. The main problem was their knowledge of baseball, where, as soon as they hit the ball, they throw down the bat – them's the rules. Someone chucked the ball at them – 'bowled' is just not the word to describe what they did with the ball – and if they hit it, they ran like blazes, hurling the cricket bat to the ground. Cricket was never more debased and disorganised, but everyone had a wonderful time.

There was one small disappointment. In a corner of his land, Richard had tethered his huge hot-air balloon, the prototype of the famous one in which he made his almost disastrous transatlantic flight. It had been hoped to give his guests a ride about 200 feet into the air. Sadly, the weather did not allow this as the wind was blowing too strongly and he had not received permission from the flying authorities to get it off the ground. Alas! all we could do was stand and gaze up at this leviathan floating above us.

Chapter 22

Through the Keyhole

"Hello... good evening... and welcome."

Sir David Frost

Whilst Ann and I were on holiday in Florida, my mother telephoned very excited about something, which was unusual as she never usually showed much enthusiasm – probably a throwback to the days when life was tough and many promises of great things never came to anything. There was a standing joke in our house about the expression, "Well, the Mayor's going to be there!" when a booker or agent wanted Dad to drop his fee below what he would normally charge – the implication being that the event was so high-profile that work would flow in abundance from it. It never happened, so when anyone mentioned this, we simply ignored it.

Mum was on the end of the line from England, which must have been special as she was still watching the pennies on the telephone. She said, "A bloke named Frost has just rung about something to do with a keyhole. Don't really know what he means, but he wants you to ring him. Can you do it from there? You don't want to lose it, whatever it is." I rang this bloke named Frost. It turned out to be Sir David of that ilk, for the programme, *Through the Keyhole*.

I had known David Frost for many years. Indeed, he came to my fortieth anniversary party. The lady told me that he wondered if I would be interested in being a guest celebrity on *Through the Keyhole*. Being self-employed, as I am, I take the view that you are only ever as good as the bookings you have in your diary, and the chance for a bit of free publicity is never to be overlooked. This would also be a bit of fun, so I jumped at the opportunity.

Back in England, I called them again and was told the format. Dates were fixed for Loyd Grossman to visit our house in Enfield to do his tour. He brought with him his usual production team of about eight people, a producer, couple of cameramen, lighting and sound technicians, all highly experienced having done dozens of these programmes, but very charming. Ann and I try to be hospitable and go to great lengths to see that any visitors are both 'well fed and well drunk'! We were both fascinated by the fact that the producer brought with her a large cool box full of their own refreshments and ate very little of the extensive spread we had laid on.

Loyd Grossman and the cameraman went through various rooms in the house which, of course, were tidier than ever, to select what would be filmed. They asked if I had any books or items which would give a hint to my profession. I had put away anything that would give the game away completely, but left a few clues around the house. They were there for about two hours setting up lights and camera angles, and filming different sections. Loyd Grossman then walked from room to room with the usual dialogue, hinting at items which would help the eventual panellists. They were kind, charming and extremely pleasant but one sensed that it was simply just 'another' *Keyhole* and left.

Several weeks later, I was phoned and given a choice of dates when the show would be filmed, and Ann and I duly travelled to the TV studios in Leeds for the big day. We were taken by a route different from the audience and put in a room with others who were to appear on the show that day. As you can imagine, for financial reasons, they do several programmes in a day, which lasts from about 11.00 am until well into the evening. It really is very hard work for the whole production team as well as the panel of judges.

A celebrity I ain't, and my main worry was that nobody on the panel would have heard of me. We had watched loads of episodes of the programme and there were many panellists of whom I had never heard and who certainly did not know some uppity toastmaster

326

from London purporting to be famous! It really did concern me that I would not be guessed, as had happened to many before me. I spoke to the studio manager about that when I arrived and asked who was on the panel. There were two ladies, one of whom was Caryn Franklin, a fashion expert unknown to me. The other, Ann Greig, I had seen on the box presenting a travel programme, but she would certainly never have heard of me. The third panellist was Tom O'Connor! BLISS! Great! We were mates and had worked together loads of times. I felt much better.

There are always two homes featured on the show and the first was that of a fairly well-known Irish men's fashion designer. He went first and was sussed out fairly quickly. David Frost then interviewed him and went to a break. Ann remained in the reception room to watch on television whilst I was led away to a private studio where I sat with an assistant floor manager to watch the Loyd Grossman bit. To say I was astounded is a huge understatement. I was absolutely bowled over by his tour of our house. It looked fabulous and almost unrecognisable. I remember making a very weak joke to the girl beside me when I said to her, "WOW! What a fabulous place. I wish I could afford to live in a house like that!" Ann and I have always tried to live in a nice home but the camera flattered this one beyond belief.

David then had the camera show me to the audience and threw it open to the panellists who asked the usual questions suggested by the house. As I suspected, the first two ladies really had no idea as to either what or who I was. When it came back to Tom O'Connor, he said, "Did I spot a gavel on the corner of a table?" Applause from the audience. "Could it possibly be a toastmaster?" Again, much louder applause. David then said, "Well, you've got the profession. If you can get a name, then you will get two more points to your total!" Tom replied, "Now, I'm going to be hated by all the others I know... but... pause... is it Bryn Williams?" The roar from the audience confirmed his answer, and you cannot possibly imagine the huge relief I felt at being 'got'. Tom went on to say a few nice things about me to the studio audience as well the viewers.

After you have been 'guessed' by the panel, David interviews you and asks the usual questions to entertain the viewers, and I told him of something that had happened to me just a week before. India was celebrating its fiftieth anniversary as an independent state and held a large banquet at The Grosvenor House. The High Commissioner for India was presiding and the list of top table guests was very impressive. Regrettably, our Asian friends are not the most consistent of organisers – and changing their minds and not telling the people concerned is just one of their problems.

The principal guests were HRH Prince Charles, Prime Minister Tony Blair, Tory Leader Williams Hague, the Archbishop of Canterbury, the Bishop of London and a plethora of ministers, high commissioners and other people who think they are important! I had an assistant toastmaster colleague, Mike Jacobs, whose task it was to try to keep the Indian ladies away from Prince Charles and some of the others – a difficult chore as they hang around him like leeches. Not only are the organisers extremely informal, but they do not do things quickly, and it took Mike and me ages to get people to their seats. Eventually, the guests were all down in the hall and I had a line-up for formal procession to the top table. It took a supreme effort but we had managed, almost literally, to tear the women away from the distinguished guests.

Now, line-ups take two forms. Either the President leads and the VIPs follow in order of seniority, or you line them all up from one end of the top table to the other so that the first one in goes straight to his seat and the others follow. This is much simpler but less formal as it means that the President is not leading his guests, but is in the middle. It was this method we chose. Following my announcement, Mike duly led them all down the sweep staircase at one end of the Great Room to the table, all neatly in order. This was on a long, raised platform overlooking the other guests. The stupid arrangement they had made was that the lectern for all the speeches was on a stage opposite, on the other side of the Great Room. Frankly, it was utterly daft, but I could do nothing about it.

When I arrived, contrary to previous instructions, I was told that the Archbishop of Canterbury was not, now, going to say Grace.

That job had been given to the Lord Bishop of London. When all were assembled, I began my announcement. "Pray silence for Grace by…" at which point, out of the corner of my eye, I spotted the Archbishop of Canterbury rising from his chair with the obvious intention of coming to my microphone to say Grace. The plans had changed, but he had not been informed! So, as slowly and as deliberately as was expedient, I continued my announcement with the precise introduction for the Bishop of London, which is quite different from one for an Archbishop. I intoned very precisely… "by… The Right Reverend and Right Honourable Lord Bishop of London!" who, strangely, was not on the top table. I had dispatched Mike Jacobs to stand beside the Bishop of London with a radio microphone, which he duly shoved under his nose as he delivered a blessing in Sanskrit – a brilliant gesture. When all had sat down, I went to George Carey, the Archbishop of Canterbury, and apologised for an apparent mistake, saying that I had only heard about the change a few minutes before dinner. He was quite charming and said, "Oh, please don't apologise, I really do not mind. And anyway, my London colleague did such a splendid job speaking in Sanskrit. You would have had a simple Grace in English from me!"

My further instructions were that, immediately after Grace, I was to plough my way through all the crowded tables to the other stage housing a lectern and microphone, to introduce the Prime Minister to speak before dinner. He too, struggled through the tables and spoke for about ten minutes.

As I clambered through to make the announcement, a piece of paper was thrust into my hand from one of the Indian committee which I had neither the time to read nor to check. A quick glance told me that it concerned the PM and I was able to read it as he was speaking. When he had finished, I said, "Prime Minister, can I please ask you to wait just a moment?" I then read the following words from that grubby bit of paper.

> Prime Minister, as a token of the love and
> respect in which you are held by His Excellency
> the High Commissioner and all the Indian

Community, will you kindly accept this gift which will now be presented by Mr Keith Vaz, MP.

At this point, Keith Vaz approached the stage in complete bewilderment, covered in embarrassment and empty-handed. He said, "I'm sorry, Prime Minister, but I know absolutely nothing about this. Nobody told me," shrugged his shoulders and returned to his seat, and I was left in front of 1,000 Indians, Royalty and other influential guests with a certain amount of egg on my face. Absolutely nobody on the committee had thought it through and we were all left in complete darkness. It is then that donkey's years of experience come to the rescue. There was Tony Blair, smiling like a Cheshire cat, obviously highly amused by my discomfort that things really had gone pear-shaped and looked at me to see what I was going to do or say.

After a split second, and still with a radio microphone in my hand, I said, "Prime Minister, I am sorry about this situation. But I happen to know that your gift is not only extremely valuable but also very heavy. Because of its value, it is still locked in the safe at The Grosvenor House for security," I lied. "However, Sir, I will guarantee that tomorrow it will be delivered to Buck... (here I had a Freudian slip of the tongue but recovered just in time) ...Number Ten Downing Street." He loved it, was greatly amused, shook my hand and we both struggled back, he to the top table and me to my little table in the corner with Mike Jacobs, where I simply collapsed. I was delighted to have been able to bluff my way out of an almost impossible situation with half a pack of lies, 'cos the bloody gift was neither very valuable nor was it in the safe; it had been forgotten! But it was heavy.

When I saw *Through the Keyhole* weeks later, I noticed that they had edited it and 'cleaned it up', removing the obvious reference to that particular function with the intention of saving embarrassment to the Indian community.

There was an amusing sequel to the Prime Minister story. The following day, I was again working at The Grosvenor House in the smaller ballroom, for a cocktail party to which Tony Blair had been invited. It was very informal; he arrived, circulated for about fifteen minutes, had a little refreshment and went to a podium to speak. He was to be given a gift, and this time had been informed in advance. The moment I introduced him, he looked down from the podium to me, gave a huge grin, laughed, and quietly said to me, "I hope you've got the thing THIS time!" I enjoyed the private joke, not least because he could see I was holding the present in my hands.

The power of appearing on television can also have its problems. People often ask if I have ever had any embarrassing moments throughout my career. The obvious answer is, yes, of course, but I try to avoid telling them because, while they certainly were embarrassing at the time, they are rarely funny or amusing, and in no way entertaining. Furthermore, as any toastmaster becomes more experienced, he is frequently able either to anticipate an embarrassing situation about to occur and fend it off, or deal with it in such a way that those involved do not feel too bad about their experience. However, referring to the power of television, I vividly recall a situation which led to acute embarrassment.

David Nixon was a wonderful conjuror and illusionist. I had known him and his second wife Paula Marshall for years as they were both on the Masonic circuit and I had engaged them both very often. David hit fame and fortune with *What's My Line?* – a programme upon which he appeared for very many years with Lady Isobel Barnett, Barbara Kelly, Gilbert Harding, and which was chaired by Eamonn Andrews. David was the luckiest conjuror in the business as he appeared weekly on the TV for years without picking up a single playing card or cutting a piece of string. He became a Water Rat and eventually achieved the distinction of being King Rat for two consecutive years. He was a very tall, gentle, giant of a man and everyone who knew him loved him. I spent many happy and successful functions with him and we became great friends.

When *What's My Line?* closed, David was given a magic show, and later in life, a late evening chat show before a studio audience. He asked me if I would like to appear and, again, I jumped at the chance. The show took the form of an informal chat with various guests, interspersed with a little magic.

His scriptwriter was another Past King Rat mate, George Martin, a regular broadcaster towards the end of the war, extremely funny and a lovely guy. I had been asked by the producer to send in a couple of anecdotes of my career which David could lead me to relate, and George told me the one they had selected. It concerned a golf club annual dinner, which I did at The Savoy Hotel for very many years.

It had never been the custom to have presentations as they were considered boring. However, one year a rather sycophantic man decided that he wanted publicly to thank his wife for 'allowing' him to be the club captain that year, and he asked a past captain, Maurice (whose surname I withhold to save any discomfort although I believe he now plays on that great celestial St Andrews above!) to make this presentation. I duly introduced him and he began praising the virtues of the captain's wife Mary, thanking her for all the long lonely hours she spent at home whilst her husband ran the golf club. He went on for about ten minutes, ending by saying, "And so, Mary, as an appreciation of our love and gratitude for all your sacrifices, will you please accept this little gift?" …and he promptly gave it to the wrong woman! It was hilarious at the time and rather embarrassing, but was soon glossed over and the evening progressed.

David Nixon and George Martin latched onto that story like leeches and I told it in all its glorious detail to a studio audience as well as millions of viewers. It received a huge laugh and they were all delighted. It was only six months later, at the next golf club banquet, that I rued the error of my ways. It hit me when I arrived. Virtually the entire club had seen the David Nixon programme, and as people queued to be introduced to the new captain, almost without exception they said to me, "Oh boy, Bryn! What have you done? Maurice is gunning for you!" The whole club had seen the show because, as soon as I appeared on the screen, they telephoned around and said, "Watch TV, Bryn's on!"

Maurice and his wife duly came to me and I have to say that they were both perfectly delightful about it. During the meal, I publicly apologised to him and the Club for the story, explaining that David Nixon had chosen that story out of the half dozen I had given him. They all roared with laughter and applauded. I had been forgiven, but not without some anxiety.

Talking of David and George, I recall a charity occasion that was held at the Lakeside Country Club, in Frimley Green, Surrey. At this event, there were loads of famous performers and the guest of honour was HRH Princess Anne and her then husband Captain Mark Phillips. They had both been training heavily for the Olympic equestrian team, in which I believe they both did very well. However, Mark Phillips had recently had a bad fall from a horse in practice.

I had formed the official line-up in the foyer of Lakeside, and as there were many, it was a wee bit tight and they all had to squeeze together. David Nixon and George Martin were side by side – both were tall and quite well built, so it was a bit like a brick wall. George Martin was also the writer for Basil Brush, a glove puppet handled by Ivan Owen, and Ivan was hiding behind those two giants.

As Princess Anne came along the line of celebrities, she reached the two and, having shaken hands with them, right on cue, up popped Basil Brush over their shoulders. In a very loud voice, Basil said to the Princess, "Hello, your Royal Highness... Boom, Boom, Haw, Haw, Haw!" She was a bit taken aback by this and recoiled a little. Basil went on to say, "Fallen off any good horses lately, Your Royal Highness? Boom, Boom, Haw, Haw, Haw, Haw!" To which her instant reply, with split-second timing, was, "You don't fall off *good* ones." Laughter and as quick as a flash, "But you ask my husband... He does!" It brought a huge roar from the crowd and storming applause.

There used to be two entrances onto the very large balcony of The Grosvenor House Great Room through a row of glass swing doors. Prince Philip was to be the guest of honour at a 1,000-strong banquet and I had been given the unusual instruction to get everyone down to their tables before his arrival – something I have always been reluctant to do in case the royal guest is delayed, which has been known to happen.

We had been notified by the police that he was on his way and would arrive on time. So, dutifully, I got all the guests to their tables and awaited the royal arrival. The delay was longer than I expected and I was peering over the balcony looking down upon the tables. I called out, rather casually, over my left shoulder, to no one in particular but in a rather loud voice, "Is 'e 'ere yet?" To which a royal voice I instantly recognised over my right shoulder said, in an equally loud voice, "YES 'E IS!" There to my horror and chagrin was a larger-than-life, broadly grinning, Prince Philip, Duke of Edinburgh! They'd brought him in the other way! B******s!

Chapter 23

Family Matters

"...Nor all the piety nor all the wit shall
lure it back to cancel half a line,
nor all thy tears wash out a word of it!"

The Rubáiyát of Omar Khayyám
Edward Fitzgerald

When Tim and Tracy were still growing up, and because Ann and I were both very busy in the evenings, we needed to find regular babysitters. Thus began our ongoing dealings with the National Council for the Unmarried Mother and Her Child run by Pauline Crabbe, a wonderful woman. We had been introduced to her as a source for an *au pair* or live-in babysitter, as Pauline needed to find homes for pregnant, unmarried girls. The stigma of out-of-wedlock pregnancy in the 1960s and '70s was still very serious, and it was generally felt that many needed to be away from their homes and protected until the baby was born, after which time they would return to their normal existence. As we had a spare bedroom, Ann and I thought that this was a great idea in so many ways.

Over the years, we gave a home and comfort to sixteen pregnant young girls, mostly from England, but with one from New Zealand and one Irish girl. As guardians of our children, they were quite superb – each one was different, and they really enriched our lives. It is interesting to reflect what happened to their babies when they were born: did they keep the baby or have it adopted? The answer was exactly 50% – eight kept them and eight handed them to adoption societies. We remember each with affection, although

335

almost as soon as they left us we were forgotten; we were part of their lives they wished to leave behind.

Things were improving for our family. I was averaging over 300 functions annually, Ann was immersed in *The Beefeater*, the children were receiving good educations and we felt the need to find a better house; so we went house-hunting away from Muswell Hill, towards Southgate. We saw over sixty houses but found nothing we liked until we received details of a property which looked wonderful and appeared to be within our price range. We went to see it, and as we entered the hallway, Ann looked all around her, up and down, and uttered the immortal words, "I want this house. I want to live here. It's wonderful!" The house was owned by Mr and Mrs Jack Lennard, who showed us around and told us that they had already bought a new flat so there was no rush to sell. We hit it off immediately and they became good friends.

We telephoned the estate agent and made an offer, only to have our hopes dashed when we were informed that there was a typographical error in the specification they sent and that it was actually £20,000 more than stated. This was way above our budget and it looked as though we would lose the house. Ann was heartbroken. I was keen that we should not over extend ourselves financially, but we looked at the sums again and somehow managed to find the difference. We went back to Jack and Juliet Lennard with a revised offer. Being kind, generous and helpful, they accepted it and made it quite clear that we could take as much time as we needed to get our finances together.

In June 1975, we moved into *The Elms*, Cannon Hill, one of the loveliest houses in the whole borough of Southgate. Our cup of joy was filled to overflowing. It is interesting to recall that in both our major house purchases, the vendors appreciated our financial difficulties and very kindly gave us time to sort them out with no pressure or coercion.

Since childhood, I had been terribly allergic to dogs, cats and any form of dust. I could tell instantly whenever I entered a house with a dog, as I would begin to sneeze, wheeze and cough, my eyes would water, and life would be miserable; it was obvious that dogs and me would never get together. Peter was a gorgeous, seven-year-old mongrel who lived at *The Elms*. The Lennards had been hoping to bestow him on us as part of the sale as they could not take him with them to their new flat. Sadly, my allergies meant that this would not be possible and we told the Lennards that they would have to find him an alternative home. They tried and tried, but to no avail, and on the day we went to collect the keys, that lovely brown-eyed, gentle, adorable mutt was lying on the floor, front paws crossed, staring up at us. They had not been able to give him away and the last resort was to have him put down, at which Ann almost went potty! "No way," she said. "Under no circumstances is that lovely dog going to be put down. Don't even think about it. We'll keep him!" – and we did. Not rating my chances if it came to a choice between the dog or me, I accepted Ann's decision.

For three to four weeks my life was misery. With all the house dust, the dog, the excitement of moving and everything else, I was a physical wreck, but miracles do happen and suddenly all my symptoms cleared up; all my allergies simply disappeared – totally. Peter stayed with us until he died naturally at the age of 16½ and we had nine glorious years of his company. We have had two dogs since then which we adored and who broke our hearts when the inevitable happened. We actually mourn far more tearfully over the passing of dogs than we do over humans. Odd, ain't it?

We lived for twelve wonderful years at *The Elms* and life continued to be blissful. Timothy graduated from Brunel and started out on his career in marketing, initially with the *Ford Motor Company* before establishing his own partnership, while Tracy got a job in a firm called *Sea Containers*, in their huge building on the South Bank. After a couple of brief sojourns elsewhere, she returned to become the Personal Assistant to the Legal Vice-President, Ned Hetherington, where she remained for about twenty years until she left the company to live in France.

It was at St Godric's College, Hampstead, that Tracy met a lovely girl from Llangollen named Chloë Diggory, whom she regularly brought home. It was inevitable that Chloë met Timothy and, to quote two horrible phrases I hate, they immediately hit it off, and the rest is history. They are very happily married with two gorgeous children, Joscelyne Sophie Elizabeth and Cameron Jamie, both of whom we adore.

Tracy met and married Paul Faulkner after mutual friends had deliberately put them together on a blind date. They are perfectly suited. In 2000, both families decided that they were fed up with England and all its attendant problems. Being Francophiles, they all decided to team up and seek a living in France. After much searching and scouring the French countryside, they happened upon a mini-hamlet in the Charente region, which they bought. They pooled their resources and moved to the Charente where they have three *gites*, three swimming pools, and a huge house which they shared with Chloë's mother Wendy. They work very hard indeed and would not return to the UK for all the money you could pay them, and we always enjoy our rather infrequent visits. Sadly, Wendy caught a virus in 2004 and was dead within three days. She was lovely, warm, slightly scatty lady and great company. Her death was frighteningly sudden – on a Christmas break in Spain she caught a cold and a virus on the last day, dying when she got home. We all miss her lots.

Ann and I have always enjoyed celebrating – well, to be truthful, I have and Ann has, generally, come along for the ride quite happily. We had many parties at *The Elms*, with, on occasions, well over 150 people present, and Ann always catered for the whole lot. She is a brilliant cook and took that kind of enterprise in her stride, producing many wonderful buffets and meals. In later years, when she was at the *Beefeater*, she persuaded Barry, the very skinny chef (never trust a skinny chef!) to come along and add the professional touches which made them pure magic. Ann became renowned for our parties around the New Year, and as a thank you to the profession, I would invite a bunch of banqueting managers, head waiters and chefs to a Sunday buffet lunch at home, thus throwing Ann in amongst the pros. She never failed, and many of them still talk about our luncheons.

We have also celebrated various anniversaries and birthdays with parties and get-togethers all over the place. We celebrated our

Silver Wedding anniversary with a dinner at the Café Royal. I was very well 'in' there with the management and decided that it would be nice to have a small dinner party in the wine cellars. For special clients, they would lay out a large table for forty people amongst the wine racks, light candles all around and serve dinner. We invited our family, and amongst our guests were Henry Cooper and his lovely Italian wife Albina, together with the founder of the British Safety Council, James Tye. The press got hold of the story with the headline, 'Who sits the head of the BSC next to a boxing champ?' and a photo of the two of them was published.

I was also very friendly with Charles Forte, for whom I have the greatest affection and admiration, and his family. The night of our party was the final of the World Cup in which Italy were playing. During the meal, I noticed that Charles was missing – he had gone into the tiny wine cellar office with all the Italian staff, excitedly watching the match on TV. Italy won and he rewarded me with the largest bottle of champagne I had ever seen.

As a surprise to Ann, I had asked the Gwalia Welsh Male Choir to come and sing for us. You can imagine the crush. There were forty guests squashed around a very large table, and about forty Welsh choristers singing their hearts out wedged between the wine racks and stores. It was heavenly and the sound was quite awe-inspiring.

Our next celebration was for my fiftieth birthday in 1983. Paul and Mary Sparks had run the banqueting at *Derry and Toms* until it closed, after which they bought the delightful Malvern View Hotel on Cleeve Hill, near Cheltenham. I asked them if they would agree to cater my fiftieth birthday and make over the whole hotel to me and my guests. We dined 36 in their small restaurant and had a wonderful evening. Just before dinner, I gave each of the men a small card stating, 'During the meal, I will call upon you to speak for a maximum of two minutes. It can be on any subject you choose excepting me, sex, religion or politics.'

After the first course, I stood up and told them what I had planned, picking on the first three: Tim and his father-in-law, Dig, plus one other; the audience loved it. The final two speakers were my colleague, Martin Nicholls, a very funny professional after-dinner speaker, and the aforementioned Joe Dindol. Nobody at the party knew him, and after the pudding and coffee, I said to them that I was terribly sorry, but I had left one man out from speaking; I had forgotten all about him and hoped he wouldn't mind. Of course, it was all a scam and Joe Dindol gave us all the funniest forty minutes anyone could remember. Incidentally, towards the end of the meal, I asked Mary to get Paul to recommend a good port. When she returned, she said, "West Hartlepool."

In 1987, Ann and I celebrated our thirtieth wedding anniversary. Ian Martin, a friend and colleague for many years, was catering director of Castle Howard in York. Ian engaged me for various functions and I came to know the Castle well, so when Ann and I had another milestone, we decided to hold it there. We chose the Grecian Room, which was perfect for about forty people.

In January we sent out invitations for the party in July, asking our guests to keep the weekend free, telling them nothing except that it would be out of London. The invitation simply asked them to come to The Royal York Hotel where they were invited to a champagne reception in our room at 6.00 pm. I arranged for a coach to take them the 18 miles to Castle Howard, but still did not tell them where they were going. On the coach, I gave Timothy a note to read out: 'Ann and Bryn have been looking for a small country retreat they wish to buy. You have all been invited to a little party to visit this new place and give your opinions!' Much laughter, as by now they were well stacked up with bubbly. As the coach turned a bend in a country lane, suddenly Castle Howard came into view. "Oh God," exclaimed Dig, "Bryn's been and gone and bought bloody Castle Howard."

The guests were directed to the small, exquisitely beautiful chapel in the Castle where, for years, weddings, funerals and holy days had been celebrated by the Howard family. Ian had engaged four choristers from York Minster to sing a few sacred songs for us as an appetiser. It was pure and ephemeral magic. However, unbeknown to us, Tim and Tracy had cobbled together a kind of slide show in conjunction with Ian, so we were led into a small room for this performance.

Now, I had developed a stupid reputation of plonking things, *anything*, on my head when handed to me – hats, scarves, medals, pots, mugs, boxes, anything – and many had been photographed. This stupid tradition was contagious and had spread to all the family. The kids had found dozens of these pictures, put them onto slides and had written a very funny script to accompany it. It was wonderful, and our unsuspecting guests were falling off their chairs at the sight of us wearing such daft headgear. The laughter was so loud that the carefully prepared script was almost inaudible. We all eventually repaired to The Grecian Room for dinner, exhausted with laughter.

Making table plans has never proved a problem with me and, knowing that my guests would be unhappy being separated from their partner, I designed a highly complicated system of seating. Everyone began by sitting with their partner, except Ann and me who sat opposite each other on the large, square table for forty. After each of the four courses, I rose and invited, first, the men to move one way, and after the next course, for the ladies to stand and move the other, thus ensuring that everyone sat with several different neighbours. I planned it so carefully that on the very last move, I was sitting beside Ann, with Tim on one side and Tracy on the other. Extremely complicated but highly successful.

Ian had engaged a Mozart String Octet to play in the background, and the York Choristers sang various songs throughout the dinner. Memories are made of this, and everyone who attended has lovely thoughts of a very special evening. Ian and Sue and Castle Howard pulled out all the stops, we had photos taken of every couple, and have blessed memories of a lovely celebration.

After twelve wonderful years at *The Elms*, in 1987 I felt pressurised to make the most difficult and traumatic decision of my life – a decision which I will take with me to the grave. I believe that it also brought on another bout of cancer for Ann, resulting in a second mastectomy, the first one occurring whilst she was still working at *The Beefeater*. There were many things stressing her at that time: it was hard work trying to get girls to work every night, and I was not the best of husbands with tremendously heavy workloads and other pressures. I was away much of the time, thus not seeing the kids growing up, or supporting them as much as I would have liked with their schooling. Then there were the usual problems of busy couples with growing families.

Ann discovered the initial lump in her breast, which proved malignant, and a mastectomy was advised. The operation in University College Hospital was a success and her recovery was swift. We had kept it quiet from her bosses at *The Beefeater*, but they found out. Tony Gorbutt and Joe Lewis were absolutely furious with her that she had not told them. One day in the public ward – her specialist refused to allow her to go private for all kinds of reasons – the largest planted arrangement of flowers was brought in; it was huge and the message was so kind and encouraging, telling her that they really needed her back at *The Beefeater*, but only when she was ready. Despite their power and influence, they were both super blokes.

I have never been a brilliant money manager, being ignorant of how to arrange my finances sensibly. *The Elms* was a wonderful house, its value had gone up eightfold and we just loved it, but our finances were seriously bad – or so I thought at the time. I am much wiser about these things now. Oh sure, we had a mortgage with which we were comfortable, but cash-flow was seemingly disastrous and I could see no way out. It was this that made me make the decision to sell *The Elms*, something that neither of us had contemplated at any time. To say it broke Ann's heart is the understatement of the year. We were both devastated but really could see no solution to our problem.

We sold *The Elms* in possibly the worst month in my calendar, October. I was out night after night, day after day, and was totally useless in helping with the move. Ann was there packing up things just to leave the home she adored, and every night when I telephoned her she was in floods of tears. It was unquestionably the worst period of our lives and one which I fervently wish I could bury. But I remain convinced that it was inevitable if we were to avoid financial difficulties.

I feel strongly that psychosomatic traumas can bring on physical illnesses, and I am totally convinced that that dreadful period in Ann's life activated a cancer in the other breast resulting in the second mastectomy. I blame myself unequivocally for that period in our lives, which I would give a King's ransom to alter, as I know it brought Ann great unhappiness which I so deeply regret.

However, God works in a mysterious way his wonders to perform, and despite our angst and devastation at having to leave our wonderful Southgate home, things eventually improved in every possible way. We moved to *Tanglewood*, The Ridgeway, Enfield – a very boring, ordinary house, but it was adequate for our needs, especially as Timothy was now married, and Tracy was soon getting a place of her own. I promised Ann that we would only live there for, at most, five years and move on. Twelve years later we sold it.

In 1999 we moved to our present home in Cuffley, Herts, a house every bit as lovely as *The Elms*, and upon which Ann has been able to impose her good taste and influence over every facet of furnishing and decoration. We love this house as much as any of the others and life is very good.

In selling *The Elms*, we released some equity with which we were able to help Tracy buy a flat, assist Timothy in his business, buy a home in Florida and enjoy a degree of comfort that my impecunious upbringing could never have envisaged. It took a long time to get *The Elms* out of our system, but some years ago I met the owner who invited us back to see it. Apart from a few downstairs improvements, they had destroyed the upstairs by putting a 'flat' in the loft and virtually covering the lovely garden with an indoor swimming pool. We left, feeling that it was not the home we had known and the yearning to return faded.

It came as a great sadness but no real surprise that, whilst I was penning this *oeuvre*, my mother died at the age of 94. No surprise, as for over two years she had been vegetating in a retirement home and had become senile; in the last year of her life, she showed absolutely no recognition of either Ann or me and did not utter a single word – we paid regular visits out of loyalty. All the staff at St Theresa's Retirement Home were quite magnificent, kind, gentle, caring, loving and tending to her every need with genuine affection. It was warm, clean, and comfortable, and the food was excellent. Ridiculously expensive, as the fees ate voraciously into her meagre capital, but the staff there gave us great peace of mind that she was being well cared for. Throughout her life, my mother loathed the thought of going into one of these places, but as she grew older, frailer and more accident-prone, there really was no option. She could not live alone and we could not care for her in her deteriorating condition, so a home it was, which proved to be the right choice.

My mother had a variety of names, *noms de plume,* aliases and other titles, and dependent upon whether you were family, friend, client, enemy or simply her son, they all differed. As a child it was 'Mummy'. 'Mum' was reserved for her mother, my maternal grandma, and 'Mother' was a joke. So, for me, 'Mummy' it was. When I married Ann, she had absolutely no idea what to call her, and for the first two years of our marriage it was more or less "Oy, You!" But I jest; Ann simply did not call her anything, not Mrs Williams, not Billie and certainly not mother-in-law. The embarrassment was saved when Timothy was born as she then automatically became Grandma, and that was that. Even I called her that for the rest of her days as it seemed somewhat twee for a middle-aged man to call an old lady 'Mummy'.

My mother was christened Ivy Heffer, married and became Ivy Williams. As she was a bus conductress during the war with another Ivy Williams in the team, she immediately became Billie Williams. My father's professional name was Hugh Owens, and in 1939 she became his 'secretary' and assumed the name of Billie Owens, by which she was known to everyone outside the family. It's amazing how families cannot adapt to changes of a relative's professional name. To the family and those friends, Dad was always Jim Williams. To all professional colleagues for the rest of his life he was Hugh Owens. Even today some of my cousins insist upon calling me Brian – yuk!

As our secretary, my mother answered the telephone and, when asked who she was, she took the first name that came into her head and instantly said, "Miss Brown!" To hundreds of our clients she was Miss Brown – which meant absolutely nothing. But as Mr Shakespeare once said, "What's in a name? A Rose by any other..."

My mother was a maverick; born in July, she was a typical Leo with all its fiery attributes. Born in August, I, too, am a Leo, and as a result we argued furiously over many trivial matters. She was feisty, quick to anger and incredibly outspoken if people offended her. She made a bad enemy and anyone in our business who crossed her felt the length and sharpness of her tongue and was never forgiven. Many of my colleagues have experienced her wrath, but to their credit we have remained friends.

The poverty syndrome never left my mother and much of her time was spent cutting corners to save the ha'pennies; her worst economy, and one which made me seethe, was re-using old envelopes. Here was I, trying to build a respectable professional standard in all my work, and there was she, in the office, steaming stamps off envelopes, sticking labels over the addresses and sending envelopes out with bits stuck all over them. The more angry it made me, the more she chose to do it. I don't suppose we ever saved more than a few quid, but it gave her satisfaction.

But she was not all mean, having a soft, generous streak if she thought the need was genuine. Earlier in this book, I tell of the many lame ducks she gathered around her. She would help all kinds of people in need, the proverbial shoulder to cry on, and would spend hour after hour talking to them on the phone. I frequently arrived home around 1.00 am to be greeted with the delightful expression, "I 'aven't lifted my arse off this bloody chair all day!"

My mother never forgave anyone she felt had seriously misbehaved, and she did not care that they knew it. One acquaintance 'buggered off' (her words) with another bloke. Mum was furious. As a placatory gesture, that lady sent her a Christmas card. My mother took delight in telling everyone that she sent it back, in the same envelope, having written 'Arseholes' all over it.

On another occasion, my son Timothy, with his then fiancée Chloë, took 'Grandma' back to her flat in their car. The owners had redecorated the whole block and had finished it off in the most awful, sickly, sludge brown. On seeing it, her immediate comment was, "I bet they've been all over London looking for this shit colour!"

She was not a lover of babies, but – on sufferance – would babysit for us… but only at her house, not ours. When Chloë told us that she was pregnant, my mother's immediate comment was, "Poor Cow!" but she came to adore her two great-grandchildren.

Although not an overtly religious person, my mother became deeply involved with Christian Science and joined a local Christian Science Society (too small to be called a church), becoming its clerk. Christian Science does not have ministers but uses two 'Readers' at each Sunday service, and defying all nerves of speaking in public, for several years she became a 'Second' Reader. The congregation was always small, with barely a dozen people present, but many recalled one particular Sunday with a degree of awe and admiration. My mother was reading her portion of the Bible when a very noisy Doodlebug flew overhead. As the noise faded away, it suddenly stopped and seconds later in the far distance, they all heard the 'GERRRUMPPHH' of its crash. My mother didn't stop, or hesitate, or give any indication that it was there, and just continued to read as though nothing was amiss. It was mildly inspirational and later intelligence revealed that the bomb landed harmlessly in a field. Despite several testimonies of Christian Science's alleged healing powers over the years, sadly, her beliefs altered in later life about which she seldom spoke; but I owe my feelings for that religion to my early years for which I am eternally grateful.

My mother was a good golfer with a handicap of 18, and represented Muswell Hill in many matches, but she was not fiercely competitive. During the war, she spent days in her brother's butcher's shop, plucking, trussing, stuffing and delivering poultry, as he was in the RAF and away from home. She was a good car driver, but a lousy golf-cart driver; on one occasion smashing the thing into a tree – being a links, it was the only tree on the course!

I suppose that my mother could be considered a character in the real sense of the word. She was kind-hearted and extremely hardworking and there is no doubt that much of my success is due to her conduct of my affairs in my formative years. Mum, 'Grandma', will always be remembered fondly and with gentle amusement. I will never forget my father's last words, when dying from a stroke in hospital. I had told him that Mum couldn't find the ward; his last whisper was, "…Well, she'd get lost in *Woolworths*!"

Having left the Royal Academy, Dad had begun a singing career in 1921 and through lean and fat years continued until the end of WWII when he moved easily from singer to toastmaster. He was hugely popular and highly successful with no thought of retirement. Born on 6th June 1900, in 1983 he was amazingly still in demand. On 19th February he worked and went to bed as usual. The following night Mum was pottering around chattering away but getting no response from Dad. Worried, she called me and asked if I would come down to Gladstone House to see him. When I saw him lying there it looked for all the world as if he had suffered a stroke, a fact which the doctor later confirmed. Dad was rushed to North Middlesex Hospital where, three days later, he finally went to sleep. No pain, no discomfort, just very tired and he breathed his last.

Dad was a kind, generous and loving man who didn't have a nasty or vindictive thought in his head. If he needed a legacy for his 83 years it would be that he spent his whole life amusing and entertaining everyone with whom he came into contact, either with his lovely baritone voice or as a dance M.C. I once saw an epitaph on an American gravestone proclaiming, "He did not know anybody whom he did not like!" That could easily have applied to my Dad. He may not be around physically but he is still around spiritually, as I think about him every day of my life. Dad was very special.

Having reached this far in my story carefully eschewing clichés as far as possible, it seems fitting to end with one. Most successful folk indulge in ecstasies over the influence their parents have had on their lives and fortunes. I take pride in joining that bunch and confirm, unequivocally, that apart from a talent with which God seemed pleased to endow me, I owe so much of my happiness and success throughout my life to my parents – and I thank God for it.

In the very early days of my career, most of the head waiters and waiting staff were Italian and I knew many of them. The President of Italy was paying an official State Visit to London, and to repay the traditional royal hospitality, he invited the Queen, the Queen Mother and Princess Margaret to a dinner at The Italian Embassy in Grosvenor Square. The organisers knew me from my work at the Café Royal and invited me to officiate. I have never seen such a breathtakingly beautiful table *mis en place* as they had prepared for this banquet. About 45 people had been invited, and the dining room contained an extremely large elliptical table with high-backed armchairs.

Everything on that table, except the crystal glassware, was made of gold – all cutlery, the side plates, the liner plates and fingerbowls were solid gold. In front of each place was an individual cruet set with the tiniest spoons I have ever seen. Nothing was out of place; it was magnificent. When the royal guests arrived, they mingled informally in the reception rooms before coming into dinner.

Now, the lovely Queen Mum was not the slimmest of ladies, and on this occasion had elected to wear a very full crinoline dress. Alas! the armchair upon which she was to sit was not very wide – they needed to be rather narrow to get 45 around the table – and was considerably narrower than she and the dress together! So, when I came to push the chair under her bottom for her to sit down, she couldn't get in and was wedged. In any other scenario it would have been hilarious, but with such a regal and elegant lady, it was potentially embarrassing.

I resorted to the simple expedient I had performed on countless brides with full, multi-skirted dresses, of literally tucking them around and under their chair. I 'stuffed' the Queen Mother's gown down between her and the sides of the arms of the chair – I sort of tucked her in. Believe me, it was not easy, and I was running the risk of becoming a Crazy Gang farce. I persevered with this 'stuffing' nonsense when she turned and looked up at me with those clear blue eyes and said, in a very sad voice, "Oh dear! I'm such a nuisance, aren't I?" To which I replied, "No, Ma'am (to rhyme with jam), you're lovely," and added in a very quiet voice that nobody heard, "Now Sit Down!" The devil in me tempted me to put my hands onto her shoulders and push... but caution and delicacy prevailed and I desisted. After all, I wanted to work again and did not wish to be sent to The Tower! Eventually, all went off smoothly and the dinner passed without incident.

It was the end of the evening that remains so vividly in my memory. There was no way that the Queen Mother could ever have prised herself out of the chair without help, so I hung around, watching for departure signs, and when she did try to stand, I had to put all my weight on the back of that damned chair otherwise she would have taken it with her; she literally had to squeeze her way out of it. The thought of our beloved Queen Mum walking out of the Italian Embassy wedged into an expensive armchair, trying to climb into the back seat of a *Roller*, and needing the assistance of a carpenter to pop her out of it, is mind-blowing.

Around 10.00 pm, it was time to go; but never forget, nobody leaves before the Queen, who was quietly saying goodnight to her hosts. The Queen Mother was just in front of me, standing with her private secretary near the door. The Queen spotted her and went over to give her a kiss on the cheek, during which I heard her mutter the immortal, but unexpected and unqueenly words, "Goodnight Mummy. I'll ring you in the morning!" This brought home to me the fact that, despite their lofty position in our lives, they are a close and loving family. And, after all, there is nothing more important in this world than the true love of one's family.

And Finally...

Home Thoughts from A Broad
(With apologies to Robert Browning)

by Ann

If you have read this book so far maybe you feel that you know This Man; but what is he really like at home? Well, let me tell you.

He has a pathological hatred of traffic lights, having been known to drive nearly ten miles further than necessary to avoid two sets of them. He hates parking meters, unnecessary speed cameras, traffic calming bumps and the congestion charge. He is paranoid about punctuality, preferring to arrive two hours early rather than half a minute late. He dislikes unfairness, deceitfulness, cruelty, hypocrisy, thin women and broccoli.

He loves classical music, jazz, Victorian ballads and old musicals when you can come away from the theatre singing the songs and not just the scenery. He enthuses over Max Bruch, Beethoven, Tchaikovsky, Moszkowski, Eric Coates, Cole Porter, Irving Berlin and George Gershwin and anything that used to be called light music; he drools over Art Tatum, big bands, Vladimir Ashkenazi, Oscar Petersen and positively loathes 'My Way', 'You'll Never Walk Alone' and 'Amazing Grace', threatening to haunt anyone if they dare to play them at his funeral. But above all he absolutely detests Rock & Roll, Heavy Metal, over-amplified rubbish and a thump, thump rhythm with no melody.

He likes the English language spoken articulately and with beautiful modulation, but with no 'estuary' English, glottal stops, poor diction and especially split infinitives which make him spit feathers. He loves to read poetry and books by the bucket-load, John Betjeman, Dylan Thomas, Dick Francis, Jeffrey Archer and anything to do with Hornblower.

He has a passion for potatoes; indeed no meal is complete without potatoes – preferably mashed. Any kind of nursery food is OK, although he is not at all keen on the current gastronomic trend of pretty pictures on plates and what he calls "poncey piles of food with pretentious presentation".

He can be charming, argumentative, belligerent, explosive, helpful, flirtatious, kind, annoying and sexy, sometimes all in the space of a morning! He is not very 'blokey' when it comes to sport, never watching tennis, rugby, snooker, darts or football – despite being a Spurs supporter since a kid – yet strangely he somehow always manages to know the results of matches and especially the nitty-gritty of cricket scores. Golf is another matter. When watching it on television, he has an expansive knowledge of all the players and the game and always manages to comment on them just before the commentator does. Apparently he knows every minute detail about the players ranging from dates of birth to their inside leg measurements – and what their caddy had for lunch.

He enjoys wearing shorts as soon as the sun peeps out. He loves gardens – but not gardening, cooking – but not clearing up, a clean, shiny car – as long as someone else washes it. He wrestles with word puzzles, crosswords, anagrams and bridge problems. His favourite fruit is chocolate and his favourite dessert is bread and jam.

He likes long chats with old friends, reminiscing, giving advice – whether asked for or not – and giving and receiving surprises of all sorts. His greatest joy is driving his precious new Jaguar – anywhere – and he is even quite happy to drive my little Nissan run-around, but wouldn't dream of praising it.

He can't cope with modern technology and is a genuine 'Grumpy Old Man' when trying to get his head around it. The TV, the DVD, the video, the burglar alarm, the cordless phone, the boiler programmer, the Internet are a closed book to him, but he's awfully good at buying me flowers.

He regularly loses his mobile phone (three to date) – of which he has not the faintest idea of the number or how to get his messages back – his reading glasses, important bits of paper, swearing that he had them in his hands "not five minutes ago" and gets furiously frustrated when any of these things go wrong blaming everybody else and muttering rude words under his breath. But he can just about manage his newest digital camera which he deems a miracle. (Oh dear, I spoke too soon. He's lost it again!)

He doesn't 'do' electricity, plumbing or DIY of any sort but knows the phone number of every handyman in the district. He's great at putting out the dustbins, arguing on the doorstep with Jehovah's Witnesses, undoing screw-top jars and sewing on buttons.

He is scrupulously honest and equally fair in his deliberations and hates injustice of any kind. He has a knack of writing wonderful letters – composing poetry – and creating personal pre-dinner graces, bringing smiles to the diners. He makes me cheerful when I'm feeling sad or depressed, can snore for England and makes the finest tea and toast this side of the Welsh Border.

He is fiercely proud of what he has achieved – especially following his very modest beginnings. He loves his home... and Florida, his children... and Florida, his two lovely grandchildren... and Florida, golf... and Florida, me... and Florida, playing the piano... and Florida, fish and chips... and Florida, sexy and beautiful women (thankfully from afar)... and Florida, and the house we used to own in Florida, but not necessarily in that order.

He has a great sense of humour and fun – and a hideously annoying habit of opening his big mouth when he should keep it shut and frequently saying the wrong thing; which, even more frustratingly he never ever regrets. He can be generous to a fault (and hates anyone who is not). He can also be difficult, annoying, irascible, persistent and persuasive. With so much energy, drive and enthusiasm for everything he undertakes, it is sometimes like living with an endearing and lovable volcano waiting to erupt.

After more than 50 years with this altogether surprising, complex man... I still love him to bits.